Journalists, Sources, and Credibility

Routledge Research in Journalism

**1. Journalists, Sources,
and Credibility**
New Perspectives
Edited by Bob Franklin and
Matt Carlson

Journalists, Sources, and Credibility

New Perspectives

Edited by Bob Franklin and Matt Carlson

Routledge
Taylor & Francis Group
New York   London

First published 2011
by Routledge
711 Third Avenue New York, NY 10017

Simultaneously published in the UK
by Routledge
2 Park Square, Milton Park, Abingdon, Oxon OX14 4RN

Routledge is an imprint of the Taylor & Francis Group, an informa business

© 2011 Taylor & Francis

The right of Bob Franklin and Matt Carlson to be identified as the authors of the editorial material, and of the authors for their individual chapters, has been asserted by them in accordance with sections 77 and 78 of the Copyright, Designs and Patents Act 1988.

Typeset in Sabon by IBT Global.

Library of Congress Cataloging-in-Publication Data

Journalists, sources and credibility: new perspectives / edited by Bob Franklin and
     Matt Carlson.
         p. cm. — (Routledge research in journalism ; 1)
     Includes bibliographical references and index.
     1. Journalism—History—21st century.   2. Attribution of news.   3. Journalistic
ethics.   4. Citizen journalism.   I. Franklin, Bob, 1949–   II. Carlson, Matt.
     PN4815.2J68 2010
     070.4'3—dc22
     2010023997

ISBN13: 978-0-415-88426-6 (hbk)
ISBN13: 978-0-203-83570-8 (ebk)

Contents

PART III
Citizens and Sourcing: Finding a Way Forward

Tables

Figures

Introduction

Matt Carlson and Bob Franklin

NEWS SOURCES AND SOCIAL POWER

What would it take to believe news of a dragon? Such is the burden borne in 1614 by the author of a written account of a local dragon residing near Sussex, England. While 17th-century audiences may be more accepting of the supernatural, this writer did find himself compelled to provide a particular form of evidence—news sources: "Three persons, whose names are hereunder printed, have scene this serpent, besides divers others . . . and who can certifie the truth of all that has been here related" (Stephens, 1988, p. 126). The installation of these named witnesses serves to forestall incredulity from the bulk of readers who themselves, we may assume, have never seen a dragon sauntering past their doorstep. Or more schematically, named sources provide evidence of activities that occur out of sight of the audience. While this example is nearly four centuries old, we find the familiar ploy of shoring up credibility through sources.

Modern news is unimaginable without news sources. Within all but the most trivial news stories, information arrives linked to the individuals and institutions that provided it. Unattributed statements draw suspicion, putting both journalists and readers ill at ease. Instead, stories "intermesh fact and source" (Tuchman, 1978, p. 90), often through direct quotations or recordings. By emphasizing sources, the role of the journalist comes to seem comparatively minor (McNair, 1998, p. 6). From the view of journalism gleaned from news stories, the reporter's task becomes one of assembly rather than the construction of meaning (Bell, 1991). This has become such an ordinary structure that it often escapes our casual scrutiny.

Yet the dominant journalistic practice of attributing information requires vigilance. If we situate journalism as a key facilitator of the public sphere (Habermas, 1991)—as journalists themselves do—then we must ask who speaks through the news? Which voices get heard? To analyze patterns of news sources, in this way, is to reflect on who has social power and who does not (Cottle, 2000). With corresponding inquiry extending to what patterned source-journalist interactions mean socially and culturally, the focus falls on the question of who speaks and who does not (Sigal, 1986). The outcome of interest becomes not merely the short-term ability to provide facts, define events, and shape public opinion, but also the long-term capacity to establish authority and assign cultural meaning (Berkowitz, 2009).

In adding power to the source-journalist-audience equation, three related-yet-separate understandings of power arise. First, to be a news source is to have the power to speak publicly. Here, our concern falls on the question of access to the news and the mixture of voices that regularly appear—as well as who is left out. But there is more than presence; to be a news source is to have the power to define the world. Providing factual information carries with it the interpretive choices a source makes about what is important. Finally, the ability to act as a news source is also the power to respond. Sources may counter other sources either with a differing interpretation or a direct refutation. Of course, it is worth mentioning at the outset that competition and complexity run through the scholarly findings on news sources.

With these critical issues in mind, this introduction picks out patterns within decades of literature on news sources. Scholars have long wrestled with defining both the dynamics at play and their implications for democratic life. This primer provides a solid foundation for the chapters that follow as the authors confront a changing media landscape. As news continues to evolve in the opening decades of the twenty-first century, so will vital questions of who speaks through the news.

WHAT WE STUDY WHEN WE STUDY NEWS SOURCES

When considering news sources, two interrelated focal points emerge around news practices and news content. On the one hand, the study of sources centers on the interactions between journalists and sources. For example, how are these interactions structured? What source-journalist interactions regularly occur? The sociology of news has long focused on journalist and source interactions. Early work focused on routines in which journalists acted as gatekeepers controlling entry into news discourse (White, 1950) or the functional roles of sources and journalists (Geiber and Johnson, 1962). In the 1970s and early 1980s, a number of now seminal works employed a variety of more sophisticated methodologies—including content analysis and ethnography—to better understand source-journalist relations (Chibnall, 1977; Fishman, 1980; Gans, 1979; Schlesinger, 1978; Sigal, 1973; Tuchman, 1978; Tunstall, 1971). The view that emerges from these works is one of mutual dependence between journalists needing material and sources desiring access to the public. But beyond this give-and-take, deeper connections obtain. Since all sources are not assumed to be equal, what develops is "structured access" (Chibnall, 1977, p. 37) or a system of recurring discrimination that orders the universe of potential news sources. Fishman (1980) points to what he labels "bureaucratic affinity" (p. 143) to mark the homophily between complex public institutions and journalists' own rigidly structured bureaucracies. This adherence to a common organizational structure lends itself to easy transfer while groups or individuals outside of such institutions find a harder time gaining entry into news discourse.

Sigal's (1973) classic study of news sources in the *New York Times* and *Washington Post* found overwhelming support for the reliance on official sources and routine channels. This pattern reflects organizational and journalistic norms encouraging both the repetition of practices and a privileging of those sources seen as having power. While Sigal does not view journalists as powerless, ultimately he concedes that sources have the upper hand. This is partly due to a competition among journalists to get scoops in an environment—Washington-based national and international reporting—with a great deal of news competition. "The incentive to get the news first makes reporters willing to play along with their sources in order to obtain disclosures on an exclusive basis" (p. 56). However, Sigal finds journalists are reliant on routine channels to gather the news efficiently, which puts reporters at the mercy of sources (p. 130). This is more than an exchange of information, as the beat reporter "absorbs" the viewpoints of whom she covers through repeated contact.

Like Sigal, Gans (1979) explores the complexity of the relationship between journalists and sources, noting that: "sources, journalists, and audiences coexist in a system, although it is closer to a tug of war than a functionally interrelated organism" (p. 81). Still, both journalists and sources stand to gain from participation. Journalists seek out sources that are both available and suitable, which serves to reinforce patterned sourcing practices. As a result of repetition, the authority of some sources is bolstered—making them likely to be called on as sources again—while other voices are continually excluded. This occurs even as journalists "harbor a pervasive distrust of their sources, since so many come to them with self-serving motives that they are not always inclined to be completely honest" (p. 130). Yet a reliance on routines compels them to return to these sources.

In light of such patterns, sourcing practices have long drawn complaints concerning the cunning of sources and their representatives to shape news content. As early as the 1920s, during the same decade Edward Bernays would help define public relations with his book *Propaganda* (1928), Lippmann expressed dismay at the outsized ability of news agents to influence the news. As a barrier between reporters and individuals within institutions, the press agent acts as "censor and propagandist" by presenting information not as disinterested, but as interpreted according to the whims of the institution being represented (Lippmann, 1922, p. 218). Public relations has grown up around the understanding that journalists possess a constant appetite for material—the more closely resembling news, the better. Gandy pushed this further by labeling material created for easy entry into news content as "information subsidies" (Gandy, 1982). This is not meant to be a conspiratorial view of journalist-source relations, but rather a pragmatic reflection of the working conditions journalist confront each day. Indeed, organizations strive to create information subsidies to take advantage of the unending need for news material.

Public relations became more than a response to reporters' inquiries or a reaction to controversies; it became a practice of grabbing journalistic attention. This is best epitomized by what Boorstin (1962) calls a "pseudo-event" (p. 6), an event held expressly for attracting media attention. It is the orchestration of attention to reach a diffuse public. Managing reporters became a key activity, made simpler by the tendency of journalists to function as a "pack" (Crouse, 1973). The general trend toward the greater prominence of public relations in shaping and augmenting news coverage continues (Davis, 2002). The importance of media relations has even transformed strategies of smaller organizations that have become increasingly adept at crafting journalistically friendly messages (Anderson, 1991). However, as Reich (2009) discovered, despite this apparent surge in public relations activities, the amount of news content directly stemming from such efforts has not likewise increased (p. 56). If anything, the pervasiveness of public relations results in a flood of competing messages fighting for the limited attention of journalists.

Research on news sources has revealed the mutual reliance between journalists and their sources. But while they rely on each other, it is not necessarily an egalitarian relationship. Put simply, certain sources have an easier time getting access in news content than others. And while enhanced publicity skills have allowed for some voices on the margins to get heard, patterns still exist.

WHOSE VIEWS ARE PRESENTED?

The patterned practices of journalist-source interactions relate to a second concern regarding the incorporation of sources into news texts. What does it matter which sources appear in news stories? In order to make sense of this question, it is important to begin by considering their function to be not only pragmatic in supplying information, but also symbolic in supplying legitimacy and authority. The latter occurs on three levels: being present in news texts highlights the legitimacy of the quoted source, tying assertions to identifiable sources signals the credibility of the news item, and having access to sources underscores the authority of the individual reporter and her news outlet.

Deriving authority from the sources of a news story more so than the author has roots in larger shifts regarding how journalism works. In the US, attribution fits squarely within what Schudson (1978) identified as the rise of the "informational ideal in journalism" (p. 90) during the end of the 19th century. The explicit use of sources dovetails with efforts to situate the journalist as being an ideal objective observer. This move can be understood within larger efforts to transform journalism from a craft to a profession in the period from the 1890s through the 1920s. Journalists sought to promote a cultural view of news as accurate, verifiable, independent and systematic. Aside from the cultural authority accompanying the status of professional (Abbott, 1988), the meteoric circulation gains of the *New York Times* proved the informational ideal could also be profitable (Schudson, 1978, p. 114). As part of this transition, sourcing practices began moving to direct quotation and the use of the once disparaged interview as a method for gathering and attributing information to help bolster their own standing: "Reporters publicly demonstrate through interviews their proximity to news sources and thereby increase the authority of their writing for the audience" (Schudson, 1995, p. 91). However, the shift to the modern emphasis on attribution was slow going and uneven. Even by 1914, large papers did not regularly incorporate direct quotations into news stories (p. 83). But by the latter half of the 20th century on, the expectation of including sources in news stories had solidified.

As the studies above indicated, the normalization of attribution led to patterns in which elites came to be privileged over non-elites. Yet this finding does not, by itself, settle the question of what impact this unequal access has on news or society. What matters more than a mere quantitative census of the types of sources in news content is how the range of voices allowed into news discourse shapes public understandings of the world. One conceptual shift taking up these concerns supplanted the interaction-centered journalist-source "tug of war" depicted by Gans with the text-centered perspective of elite sources as "primary definers" (Hall et al., 1978). These sources attained interpretive rights unrealized by journalists conscious of minimizing their own voices or other sources deemed to be lacking the requisite authority to speak. In this arrangement, journalists are neither in cahoots with sources nor acting malevolently, but handcuffed by the combination of a professional ideology preaching impartiality, a style of news heavily reliant on direct quotation, and a need to work efficiently and swiftly. In the study by Hall and colleagues, this resulted in the making of a crime wave not through an appeal to criminal activities but through its construction by elite sources. Their views simply received more attention.

Around the same time, Gitlin (1980) connected news content with political hegemony in the US. Echoing the primary definers model espoused by Hall and colleagues, Gitlin writes, "Simply by doing their jobs, journalists tend to serve the political and economic elite definitions of society" (p. 12). In denoting the happenings of the world through the voices of its sources, the news inextricably produces lasting connotations conferring importance and insignificance, normalcy and deviancy, acceptability and unacceptability—even right and wrong. This formulation characterizes the power of sources as nothing short of the power to define reality, strengthened by journalism's own claims of objectively mediating reality.

Over time, the ability of a ruling elite to dictate meaning within news has been usefully challenged and modified to recognize competition between news sources (Schlesinger, 1990; also Eldridge, 1993; Miller, 1993). Most pointedly, Schlesinger and Tumber (1994) call attention to ambiguities arising in the primary definers' model, including its assumptions of elite consensus, invariably passive journalists, and static, atemporal boundaries of who may be a societal elite. By complicating earlier models, these criticisms are not meant to vacate inquiry connecting sourcing patterns with social control. More productively, this view replaces the assumption of power with an interest in the process by which sources acquire dominant positions within a story against other possible sources or positions and how they sustain or lose this place over time. What we gain is a set of variables and conditions to think with when we think about sources.

Ericson, Baranek and Chan (1989) move away from a newsroom-centered approach to studying journalist-source relations and instead seek to understand the perspective of the sources. Through a comparative analysis of the courts, police, legislature, and private sector in Canada, they conclude sources possess power in shaping meaning through various tactics by which they promote their version of reality. As a result, these institutions have come to be viewed as authoritative. "News is a representation of authority. In the contemporary knowledge society news represents *who* are the authorized knowers and *what* are their authoritative versions of reality" (p. 3, original emphasis). News reaffirms the unequal distribution of knowledge within a society by promoting some sources as authoritative while ignoring other voices. Yet the relationship between sources and journalists is presented as one of conflict and negotiation (p. 2). Journalists retain meaning-making power through controlling the presentation of source information through the construction of a news text (p. 339). So, while sources do have influence on the news, they cannot determine its final form.

In many ways, scholars in the US underwent a similar conceptual demassification of elite sources. Rather than assume coherence, scholars such as Hallin (1986) and Bennett (1990) track how elite dissensus affects news coverage. Hallin found that growing disenchantment with the Vietnam War within the government, rather than grassroots efforts or a cynical news media, led to wider debate about the conflict. Similarly, Bennett's "indexing" model relates the degree of agreement or disagreement displayed in news texts to the degree to which an issue is debated among elites. This pattern reinforces the claim that journalists rely on definitions and interpretations of sources to define the contours of reality. The impact of this structure can be seen in later work by Bennett and colleagues (Bennett, Lawrence, and Livingston, 2007) documenting reportorial decisions in the US press concerning the foreign policy actions of President George W. Bush's administration. Even the selection of basic vocabulary—for example, whether the scandal at Iraq's Abu Ghraib prison constituted 'abuse' or 'torture'—became a point of major contention in which elite sources influenced the very words available to describe what happened.

In the end, the question of power remains an integral part of studying news sources. Over the years, a more nuanced vision of sources in perpetual competition has strengthened the conceptual tools available to researchers. No source is guaranteed definitional control, but it should also be reiterated that the ability to characterize a situation within a news story has consequences in constraining the perspectives audiences have available to view reality.

NEWS SOURCES IN A TIME OF CHANGE

A casual glance at the preceding section reveals that much of the academic literature on news sources emerged during the golden era of mass communication. In the late 1970s, while the study of journalism flourished in the US and UK with a wave of empirical studies, the mass media also flourished. The US news diet consisted of popular evening news broadcasts on the three national television networks, a few news magazines, and strong local newspapers. In Britain, the BBC remained powerful in television and radio while national and local newspapers competed vigorously. Decades later, audience fragmentation and the rise of the Internet has created new venues for news exhibition, opened the door to non-elite media, and birthed new forms that, in many fundamental ways, are incommensurate with how news was envisioned a short while ago. The question inevitably follows: what does this mean for how we understand news sources?

The rise of "convergence culture," to use Jenkins' term (2006), portends a shift from the authority of a singular author and the fixedness of a text to a view of texts as collaborative and unstable. The borders between producers and consumers, a hallmark of mass communication, begin to give way to a new hybrid identified alternatively as "prosumers," "citizen journalists," and "writer-gatherers" (Couldry, 2010, p. 139) creating "user-generated content." Putting aside the nuances behind the blossoming terminology, the underlying movement is one away from the privileged position of the professional journalist to that of a more open system of public communication.

Many have trumpeted the democratizing potential of expanding the ability to participate in the mediated public sphere. As technology writer Dan Gillmor (2004) puts it, "For the first time in history, at least in the developed world, anyone with a computer and Internet connection could own a press. Just about anyone could make the news" (p. 24). Technology has altered the conditions of access, which gives rise to "'ordinary' voices" (Atton and Hamilton, 2008, p. 90). In contrast to the practice of inviting non-elite sources for brief comments, alternative journalistic forms radically realign the universe of preferable sources, treating individuals and groups normally outside of news "as voices that have as equal a right to be heard as do the voice of elite groups" (p. 93). More than just an alternative media space, proponents of non-professional online journalism view their work as a check on the power of elite media. In the US, this claim was fueled by a number of well-publicized victories claimed by bloggers, including the retraction by CBS News of a story critically assailing the military service record of President Bush (Carlson, 2011). Such challenges extend to a general normative thrust in favor of transparency.

While new opportunities exist for mediated self-expression, the impact on journalism is certainly more mixed in ways that are not necessarily positive. Enhancements in technology have complicated journalistic work through the greater emphasis on speed. When once publication or broadcast deadlines set the rhythm of the day, new distribution opportunities encourage the constant drive to publish early and often. Without an infusion of concomitant resources, journalists must make due, which often requires falling back on regular, common news sources (Phillips, 2010). Unsurprisingly, a continuing explosion of public relations materials exists to supplement news outlets needing a constant stream of materials (Lewis, Williams, and Franklin, 2008). Thus, while new technologies allow non-journalists greater ability to circulate messages, journalists find themselves even more entrenched with tried-and-true sourcing practices in order to meet the unceasing demand for content (see Kovach and Rosenstiel, 1999).

It is unclear what the trajectory for news sourcing will be. New technologies give rise to altered working conditions while not erasing old patterns. Media consolidation remains as strong as ever and most major news outlets remain under the auspices of for-profit companies. At the same time, unique attributes of digital, networked technology allow for new capabilities for both mainstream and alternative news outlets. With Web-based news, hyperlinks allow an audience to immediately connect to source material used in a story. Journalists are also able to make available raw material—be it audio, video, or a document—to audiences wanting more information than what a story offers. In sum, there seems to be great need for scholars to continue rethinking how news sourcing and access functions going forward.

RESEARCHING NEWS SOURCES IN THE 21ST CENTURY: THE BOOK IN OUTLINE

As the chapters in this volume attest, there is no shortage of questions about news sources left to answer. Changes in news technology, economics, ownership and regulation coupled with a dynamic cultural and political context require our vigilance. While we devote ourselves to this study, we must not lose track of *why* we care about patterns and practices surrounding news sources. The prevailing Western mode of journalism is one relying on attribution to convince audiences that the facts and assertions within news content are, indeed, credible and legitimate. As long as this is true, news sources not only provide details about a situation, but, more importantly, ascribe meaning to the events of the world. What is true in a news account is not the word of the journalist, but that of a source. Who are these sources? How do they get to be in the story? Which sources are left out? These questions remain vital to unraveling the connection between journalism and the reproduction and distribution of power within a society; it is these questions that are addressed by the essays collected in this volume.

The book is divided into three broad sections that deal in turn with the analysis of concepts such as credibility, transparency and diversity which are central to the discussion of news sourcing, before moving to identify and interrogate the entrenched practices of journalists and sources which foreground the influence of privileged sources in news production. The final section assesses the implications of new media technologies and online journalism for potentially more pluralistic forms of journalism practice and sourcing patterns.

In the opening chapter, Zvi Reich deploys reconstruction interviews to analyse the neglected question of how journalists assess the credibility of news sources and how these assessments influence the frequency with which particular sources appear in news reports. Reich's interviews with reporters from nine leading Israeli news organizations enabled the assessment of journalists' credibility judgments of a sample of 1840 specific news sources. He concludes that journalists employ four interrelated strategies, which he terms "A priori 'typecasting', practical scepticism, prominent presentation and distancing by attribution," in their relations with sources designed "to minimize their exposure to erroneous publications." These strategies provide a "relatively perfect shield" but reporters nonetheless acknowledge that more credible sources are treated less thoroughly, that journalists' assessments of credibility are associated with specific source characteristics and that even less credible sources receive considerable news space.

Matt Carlson redirects our focus to the important and special case of unnamed sources which provide journalists with significant information and stories but in return for anonymity. For the journalist and the reading public, this exchange delivers otherwise inaccessible information which may hold the powerful to account and promote the public interest. But in practice, restricting audiences' knowledge about news sources has triggered controversy. Carlson analyses the future viability for this particular journalism practice at a time when the key issues of 'transparency' and 'anonymity' are being renegotiated as part of the broader influence of new media technologies on news gathering, news sourcing and news reporting regimes. Carlson suggests that as journalists confront a growing crisis of credibility, the practice of anonymous sourcing "will continually come under fire" but concludes that journalists "should not lose a tool for holding power accountable."

In Chapter 3 Angela Phillips draws on interviews with UK national newspaper journalists to argue that journalists' claims to stress investigation, fact checking, and accuracy, as key elements in their professional practice that distinguish them from 'amateur' journalists and bloggers are undermined by the increasing occurrence of what she terms 'news cannibalism'—(i.e. using material published by other news organizations in their own stories and without attribution). The arrival of digital technology and online editions has prompted changes in journalism ethics and practice to the extent where Phillips' interviews revealed that approximately "a third of the *Daily Telegraph* stories discussed had been lifted directly from another news organisation." Phillips suggests that establishing new standards of transparency could help protect professional reporting in the new, networked era, as well as improving ethical standards in journalism.

Chris Atton argues that the "amateur and inclusive nature" of the editorial practices of the global online network of Independent Media Centres (*Indymedia*) offer a critique of the "dominant practices and philosophy of professional journalism." However mainstream media may also learn from *Indymedia's* journalism which happened with blogging; a practice initially associated with alternative journalism, but subsequently adopted by professional journalists. Atton's chapter explores the opportunities provided by alternative journalism to reimagine the professional practices of journalism in terms of agenda setting, sources used and discourses employed. He concludes that it is possible to "envision and encourage a professionalised journalism that takes more account of the self-reflexive lessons to be learned from alternative journalism" but adds a note of caution that "we should not be over-optimistic."

The discussion of "Entrenched Practices and Entrenched Sources" opens with Julian Petley's analysis of Nick Davies' "trenchant" critique of modern journalism in his widely read book, *Flat Earth News*. Davies formulates ten rules informing contemporary journalism which account for what he believes is its current parlous state and which bear a certain resemblance to the five filters identified by Herman and Chomsky's propaganda model. But while Davies' analysis emphasizes the debilitating consequences of journalists' reliance on sources of news, Herman and Chomsky lay greater stress on media ownership and the media's reliance on advertising revenues, an approach which Davies (who does not cite Herman and Chomsky) regards as overly "conspiratorial." Petley argues that such an approach is by no means a form of conspiracy theory and that Davies' own critique would have been strengthened by including consideration of the wider political, ideological and economic perspectives adopted by Herman and Chomsky.

Bob Franklin continues the focus on Nick Davies' influential study of *Flat Earth News* by applying the same research approach of close textual comparison of public relations news sources with journalists' published news stories to identify the extent and character of journalists' reliance on these information subsidies. Franklin argues that while the current recession, in tandem with developments in digital media technologies, have exacerbated journalists' use of PR sources, they did not create it. He complements a reprise of the research study informing Davies' findings about the impact of PR and Agency sources on UK national, 'quality' or 'broadsheet' journalism, with studies from the mid 1980s onwards that reveal journalists' earlier but extensive reliance on PR subsidies in local, regional and national newspapers. Throughout the chapter, Franklin considers the implications of this continuing trend for UK democracy in the local and national setting as the fourth estate becomes ever more in hock to the fifth estate of public relations.

Tom Van Hout offers a case study which tracks the newsroom trajectory of a single story about increased government funding of biotechnology research. Data derive from a 6-months newsroom ethnography of business reporters at *De Standaard*, a quality newspaper in Belgium, combined with the deployment of software packages which record keyboard strokes and mouse movements allowing the researcher to track the journalist's writing protocols from inception to story completion. For Van Hout, journalism is a literacy event comprised by three distinct episodes of textual mediation: story inception, negotiation and inscription. By unpacking reporters' literacy practices that shape these episodes, he reveals the complexities of news writing, how 'information subsidies' are taken up and how writing from sources is both facilitated and constrained by newsroom technologies. These findings contextualize the contingent practices through which journalists negotiate stories with sources and editors, manage newsroom technologies and accomplish routine writing tasks.

The second part of the book concludes with Lucinda Strahan's case study of the 'extensive' level of 'public relations activity' in a week's arts journalism in *The Age* and the *Herald Sun*—two daily newspapers based in Melbourne, Australia. She argues that public relations activity is central to the production of arts journalism at these newspapers to the extent where even basic arts publicity assumes the value of journalism itself. The chapter concludes by exploring John Hartley's idea of 'DIY citizenship' as a possible tool for future consideration of changing arts news values and arts journalism's role in the construction of creative identities—of the city itself and the arts-going inner-city Melbournian.

The final part of this collection titled, "Citizens and Sourcing: Finding A Way Forward" focuses on the implications of new media technologies both for journalism practice and sources, with a perhaps predictable emphasis on the role of User Generated Content in reshaping the range and diversity of sources available to news journalists.

Jeroen De Keyser, Karin Raeymaeckers, and Steve Paulussen use Jürgen Habermas' model of arenas of political communication as a starting point for their analysis of the sourcing practices of Flemish (i.e. Northern Belgian) journalists, using data from a large-scale postal survey which achieved a 31% response from a national journalist population of 2,230. Traditionally, elite sources have enjoyed privileged access to journalists while individual citizens have by-and-large been ignored as news sources. With the introduction of digital technologies on the internet, however, study findings suggest that while, "the top three [sources of journalists' information] are undeniably elite sources (i.e. government, researchers, and politicians) . . . Citizen sources (45.1%) occupy a central position . . ." and are "valued more highly" by journalists "than special interest groups, NGOs and even the business elite."

Andrew Williams, Claire Wardle and Karin Wahl-Jorgensen's methodologically rich study includes observational studies in BBC regional and network newsrooms, combined with interviews with 115 BBC journalists and editors, to explore BBC uses of user generated content in news reports, as well as the reality of claims that this audience contribution has 'revolutionized journalism' by reshaping relationships between news producers and consumers. Their findings suggest that journalists and editors perceive UGC as simply another news source, a perception which is reinforced by the organizational framework established to elicit and process audience material, as well as the BBC's UGC training programme for journalists. The authors conclude that "overwhelmingly" at the BBC, "journalists have remained journalists and audiences are still audiences" while "truly collaborative relations between the two groups remain rare exceptions."

Annika Bergström's chapter investigates audience attitudes towards UGC and user-contributions on Swedish news sites staffed by professional journalists. A survey distributed to a representative Swedish sample of 3,000 people (59% response) was designed to explore two broad research questions: first, how attractive is UGC for online news audiences? Second, which audience groups are most likely to contribute with different kinds of content? Bergström's findings suggest that the numbers of people contributing to online news is very modest and they are mostly young (50% of those who judge user contributions to news as *very* or *fairly important* are aged 15–29). Despite these "low levels of participation," user contributions "are growing" but mostly readers' "contributions are not [judged] as attractive as professionally produced content."

In the final essay, Axel Bruns moves beyond political debate—the usual focus for research on citizen participation in journalism—to consider the distinctive and more novel issue of citizen engagement and 'produsage' in the reporting of everyday community life. His case study focus is the German-based citizen journalism Website *myHeimat.de*, which provides a nationwide platform for participants to contribute reports about events in their community. *myHeimat* adopts a hyperlocal approach but also allows for content aggregation on specific topics across multiple local communities. Hannover-based newspaper publishing house

Madsack has recently acquired a stake in the project. Drawing on extensive interviews with *myHeimat* CEO Martin Huber and Madsack newspaper editors Peter Taubald and Clemens Wlokas, Bruns analyses the *myHeimat* project, examines its applicability beyond rural and regional areas in Germany and poses questions about the potential for citizen journalism beyond the realm of political issues and concerns.

JOURNALISM, SOURCES AND CREDIBILITY; CONTINUITY AND CHANGE

The contemporary world of news production is radically different from the seventeenth century when a news report announced the sighting of a dragon which was allegedly living peacefully in Sussex. But crucially, even 400 years ago, for this story to enjoy credibility with the reading audience, it required the endorsement of news sources, the "Three persons, whose names are hereunder printed," who confirmed they had "scene this serpent" and who could "certifie the truth of all that has been here related" (Stephens, 1988, p. 126 cited above). Certain aspects of the significant relationship between journalists and news sources, which also inform scholarly discussion surrounding that relationship, seem to pose what might be termed 'perennial questions' or concerns. Who, for example, has a voice in media and hence public reports about important issues? When there are conflicting views about such significant issues, whose account prevails? And how does news media's inclusion of these utterances help to shape and define the world? Who among journalists and sources decides which of the many events which occur in the world will become 'news' reported in news media, while other happenings are ignored and consigned to the dust heap of history?

These 'perennial' concerns have been joined by others reflecting developments in new media technologies and platforms? How is the carefully choreographed dance between journalists and news sources shifting as digital technologies empower a wider range of citizens, groups and organizations? And what problems arise concerning transparency, credibility and diversity given this enhanced engagement and more popular involvement with journalism?

This compendium of research-based essays addresses these questions and responds to them with findings drawn from a series of case studies from around the globe which draw on a wide range of research methods employed within the humanities and social science. While dragons may not stalk the landscape of Sussex, the relationship between journalists and their news sources remains firmly located at the heart of journalism studies. The study of news sources grows ever more significant in its implications for the changing world of news and provides fascinating and fertile ground for further scholarly research.

REFERENCES

Abbott, Andrew (1988) *The System of Professions*, Chicago: University of Chicago Press.

Anderson, Alison (1991) "Source strategies and the communication of environmental affairs," *Media, Culture and Society* 13: pp. 459–476.

Atton, Chris and Hamilton, James (2008) *Alternative Journalism*, Los Angeles: Sage.

Bell, Allan (1991) *The Language of News Media*, Oxford, UK: Blackwell.

Bennett, W. Lance (1990) "Towards a theory of press–state relations in the United States," *Journal of Communication* 40: pp. 103–125.

Bennett, W. Lance, Lawrence, Regina and Livingston, Steven (2007) *When the Press Fails*, Chicago: University of Chicago Press.

Berkowitz, Daniel A. (2009) "Reporters and their sources," in Karin Wahl-Jorgensen and Thomas Hanitzsch (Eds), *The Handbook of Journalism Studies*, New York: Routledge, pp. 102–115.

Bernays, Edward (1928) *Propaganda*, New York: Liveright.

Boorstin, Daniel (1962) *The Image: A Guide to Pseudo-Events in America*, New York: Atheneum.

Carlson, Matt (2011) *On the Condition of Anonymity: Unnamed Sources and the Battle for Journalism*, Champaign, IL: University of Illinois Press.

Chibnall, Steve (1977) *Law and Order News*, London: Tavistock.

Cottle, Simon (2000) "Rethinking news access," *Journalism Studies* 1: pp. 427–448.

Couldry, Nick (2010) "New online news sources and writer-gathers," in Natalie Fenton (Ed), *New Media, Old News*, Los Angeles: Sage, pp. 138–152.

Crouse, Timothy (1973) *The Boys on the Bus*, New York: Random House.

Davis, Aeron (2002) *Public Relations Democracy*, Manchester, UK: Manchester University Press.

Eldridge, John (1993) "News, truth and power," in John Eldridge (Ed), *Getting the Message: News, Truth and Power*, London: Routledge, pp. 3–33.

Ericson, Richard, Baranek, Patricia and Chan, Janet (1989) *Negotiating Control: A Study of News Sources*, Toronto, ON: University of Toronto Press.

Fishman, Mark (1980) *Manufacturing the News*, Austin, TX: University of Texas Press.

Gandy, Oscar (1982) *Beyond Agenda Setting*, Norwood, NJ: Ablex.

Gans, Herbert (1979) *Deciding What's News*, New York: Pantheon Books.

Gieber, Walter and Johnson, Walter (1961) "The City Hall 'beat': A study of reporter and source roles," *Journalism Quarterly* 38(3): pp. 289–297.

Gillmor, Dan (2004) *We the Media*, Sebastopol, CA: O'Reilly Media.

Gitlin, Todd (1980) *The Whole World is Watching*, Berkeley, CA: University of California Press.

Habermas, Jürgen (1991) *The Structural Transformation of the Public Sphere*, Cambridge, MA: MIT Press.

Hall, Stuart, Critcher, Charles, Jefferson, Tony, Clarke, John, and Roberts, Brian (1978) *Policing the Crisis*, London: Macmillan.

Hallin, Daniel (1986) *The "Uncensored" War: The Media and Vietnam*, New York: Oxford University Press.

Jenkins, Henry (2006) *Convergence Culture*, New York: New York University Press.

Kovach, Bill and Rosenstiel, Tom (1999) *Warp Speed: America in the Age of Mixed Media*, New York: Twentieth Century Fund.

Lewis, Justin, Williams, Andrew and Franklin, Bob (2008) "A compromised fourth estate? UK news journalism, public relations, and news sources," *Journalism Studies* 9: pp. 1–20.

Lippmann, Walter (1922) *Public Opinion*, New York: Macmillan.

McNair, Brian (1998) *The Sociology of Journalism*, London: Arnold.

Miller, David (1993) "Official sources and 'primary definition': The case of Northern Ireland," *Media, Culture and Society* 15: pp. 385–406.

Phillips, Angela (2010) "Old sources: New bottles," in Natalie Fenton (Ed), *New Media, Old News*, Los Angeles: Sage, pp. 87–101.

Reich, Zvi (2009) *Sourcing the News*, Cresskill, NJ: Hampton Press.

Schlesinger, Philip (1978) *Putting 'Reality' Together*, London: Constable.

Schlesinger, Philip (1990) "Rethinking the sociology of journalism: Source strategies and the limits of media centrism," in Marjorie Ferguson (Ed), *Public Communication: The New Imperatives*, London: Sage, pp. 61–83.

Schlesinger, Philip and Tumber, Howard (1994) *Reporting Crime*, Oxford, UK: Clarendon Press.

Schudson, Michael (1978) *Discovering the News: A Social History of American Newspapers*, New York: Basic Books.

Schudson, Michael (1995) *The Power of News*, Cambridge, MA: Harvard University Press.

Sigal, Leon (1973) *Reporters and Officials*, Lexington, MA: D.C. Heath.

Sigal, Leon (1986) "Sources make the news," in Robert K. Manoff and Michael Schudson (Eds) *Reading the News*, New York: Pantheon, pp. 9–37.

Stephens, Mitchell (1988) *A History of News*, New York: Penguin.

Tuchman, Gaye (1978) *Making News*, New York: Free Press.

Tunstall, Jeremy (1971) *Journalists at Work*, Beverly Hills, CA: Sage.

White, David M. (1950) "The 'gatekeeper': A case study in the selection of news," *Journalism Quarterly* 27(3): pp. 383–390.

Part I

Credibility, Transparency and Diversity

1 Source Credibility as a Journalistic Work Tool

Zvi Reich

One key determinant of who becomes a news source and thus acquires voice and involvement in news content is the extent to which different agents are perceived by journalists as credible (Detjen et al., 2000; Gans, 1979; Goldenberg, 1975). Source credibility in journalism, that is always a perceived phenomenon (hence hereinafter "credibility" is used to mean "perceived credibility"), extends far beyond the believability of one actor or another, as human agents stand behind virtually all news (Reich, 2009; Sigal, 1986; Strömbäck and Nord, 2005) and credibility is interwoven into the wider logic of news making, outlining the borderline between versions and facts, trust and skepticism, objectivity and bias, high exposure and news deprivation (Cottle, 2000; Reich 2009; Schudson, 2001).

Journalists ranked credibility as the most influential factor in source selection, followed by source accessibility and time pressure (Powers and Fico, 1994), describing it as a factor that aids in determining whether the journalist or sources control the story (Altheide, 1978).

Despite its importance, however, very limited research attention has been devoted to source credibility in journalism (Tsfati, 2008). Most of the so-called "plentiful" (Self, 1996, p. 421) credibility literature focuses on audiences and their perceptions of sources, media and messages (Gaziano and McGrath, 1986; Johnson and Kaya, 2000; Rouner, 2008, pp.1040–1041; Wanta and Hu, 1994). The applicability of these studies to journalism may be limited. Journalists are probably unique administrators of doubts, as practitioners who constantly juggle between losing time when being over-suspicious and losing face (and sometimes even losing their jobs) when being under-suspicious. They are more intensive and proficient judges of credibility than lay-people. For journalists, credibility is a major professional value and a central tenet of codes of ethics, playing a quadruple role "as a goal, a tool, an asset and a rationale behind most professional creeds" (Tsfati, 2008, p. 2598). From the point of view of their sources, journalists perform a triple role as an audience, medium and gatekeeper (Aronoff, 1975, p. 45).

Even the minority of studies that have focused on journalists have asked them to rank hypothetical, generic and decontextualized types of sources; such as senior officials, public relations practitioners, commercial or academic sources; while in real-life situations journalists encounter specific personae who offer specific information under specific contexts of newsworthiness, competition, risk of error and the availability of time, resources and accessibility, that are required for cross-checking suspected sources or details in advance. In some studies, journalists were even asked to rank the credibility of entire organizations (Yoon, 2005) or clusters of sources (Detjen et al., 2000; Powers and Fico, 1994; Rouner, Slater, and Buddenbaum 1999), each of which may incorporate, side by side, notorious liars and reputable truth tellers.

The purpose of this chapter is to elicit the role of source credibility in journalism, demonstrating how news reporters actually assess the credibility of specific news sources in a specific sample of items. Furthermore, it attempts to detect productive associations between credibility and other aspects of newswork: source map structure, patterns of journalistic treatment of sources with different levels of perceived credibility and the characteristics of more versus less credible sources.

Data were gleaned in a series of face-to-face reconstruction interviews in which reporters ranked, contact by contact, the credibility of a sample of 1,840 news sources on which they had relied recently, testing several generalizations suggested in the literature.

CREDIBILITY AND NEWSWORK

Although interest in source credibility is at least as ancient as Greek philosophy (Self, 1996), modern credibility studies only began to appear during the 1940s. The topic soon became one of the most widely studied concepts in communication (Rouner, 2008), with hundreds of published empirical studies (Metzger et al., 2003). Nevertheless, in the specific context of journalism, credibility studies remain scarce (Flynn, 2002; Tsfati, 2008).

Most research outside journalism, beginning with interest in propaganda (Rouner, 2008; Self, 1996), focuses on audiences as addressees of different speakers, writers, messages and media (Metzger et al., 2003; Rouner, 2008; Self, 1996). The applicability of this rich body of research to the specific context of journalism is probably limited.

In the specific context of journalism, credibility is perceived as having a "visceral nature," as "an assumption rather than a judgment to be made about a source [. . .] not a quality inherent in a source but instead . . . levied onto a source by the media" (Dunwoody and Ryan, 1987, p. 21). Categorizations of source credibility among journalists are based on cognitive biases (Stocking and Gross, 1989, cited by Self, p. 429) and their criteria are debated by journalists, academics (Tsfati, 2008, p. 2597) and other professionals (Salomone et al., 1990).

Critical approaches assert that "[. . .] it is style and presentation rather than truthful information which gives some sources more control over their messages. In this context, journalistic truth is but a by-product of familiarity and legitimacy" (Altheide, 1978, p. 375).

Source credibility is seen by its critics as a "higher order resource" of organizations and institutions, resulting "in part from other resources such as size, cohesion, knowledge, intensity of feeling and perhaps money or votes" (Goldenberg, 1975, p. 46).

Three main aspects of source credibility and journalism may be found in the literature: Structural, practical and contextual, each of which will be accompanied by a specific research question.

Structural Aspects

Common wisdom asserts that journalists rely heavily on credible (Manning, 2001) and familiar sources (Gans, 1979; Tuchman, 1978) and that familiarity and credibility are somehow associated (Altheide, 1978; Gans, 1979; Yoon, 2005). This association is consequential, because it may structure the actual mix of sources according to their "hierarchy of credibility" (Becker, 1970), resulting in a highly disputed discrimination of "news access" (Cottle, 2000; Goldenberg, 1975; Hall et al., 1978; Manning, 2001) in which "upper"-class sources receive regular coverage and whose "distrust must be earned" whereas "lower"-class sources, constantly deprived of coverage, are considered "illegitimate until proven innocent" (Altheide, 1978).

Against this backdrop, we may formalize the first research question:

RQ 1: To what extent do journalists consider their sources credible and rely on them regularly and how strong are the associations between regular use and credibility?

Practical Aspects

In its basic function, source credibility is a major criterion for source selection (Gans, 1979; Goldenberg, 1975; Manning, 2001) in a manner that "avoid[s] engaging in arduous investigations to find evidence for the trustworthiness of a specific source" (Jackob, 2008, p. 1045). According to this perspective, journalists apply source credibility as an efficiency measure: the more credible the source, the less strict the attendant production practices (Fishman, 1980; Gans, 1979). Strictness, in this case, refers to a set of journalistic practices, including cross checking, relying on additional sources (not necessarily for corroboration of previous information) and less anonymity in an attempt to delegate some responsibility to the attributed source (Allan, 1999). A fourth impact is the allocation of less item space for less credible sources—an inevitable result of using more sources and applying more cross checking. This association is valuable not only because it was not discovered in previous studies (Flynn, 2002; Yoon, 2005) but primarily because it may help translate an abstract and evasive act of news judgment, carried out on the go, into a measurable output, suggesting a second research question:

RQ 2: To what extent are less credible sources treated with stricter sourcing practices than others, namely fewer additional sources per item, less cross checking and less source anonymity?

As an efficiency measure, source credibility fits the constraints of journalism, in which reporters cannot afford to follow their doubts too far (Fishman, 1980; Gans, 1979; Tuchman, 1978). However, they cannot overextend their efficiency considerations either, as they are employees of brands that have to preserve their own credibility (Roshco, 1975; Schudson, 2003) and whose blunders, flaws, biases, and libels are published promptly and extensively under their own names (Tuchman, 1978; Reich, forthcoming). Hence source work may be perceived as a constant effort to avoid both a prohibitive workload of excessive distrust and reckless trust of unreliable sources.

Contextual Aspects

According to the literature, journalists' perception of source credibility is associated with various source traits, such as role (e.g., senior source or public relations practitioner), sector in society (e.g., political or private sector), resources and symbolic assets and even the communication channels through which information is obtained (Gitlin, 1980; Goldenberg, 1975; Reich 2009; Schlesinger, 1990). Apparently, the most trusted sources are public officials, especially senior ones (Fishman, 1980; Machin and Niblock, 2006; Sigal, 1986), followed by not-for-profit and academic sources and medical experts (Becker, 1970; Cottle, 2000; Detjen, 2000; Rouner, 2008; Yoon, 2005). Less credibility is ascribed to business sector sources, PR practitioners, politicians and ordinary citizens (Gans, 1979; Ericson, Baranek and Chan, 1989; Machin and Niblock, 2006).

Although reliance on other persons had become the dominant method for obtaining news (Sigal, 1986; Strömbäck and Nord, 2005), the most credible sources are probably none other than . . . journalists themselves when relying on their own eyewitness reports. This practice is not only more immune to bias, but is also perceived as professionally and ethically superior (Christopher, 1998; Russell, 1999; Zelizer, 1990), leading to the third research question:

RQ 3: To what extent is credibility associated with certain source characteristics: roles, sectors in society and the channels through which they are communicated?

Methodology

The present study elicits the role played by source credibility in shaping the public news diet using face-to-face reconstruction interviews. This method allows for contact-by-contact testing of the credibility assigned to a given sample of sources by a specific group of reporters who relied on them recently. It enables coverage of a representative sample of news items that were subsequently published or aired, based on detailed testimonies of the reporters who authored them.

The reconstruction interview method proved its ability to identify the contributions of different entities to the published news (Bustos, 2008; Reich 2006, 2009) and was adopted here because of the shortcomings of traditional methods in the context of credibility research.

Theoretically, contextual examination of source credibility judgment could be achieved by newsroom observations, some of which contributed the most substantial insights (Altheide, 1978; Domingo and Paterson, 2008; Gans, 1979; Gitlin, 1980; Tuchman, 1978). Source credibility, however, is hardly observable because it is of an abstract, evasive and fragmented nature, spread across different locations inside and outside newsrooms and across different official and unofficial channels of communication. Furthermore, observations do not allow any quantitative measurement of different levels of source credibility.

The experiments used in early studies and the interviews conducted in more recent ones (Tsfati, 2008) tend to decontextualize source credibility judgment, focusing on generic and faceless news sources. Some studies used content analysis either exclusively or as a complementary method (Flynn, 2002; Stempel and Culberstone, 1984). Although content analysis effectively indicates measures of source acceptance such as accessibility, prominence, dominance and valence, it is highly speculative in its association with source credibility, as news products rarely bear unequivocal traces of news processes (Manning, 2001, p. 48) such as credibility judgment.

Three steps precede the reconstruction interviews used in this study:

1. *Random selection of beats and reporters*: Ten parallel print press, online and radio news beats were chosen randomly from each of the nine leading Israeli national news organizations.[1] The final selection included 80 reporters from three clusters of beats: Politics and security, domestic affairs and business affairs, proportional to their overall share of reporting personnel. The majority (70%) were men, their mean age was 36 (sd=10.44, 12 did not answer) and they had a little more than 13 years of journalistic experience (sd=10.56, 5 did not answer). Fourteen reporters were replaced with others from their cluster after refusing to participate or having published fewer items than the specified minimum. The market reaches of the specific organizations at the time of research were as follows: **Print:** *Yedioth Aharonoth* (40% of readership), *Ma'ariv* (20%), *Haaretz* (6%); **Online:** *Ynet* (44%), *nrg* (23%), *Haaretz online* (12%);

Radio: *Kol Israel* (46%) *Galey Zahal* (44%) and *Channel 10* Radio (unspecified).[2]

2. *Identification of all published items*: The sampling period extended over four weeks, reflecting the attempt to achieve a fair balance between variety of stories and use of material still fresh in reporters' memories. News websites were visited four times a day.[3]

3. *Random sampling of news items*: Ten items per reporter were selected randomly, providing a sample large enough to allay any concern that stories could be matched to their descriptions but not so large as to tax reporters' focus and patience.

Further measures to maintain source confidentiality included asking reporters to describe how they obtained each of their sampled items, using general categories such as senior source or political sector, without revealing any specific details about them, as well as the seating arrangements, with reporter (with a pile of sampled stories) and interviewer (with a pile of coding sheets) sitting on opposite sides of a table with a screen between them.

Reconstruction interviews were conducted during the month following the sampling period, each lasting a duration of approximately 90 minutes. Although nearly all interviewees cooperated, the goal of deciphering 300 items per medium was not entirely achieved because of structural constraints applying to the organizations studied, such as insufficient number of business items for one of the radio stations and the need to avoid double-length interviews of *Haaretz* reporters who work for both print and online media.

Obviously, reconstruction interviews are not completely free of weaknesses, the most prominent of which are the self-reports, that are subject to biases and the limits of recollection. Furthermore, this method is blind towards items and sources that were eventually dismissed during the selection phase, which were beyond the scope of the present study. Overall however, reconstruction interviews are probably less biased than traditional methods, primarily because reporters provided testimony anchored in a sample of specific sources and items and were asked to reconstruct specific actions and categorizations rather than to evaluate their own conduct.

FINDINGS

Data elucidate how journalists use source credibility as a working tool in a (reconstructed) real-life context in which specific sources exchange specific information under specific circumstances. Furthermore, the study exploits the current method to detect associations between credibility and other source characteristics and to investigate whether information provided by more or less credible sources is treated differently in terms of news practices and routines.

All in all, the study analyzed the perceived credibility and journalistic treatment of 1840 news sources involved in a sample of 840 news items, based on face-to-face reconstruction interviews with the reporters who relied on them. I will begin with findings concerning the structural impact of source credibility, addressed in the first research question, that shape not only specific news items but also entire journalistic subfields and their news source hierarchies. These will be followed by findings pertaining to the second research question, showing how journalists actually treat more credible versus less credible sources. Subsequently I will outline the characteristics of more and less credible news sources, addressed by the third research question.

Structural Aspects

Although credibility is first and foremost a micro-level mechanism that shapes news items, it has substantial mid-level and even macro-level ramifications, as in the long run, more credibility entails more regular news access while less credibility may imply reduced access, as evidenced by overall credibility of news sources and the regularity of reliance on them.

Of the 1,840 news sources in the sample, 48% were ranked by the reporters as highly credible and 41% as credible. Only about 10% of the sources on which the published material relied were perceived as fairly credible at most. The regularity with which these sources are relied on is presented in Table 1.1:

Table 1.1   Source Credibility and Regularity of Contact between Parties

Regularity of Contact				
On a daily basis	On a monthly/ weekly basis	Several previous contacts	First in this item	Source credibility
473	896	293	166	N
2%	3%	4%	5%	Not very credible or less[a]
7%	11%	12%	13%	Fairly credible
35%	42%	44%	48%	Credible
56%	44%	40%	34%	Highly credible
100%	100%	100%	100%	Total

Notes: The correlation between credibility and regularity was significant (Spearman's $r=0.145$; $p=0.000$).

[a] including the category *not credible at all*

These findings suggest that there is an association between credibility and regularity that is most clearly evident in the line of highly credible sources. The linear rise in credibility according to intensity of contact demonstrates that credibility plays a role in shaping news access gaps between the highly covered and the deprived. It exposes the logic of credibility judgment, along with several of its weaknesses: Journalists do not hesitate to judge the credibility of their sources even when contacted for the first time regarding a given item, ranking many of them as highly credible (although less credible than older contacts).

While one may speculate whether regularity is being transformed into credibility or vice versa, it is clear that the strategic coupling of the two embodies one of the basic journalistic methods for news gathering: Covering new stories by relying on old sources perceived as credible or highly credible.

Practical Aspects

To test the second research question regarding actual treatment of sources in line with their credibility, news items were grouped into four clusters according to the weakest link (in terms of credibility), as displayed in Table 1.2. While the upper line includes no sources perceived as less than perfectly credible, the bottom line includes at least one classified as "not very credible" or "not credible at all." Table 1.2 shows the extent to which the items in each group were cross-checked and accompanied by additional news sources (that obviously exhibit some partial overlap).

Table 1.2   Sourcing Patterns According to the Weakest Link (in terms of credibility)

Clusters of items according to the weakest link	News items		Sourcing patterns	
	#	%	% of cross checking	No. sources per item
All sources are highly credible	284	34	32	2.06
At least one source credible	352	42	49	2.62
At least one source fairly credible	144	17	59	3.12
At least one not very credible or less[a]	50	6	66	3.26
Total	830	100	46%	2.56

Notes: Correlation was significant between credibility and cross checking (Spearman's $r=0.226$, $p=0.000$) and between credibility and source number (Spearman's $r=0.296$, $p=0.000$).

[a] including the category *not credible at all*

Data show that source credibility is not just a matter of theoretical skepticism but rather a practical mechanism translated by journalists into real actions to verify or refute certain source versions or at least minimize dependency on their assertions: the less credible the sources, the more cross checking they face and the more additional sources will be employed. Cross checking and number of sources per item rise inversely to source credibility, with two interesting nuances: even when all sources are highly credible, each third item is still cross checked and even when sources are perceived as having the least credibility, a third of the items are not cross checked at all. The logic behind the latter phenomenon may derive from another practice employed by reporters to protect themselves from less credible sources: clear identification of the source in the final item. While in the three upper degrees of credibility only 28% of the sources are identified, in the lower echelon of credibility, where sources are classified as "not very credible" or "not credible at all," the percentage rises to 39. The difference between the three upper degrees of credibility grouped together and the non-credible sources was significant ($t_{1819}=1.933$; $p=0.053$).

The inevitable result of more sources and more cross checking is less news space for the less credible, as shown in Figure 1.1.

The correlation between credibility and item space was small but significant (Spearman's $r=0.136$; $p=0.000$). One finding that was somewhat less expected, however, shows that reporters grant substantial space even to less credible sources (although less than they allocate to credible ones) and to those perceived as not credible at all, probably because at times, newspeople cannot be too choosy.

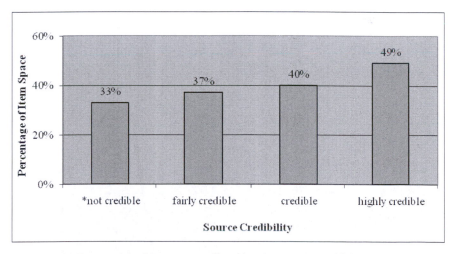

Figure 1.1   Percentage of item space allocation by source credibility.
* including the categories *not very credible* and *not credible at all.*

While percentages of space were estimated, the figures are probably more reliable than those originating in lay-persons' assessments, as journalists have to estimate word counts on a daily basis and calculations were conducted meticulously with the respective items in front of the reporters' eyes.

Contextual Aspects

To address Research Question 3, data will be presented according to the roles of news sources, their affiliation with certain sectors in society and the channels of communication through which they are contacted. Table 1.3 presents the different types of sources and the extent to which each was ranked as highly credible.

If we ignore the category "other," a mélange of miscellaneous sources, the most credible are the reporters themselves when employing their own eyewitness reports. Post hoc comparisons show that reporters' observations are perceived as more credible than any other human source (p<0.014). Despite its high credibility, however, firsthand witnessing is used in only 6% of coverage, while other human agents account for 92% of journalists' work—despite their relatively limited credibility. Senior sources are perceived as more credible than PR practitioners (p=0.002), as described in the literature (Becker, 1970; Cohen, 1963), although they maintained no credibility advantage relative to sources with less seniority. Even the inferior credibility ascribed to PR practitioners (Aronoff, 1975; Jeffers, 1977) is evident chiefly when compared with that of senior sources.

Table 1.3   Who are the Most Credible Sources?

Source Type	#	# of contacts ranked as highly credible
Senior sources [a]	536	47%
Non senior	461	44%
Spokespersons and PR	687	39%
Reporter's Observation	51	80%
Other [b]	100	78%
Total	1835	46%

Notes: The overall difference between source groups was significant. $(F_{(4,1830)}=14.453; p=0.000)$.

[a] Heads of agencies and corporations, chairmen of parliamentary committees, party and faction leaders, high-ranking officers in the army (colonel +) and police (deputy commissioner+), mayors and their deputies.

[b] Other: Media publications, newsroom updates, documents and archive.

Communication channels play a role in the credibility game as well. The overall difference among channel groups was significant ($F_{(3,1846)}$=3.343; p=0.019), although the advantage seems to rest with written materials only (typically public relations supplies, press releases, documents, e-mails, Web searches etc.) over the oral channels of telephony (p=0.029): While the oral channels scored only 44% of highly credible contacts, textual channels scored no less than 3%. These written materials are often source-initiated, but are perceived as more credible, probably because texts are less deniable than oral utterances.

Table 1.4 presents the extent to which different sectors in society are perceived as credible.

Again ignoring the "other" category, the only significant difference is between political sources and their inferior credibility compared with government (p=0.006) and public sector sources (p=0.0025). Differences between private persons and other sectors were not significant. The data do not support the assumption that journalists consider government and public sector sources more credible than those in the private sector. Distrust of political sources conforms with journalistic cynicism towards politics found by several scholars (Cappella and Jamieson, 1997; Schudson, 1999).

DISCUSSION

It is tempting to explain the overwhelmingly high perceived credibility findings as pure journalistic bias. After all, overestimating one's sources' credibility—especially after relying on them—avoids the cognitive dissonance of admitting reliance on less than perfectly credible sources. Furthermore,

Table 1.4   Highly Credible Sources, by Sectors in Society

Sector in society	#	% of sources ranked as highly credible
Government	911	46%
Political	105	31%
Public	296	47%
Private sector	293	42%
Private person	111	38%
Other[a]	96	75%
Total	1812	46%

Notes: Overall difference between groups was significant ($F_{(5,1806)}$=6.366; p=0.000).

[a] Other: Messages published by other media, academic sources, PR sources, information from the Web.

current trends in communication studies acknowledge the perceived and biased nature of credibility (Jackob, 2008; Rouner, 2008; Self, 1996; Tsfati, 2008; Yoon, 2005), as do journalism studies (Salomone et al., 1990; Stocking and Gross, 1989; Tsfati, 2008).

It should be indicated, however, that sources whose versions were subsequently published, such as the ones studied here, are naturally perceived as more reliable because those considered less reliable were dismissed during the selection stage. Furthermore, credibility judgment plays a more intensive, crucial and evidence-based role for journalists than it does for laypersons, considering the realities of news-making, the journalists' added motivation to protect themselves from erroneous publication and the "credibility literacy" they accumulate in years of daily feedback from their audiences and competitors regarding right and wrong choices of sources.

Do routine sources acquire an aura of credibility or do credible sources attract more routine reliance? Though the direction of causality remains unclear, the latter possibility enjoys greater support in the literature, as Yoon (2005, p. 295) notes: "Journalists regularize interactions with sources they view as credible." But even if the causality was in the opposite direction, source credibility would still play a key role as constant justification for journalists' decision making, especially regarding regular sources that enjoy generous space allocation, probably because journalists lack more robust criteria for source selection or more solid evidence regarding their versions, considering the numerous constraints of time, access, energy, attention, routine and epistemology (Ekström, 2002; Gans, 1978; Manning, 2001; Reich, 2009).

Findings suggest that source credibility judgment is more complex than a straightforward summation of the truth-telling track record of a particular news source. This complexity is evident when reporters allocate substantial news holes even to news sources they do not trust or avoid cross-checking items in which one source or more was ranked with the lowest degree of credibility; it is also reflected in their cross checking of items whose sources were ranked at the highest level of credibility and in their willingness to judge the credibility of news sources even when contacted for the first time. These peculiarities indicate that reporters go beyond source credibility in determining how far to go in protecting themselves against erroneous publication.

My findings indicate that sources perceived as highly credible may be relied on only rarely and vice versa. For example, reporters' firsthand witnessing is hardly used despite the high credibility of the information it may yield, while spokespersons are widely used despite their (marginally) lower credibility. As Gans suggested, credibility and other major source selection criteria are subordinated to the supreme consideration of efficiency (Gans, 1979).

No evidence was found for any substantial advantage of senior sources or disadvantage of spokespersons and PR practitioners insofar as perceived credibility is concerned. This observation calls for a thorough reexamination of the previous and current findings, as well as the common wisdom regarding these two prominent news actors. One possible explanation maintains that personal acquaintance between journalists and public relations practitioners, that applies to specific practitioners in the present study as well, changes the perceptions of each regarding the other's capabilities, ethics and general performance (Jeffers, 1977).

CONCLUSION

The study proposes a new point of view for studying source credibility as actually implemented by journalists in a real-life reconstructed context in which journalists obtained specific information from concrete personae.

According to the findings, journalists employ four interrelated strategies to minimize their exposure to erroneous publications, extending throughout the news process from pre-item stage to final presentation.

1. *A Priori "Typecasting"*: Using this most influential and controversial strategy, long before a specific item comes into being, reporters surround themselves with a tight ring of credible or highly credible sources, most of which are regulars. This "typecasting," observed among the structural aspects, may construct entire news fields, rendering journalism an occupation that covers the new primarily by relying on the old. The strategic coupling between highly credible sources and intensive reliance on them, as well as the magnitude and consistency of its implementation, can refuel the long-standing, heated debate on the role of credibility as an apparatus of discrimination. Even if not seen as a hegemonic conspiracy, preference of the same highly credible sources over time offers superior news access to resource-rich sources that are better positioned to buy their entrance tickets to the news arena and an extremely dismissive attitude towards new faces and alternative voices (Gans, 1978; Schlesinger, 1990).

2. *Practical Skepticism*: The second strategy, which uses cross verifications and additional sources in inverse proportion to perceived source credibility, as noted in the practical aspects takes place during the newsgathering phase. The lion's share accorded to credible and highly credible sources, using Strategy 1, helps reporters reduce the number of "problematic" sources—who require additional and expensive journalistic treatment, such as triangulation of their versions with a third party—to tolerable proportions.

3. *Prominent Presentation*: Reporters and their editors allocate more news space to sources perceived as credible. Although final space allocation is determined at the presentation stage, more space often requires more raw materials that must be obtained in advance. According prominence and dominance to the more credible is somewhat expected but not obvious, as previous studies did not find evidence for

an association between credibility and news hole (Flynn, 2002; Stempel and Culbertson, 1984; Yoon, 2005). The principal contribution of the correlation between credibility and volume, however, is its ability to transform a highly evasive and abstract act of credibility judgment into a measurable indication.

4. *Distancing by Attribution*: According to the fourth strategy, employed during the presentation stage, less credible sources are better identified and attributed explicitly in published items, as an attempt to distance the journalists from potentially dubious source versions.

This set of strategies appears to be a relatively perfect shield against erroneous publications, contrary to the "visceral" perceptions of source credibility judgment (Altheide, 1978; Dunwoody and Ryan, 1987; Goldenberg, 1975; Stocking and Gross, 1989), cited by Self (1996, p. 429). The current study however, exposes four deep fissures in that shield, embodying imperfections in the actual implementation of source credibility judgment and in its accompanying practices:

First, interviewees did not hesitate to judge the credibility of nearly 10% of their sources, even though they were contacted for the first time regarding the respective items and had no previously established record of believability (although they were perceived as relatively less credible).

Second, according to their testimonies, reporters and their editors allocated considerable (but still relatively little) space to source versions ranked as least credible.

Third, reporters cross checked about a third of their items, even though their own accounts indicate that the items involved only sources with the highest degree of credibility.

And fourth—and most hazardous of all—reporters avoided cross checking another third of their items, although these involved at least one source which was ranked among the least credible degrees.

Some of these fissures, especially the latter two, suggest that journalists probably employ yet another set of credibility considerations that is beyond the scope of the current study. These considerations may address the nature of the raw information itself and its perceived credibility, controversial quality and potential risk for their own reputation or that of their news organizations.

Using these strategies, reporters maneuver between excess suspicion that could swamp them with arduous verifications and excess trust that could expose them to an endless series of libel suits, job loss, retractions, corrections and denials—both of which could have paralyzed the news industry as we know it.

According to the data, reliance on sources, the dominant method for obtaining news, involves an occupational compromise, unlike reporters' firsthand witnessing that is rarely used nonetheless, probably because journalists weigh the gain in credibility against loss of time and other resources.

Findings show also that hierarchies of credibility are flatter than accepted wisdom would dictate: Senior sources have only a modest credibility advantage over PR practitioners, although political sources are perceived as substantially less credible than those in other sectors in society. Moreover, textual communication is perceived as more credible than oral.

This study uses the Israeli case to answer key universal questions regarding source credibility and journalism. Nevertheless, the representativeness of the current findings requires further study in other cultural contexts. Until further study is conducted, readers should bear in mind that the Western objective-neutral model is dominant among Israeli journalists (Meyers, Peri, and Tsfati 2006) and that Israeli national news organizations are small, centralized and characterized as free, commercial and highly competitive. Trust in sources is a central value among Israeli reporters no less than among their Western counterparts (Tsfati, 2004) and both US and Israeli journalists agree that checking the credibility of information prior to publication is the most important journalistic value (Arian et al., 2005).

Further research should focus on the blind spots of this study which focused on recollected sources whose output was eventually published. A complementary 'waste basket' study emphasizing the perceived credibility of sources for items dismissed in the gatekeeping process, is required to detect the contribution of credibility to the decision not to rely on certain sources. This is particularly important if we assume that the wastebasket contains a source mix different from those that make it to publication, with extra weight accorded to new, alternative and resource-poor sources (Gitlin, 1980; Goldenberg, 1975). Other studies should examine whether journalists distinguish between source credibility and information credibility, and if so, how they are implemented in concert and contribute to news processes and news products.

ACKNOWLEDGMENTS

This research was supported by a grant from the Israel Foundations Trustees (2006–2008). The author thanks Sharon Ben-David, Oz Carmel, Alex Nirenburg and Dror Walter for their help in compiling the data, Dr. Yariv Tsfati for his most beneficial remarks and Tali Avishay-Arbel for her statistical advice.

NOTES

1. The criteria for choosing the organizations were as follows: 1. National news organizations. 2. Market leaders. 3. Employers of dedicated reporting staffs. Beats were selected from the full lists of reporters, prepared by following the reporters' bylines over a three-month period, using the following criteria: (a) Mainstream beats in each of the nine news organizations. (b) Output

published primarily in news and business sections. (c) Covered by full-time reporters. (d) Reporters who publish at least 12 items per month. The fourth medium, television, was omitted to avoid overextending the scope of an already amply broad study and to eliminate the production and visual biases that television embodies (Bantz, McCorkle,and Baade 1980; García Avilés et al. 2004; Hemingway, 2008).

2. *Globes*, October 30, 2006, July 19, 2006; *The Marker*, August 8, 2006.
3. Following the suggestion of *The State of the News Media* (2006). Available http://www.stateofthenewsmedia.com/2006/narrative_online_content-analysis.asp?cat=2&media=4. Accessed 28, July, 2009.

REFERENCES

Allan, Stuart (1999) *News Culture,* Buckingham, UK: Open University Press.
Altheide, David L. (1978) "Newsworkers and newsmakers: A study in news use," *Urban Life* 7: pp. 359–378.
Arian, Asher, Ben Nun, Pazit, Barnea, Shlomit, and Tsfati, Yariv (2005) *The Media and Israeli Democracy from Various Vantage Points,* Jerusalem: Israeli Democratic Institute Press. Avaible:http://www.idi.org.il/sites/english/PublicationsCatalog/Pages/The_Media_and_Israeli_Society_From_Various_Vantage_Points/Publications_Catalog_7765.aspx.
Aronoff, Craig, E. (1975) "Credibility of public relations for journalists," *Public Relations Review* 2(4): pp. 43–57.
Aviles, Jose Alberto Garcia, Bienvenido, Leon, Sanders, Karen, and Harrison, Jackie (2004) "Journalists at digital television newsrooms in Britain and Spain: Workflow and multi-skilling in a competitive environment," *Journalism Studies* 5(1): pp.87–100.
Bantz, Charles R., McCorkle, Suzanne, and Baade, Roberta C. (1980) "The news factory," *Communication Research* 7(1): pp.45–68.
Becker, Howard S. (1970) "Whose side are we on?," in Jack D. Douglas (Ed) *The Relevance of Sociology,* NY: Meredith Corporation, pp. 99–111.
Bustos, Andrea (2008) "Practices and Routines of Chilean Journalists," Unpublished M.A. thesis, submitted at Department of Communication Studies, Ben Gurion University.
Cappella, Joseph, N. and Jamieson, Kathleen, H. (1997) *Spiral of Cynicism,* New York: Oxford University Press.
Christopher, Carol L. (1998) "Technology and Journalism in the Electronic Newsroom," in Diane L. Borden and Harvey Kerric (Eds) *The Electronic Grapevine,* Mahwah, NJ: Lawrence Erlbaum Associates, pp. 123–139.
Cohen, Bernard C. (1963) *The Press & Foreign Policy,* Princeton NJ: Princeton University Press.
Cottle, Simon (2000) "Rethinking news access," *Journalism Studies* (3)1, pp.427–448.
Detjen, Jim, Fico, Fred, Li, Xigen, and Yeonshim, Kim (2000) "Changing work environment of environmental reporters," *Newspaper Research Journal* 21(1): pp.2–12.
Domingo, David and Paterson, Chris (2008) *Making Online News. The ethnography of New Media Production,* New York: Peter Lang.
Dunwoody, Sharon and Ryan, Michael (1987) "The credible scientific source," *Journalism Quarterly* 64: pp.21–27.
Ekström, Mats (2002). "Epistemologies of TV Journalism: A Theoretical Framework," *Journalism* 3(3): pp. 259–282.

Ericson, Richard V., Baranek, Patricia M., and Chan, Janet B. L. (1989) *Negotiating Control: A Study of News Sources,* Toronto: University of Toronto Press.

Fishman, Mark (1980) *Manufacturing the News,* Austin: University of Texas Press.

Flynn, Terence (2002) "Source Credibility and Global Warming: A Content Analysis of Environmental Groups," Paper presented at the annual meeting of Association for Education in Journalism and Mass Communication (AEJMC), August 2002, Miami, FL.

Gans, Herbert J. (1979) *Deciding What's News,* NY: Pantheon Books.

Gaziano, Cecilie and McGrath, Kristin (1986) "Measuring the concept of credibility," *Journalism Quarterly* 63: pp. 451–462.

Gitlin, Todd (1980) *The Whole World is Watching,* Berkeley: University of California Press.

Goldenberg, Edie (1975) *Making the Papers,* Lexington, MA: D. C. Heath.

Hall, Stuart, Critcher, Charles, Jefferson, Tony, Clarke, John, and Roberts, Brian (1978) *Policing the Crisis,* London: Macmillan.

Hemmingway, Emma (2008) *Into the Newsroom: Exploring the Digital Production of Regional Television News,* London: Routledge.

Jackob, Nikolaus (2008) "Credibility effects," in Wolfgang Donsbach (Ed) *The International Encyclopedia of Communication,* Oxford, UK: Blackwell, pp. 1044–1047.

Jeffers, Dennis W. (1977) "Performance expectations as a measure of relative status of news and PR people," *Journalism Quarterly* 54(2): pp. 299–306.

Johnson, Thomas J. and Kaya, Barbara K. (2000) "Using is believing: The influence of reliance on credibility of online political information," *Journalism and Mass Communication Quarterly* 77(4): pp. 865–879.

Machin, David, and Niblock, Sarah (2006) *News Production: Theory and Practice,* Abingdon: Routledge.

Manning, Paul (2001) *News and News Sources: A Critical Introduction,* London: Sage.

Metzger, Miriam J., Flanagin, Andrew J., Eyal, K., and Lemus, R. M. (2003) "Credibility for the 21st century: Integrating perspectives on source, message, and media credibility in the contemporary media environment," *Communication Yearbook* 27: pp. 293–335.

Meyers, Oren, Peri, Yoram, and Tsfati, Yariv (2006) "What is good journalism? Comparing Israeli public and journalists' perceptions," *Journalism* 7(2): pp. 153–174.

Powers, Angela and Fico, Fredrick (1994) "Influences on use of sources at large U.S. newspapers," *Newspaper Research Journal* 15(4): pp.87–97.

Reich, Zvi (2006) "The process model of news initiative: Sources lead first, reporters thereafter," *Journalism Studies* 7(4): pp. 497–514.

Reich, Zvi. (2009) *Sourcing the News*: key issues in journalism: an innovative study of the Israeli press, Cresskill, NJ: Hampton Press.

Reich, Zvi (forthcoming) "Constrained authors: Bylines and authorship in news reporting," *Journalism.*

Roshcho, Bernard (1975) *Newsmaking,* Chicago: University of Chicago Press.

Rouner, Donna (2008) "Credibility of content" in Wolfgang Donsbach (Ed) *The International Encyclopedia of Communication,* Oxford, UK: Blackwell, pp. 1039–1044.

Rouner, Donnna, Slater, Michael D., and Buddenbaum, Judith M. (1999) "How perceptions of news bias in news sources relate to beliefs about media bias," *Newspaper Research Journal* 20(2): pp. 41–51.

Russell, Frank (1999) "You had to be there (and they weren't): the problem with reporter reconstructions," *Journal of Mass Media Ethics* 14(3): pp. 146–158.

Salomone, Kandice L., Greenberg, Michael R., Sandman, Peter M., and Sachsman, David B. (1990) "A question quality: How journalists and news sources evaluate coverage of environmental risks," *Journal of Communication* 40(4): pp. 117–131.

Schlesinger, Philip (1990) "Rethinking the sociology of journalism: Source strategies and the limit of media-centrism" in Margjorie Ferguson (Ed) Public *Communication: The New Imperatives,* London: Sage.

Schudson, Michael (1999) "Social origins of press cynicism in portraying Politics," *American Behavioral Scientist* 42(6): pp. 998–1008.

Schudson, Michael (2001) "The objectivity norm in American journalism," *Journalism* 2(2): pp.149–170.

Schudson, Michael (2003) *The Sociology of News,* New York: W. W. Norton.

Self, Charles C. (1996) "Credibility," in Michael B. Salwen and Don W. Stacks (Eds) *An Integrated Approach to Communication Theory and Research,* Mahwah, NJ: Lawrence Erlbaum Associates, pp. 435–457.

Sigal, Leon V. (1986) "Sources make the news," in Robert Karl Manoff and Michael Schudson (Eds) *Reading the News,* NY: Pantheon, pp.9–37.

Stempel, Guido, III, and Culbertson, Hugh (1984) "The prominence and dominance of news sources in newspaper medical coverage," *Journalism Quarterly* 61(3): pp. 671–676.

Stocking, S. Holly and Gross, Paget H. (1989) *How Do Journalists Think: A Proposal for the Study of Cognitive Bias in Newsmaking,* Bloomington, IN: Smith Research Center. Indiana University.

Stromback, Jesper J. and Nord, Lars W. (2005) "Who Leads the Tango? A Study of the Relationship between Swedish Journalists and their Political Source," Paper presented to the Political Communication Division, International Communication Association, New York.

Tsfati, Yariv (2004) "Exploring possible correlations of journalists' perceptions of audience trust," *Journalism and Mass Communication* 81(2): pp. 274–291.

Tsfati, Yariv (2008) "Journalists, credibility of," in Donsbach, Wolfgang (Ed) *The International Encyclopedia of Communication,* Oxford, UK: Blackwell, pp. 2597–2600.

Tuchman, Gaye (1978) *Making News,* New York: Free Press.

Wanta, Wayne and Hu, Yu-Wei (1994) "The effects of credibility, reliance, and exposure on media agenda-setting: A path analysis model," *Journalism Quarterly* 71(1): pp. 90–98.

Yoon, Youngmin (2005) "Examining journalists' Perceptions and news coverage of stem cell and cloning organizations," *Journalism and Mass Communication Quarterly* 82(2): pp. 281–300.

Zelizer, Barbie (1990) "Where is the author in American TV news? On the construction and presentation of proximity, authorship, and journalistic authority," *Semiotica* 80: pp. 37–48.

2   Whither Anonymity?

Journalism and Unnamed Sources in a Changing Media Environment

Matt Carlson

INTRODUCTION

The relationship between journalists and their sources has been a cornerstone of journalism research, yet less attention has been focused on the special case of unnamed sources in which journalists promise sources anonymity in exchange for information. Within the literature on sourcing, the dearth of attention to such arrangements has led to a blind spot not only in our understanding of news sources, but of journalism more broadly. How journalists pursue—and are pursued by—unnamed sources, the reporting that results, and challenges to this practice matter given the pervasive use of unnamed sources to dispense incompletely attributed information to the public. In assuming a particular professional position, journalists justify their need for special rights to protect source confidentiality by invoking a normative argument that encompasses the public interest while passing along rights to themselves and their sources. However, this practice also creates stress between journalists and their audiences by masking unseen alliances and hidden source motives. What emerges is a view of unnamed sources as complex and contradictory. That unnamed sources both assist and impede the ability of the public to know what is happening in its major institutions is evident in the journalistic triumphs and humiliations that result.

Our attention turns to unnamed sources at the moment of their entrenchment, but also a moment when their very viability in news discourse is being rightfully questioned outside the academy among journalists and other commentators. With many voices asking if we would be better off without unnamed sources, both the practice of source anonymity and the shape of the discourse around it deserve attention and reflection. Our concern is not simply with the presence or absence of unnamed sources, but the ideological assumptions underpinning the defense of and assault against this style of news. That is, how is anonymity being talked about and, in the process, what does this tell us about journalism? This chapter explores issues around unnamed sources and how such arrangements fit with the future of journalism given the present moment of upheaval and uncertainty.

NAMED AND UNNAMED SOURCES

Interest in the relationship between journalists and their sources has long been central in journalism research (Carlson, 2009a). Whether seen as combative or overly snug, critics have rightfully raised alarm due to the enormous power bestowed on those who speak through the news. Patterns of sourcing matter because they confer visibility and voice. News sources define not only what's worth knowing, but who is worth listening to. Yet regardless of the iteration of the journalist-source power dynamic, journalists are not blind to the motivations of their sources. Reporters harbor varying levels of trust in what their sources tell them but find these fears somewhat offset through standard attribution. Pragmatically, the patterned use of named sources yields routinized workflows allowing journalists to accomplish their assignments efficiently and reliably. Epistemologically, standard attribution clearly locates the origin of information and statements of opinion with non-journalists, which provides reporters with a strategy to present an account of the world while remaining within the self-imposed confines of the objectivity paradigm.

Yet what happens when the cushion of full attribution gives way to the veil of source anonymity? While certainly part of sourcing in a general sense, on closer examination unnamed sources differ substantively from their more common, fully attributed siblings (Carlson, 2011). They require careful analysis to identify the unique set of conditions connected to their use. To be clear, this chapter pertains to unnamed sources that make anonymity a condition under which they pass along information, whether this is an unattributable quote, unquotable background information, or a confidential document. It differs from conventional sourcing by shifting the mode of publicity from the source's identity to the content of the source's disclosure. In this shift we begin to recognize differences separating conventional from unnamed sources—and with it the inveterate problems plaguing the practice.

Unnamed sources vary from conventional practices in three key ways. First, the absence of identification entails a lack of transparency into newsgathering practices. Information—quoted or not—appears without a name, with only a vague identifier signaling the category of the unnamed source (e.g., "senior White House official") and perhaps a fuzzy—and often circular—explanation of why anonymity was granted (e.g., "spoke on condition of anonymity because he was not authorized to discuss the issue publicly" (Sang-Hun, 2009). This relates to a second difference—the assumption of extra responsibility when reproducing statements made by unnamed sources. Conventional sourcing practices allow journalists to deflect blame back to their sources when reporting comes under fire (Tuchman, 1972). Without this safety valve, journalists not only take on more responsibility for the material they use, but also become susceptible to scrutiny over what may or may not have occurred out-of-sight. Allegations easily bloom in the absence of dissuasive evidence, a topic discussed below.

A final difference pertains to the explicit agency journalists assume when granting anonymity to a source. With conventional sourcing, journalists retreat to the background by foregrounding source statements, often relayed through direct quotes or recordings. This is a strategic move, since journalists seek to downplay their authorship in order to support the metaphor of their work as holding up a mirror to events (Epstein, 1973). This self-conception locates meaning in already existing reality with journalists serving only as assemblers. By contrast, journalists deploying unnamed sources signal their active role as participants creating stories and negotiating with sources. Without quoted, on-the-record sources to hide behind, journalists encounter discord with the image of the passive reporter maintaining objectivity while collecting information for her stories. Such a shift often occurs hand-in-hand with investigative journalism modes of news (Ettema and Glasser, 1998).

Cumulatively, these divergences from standard attribution give rise to the heightened need for trust accompanying hidden news practices (Boeyink 1990). The public, confronted with a news text even more incomplete than usual, is left with little recourse to adjudicate or verify claims.

THE ASSAULT ON UNNAMED SOURCES

While conventional sources may be readily counted and categorized, unnamed sources are more difficult to examine from the traces that end up in the news. Studying this practice is further complicated by the reluctance of sources or reporters to speak about their covert relations. However, moments of controversy do allow for a public glimpse into the practices of source anonymity. At the same time, controversies involving unnamed sources become opportunities for public reflection and criticism about not only sourcing practices, but the fundamental operation and role of journalism.

One way of sorting out criticisms levied at the use of unnamed sources is to consider two separate but related levels of analysis: grounded examples of their misuse and the normative assumptions justifying their application. At the level of practice, journalists have repeatedly found themselves apologizing for and cleaning up after controversies involving some aspect of journalist-unnamed source relations. The *New York Times*, the unofficial flagship of US journalism, provides some recent examples illustrating how thorny source anonymity can be, including misinformed accusations of nuclear scientist Wen Ho Lee (Scheer, 2000) and the fabrications of Jayson Blair (Mnookin, 2005). Of the latter, the trade journal *Editor & Publisher* shifted blame from the individualized malfeasance of Blair to an organizational inability to police unnamed source use: "the *Times* has developed an addictive tolerance for anonymous sources, the crack cocaine of journalism" (*Editor & Publisher*, 2003). The prescience of this editorial could only be fully realized months later with the unraveling of the newspaper's unfounded reports of Iraq's weapons of mass destruction (Wheeler, 2007). Claims of an imaginary arsenal were hardly unique to the *Times*, but its front-page exposés received much attention in the debate over war before the March 2003 invasion of Iraq and in the aftermath of reconstructing how it had gone so wrong. More than a year after the invasion, editor Bill Keller blamed reporting failures on a newsroom-wide blindness brought on by competitive pressures (Keller, 2004). The quest for scoops made the newspaper susceptible to anonymously supplied claims by administration officials that unduly corroborated public statements. This created an echo chamber turning speculation into solid fact through sheer repetition. How the *Times*'s prewar reporting laundered faulty intelligence claims while stifling antiwar discourse demonstrates the chilling consequences when unnamed sources work against the public interest. What makes the situation worse is our blindness to unnamed source-based reporting failures until long after their damage has been done.

This is not to ignore positive reporting made possible through unnamed sources. A year after apologizing for its prewar errors, the *Times* broke the story of the US government's massive program of wiretapping citizens within its borders without warrants (Risen and Lichtblau, 2005). The front-page article informed readers that "Nearly a dozen current and former officials, who were granted anonymity because of the classified nature of the program," came forward "because of their concerns about the operation's legality and oversight" (p. A1). By exposing covert government actions, the reporting encouraged public debate over tensions between security and privacy, the limits of state power, and surveillance uses of communication technologies. While many on the right balked at the disclosure of an ongoing secret program, the reporters received professional acclaim, including a Pulitzer Prize. Such extremes demonstrate the complexity of unnamed sources and the variations of their usage. There are times when their use should be applauded and times when it should be scorned.

What makes separating unnamed wheat from unnamed chaff difficult is that the bulk of unnamed sources fall in a spectrum bounded by the award-winning wiretapping exposé and the prewar intelligence reporting failures. Echoing *Editor & Publisher*, journalists weave unnamed sources into the fabric of their work across different topics. To use the *New York Times* again, a story on the lack of successors to movie actress Julia Roberts turned to an unnamed source for its first quoted source: "'Nobody has stepped into the vacuum,' said one female producer, who spoke on condition of anonymity to protect her future hopes of casting the likes of Reese Witherspoon, Amy Adams and Scarlett Johansson" (Cieply, 2009). Here, anonymity is granted for a story not of vital public concern (the opinions of Julia Roberts fans notwithstanding) to a source providing a less than insightful and vague opinion. This certainly seems a far cry from the pledges of anonymity used only as a last resort in stories of extreme importance and never for opinion, as laid out in the *Times*'s own guidelines (New York Times Company, n.d.). Some may argue it does not matter, given its subject of the cachet of a Hollywood entertainer, not caches of Iraqi bio-weapons. Regardless, this casual implementation of unnamed sources demonstrates the degree to which the practice is utilized within the newspaper despite stringent restrictions codified by the organization.

Beyond the *New York Times*, anonymity is a common practice which elite news organizations use to lure sources both in the US and in other countries. In the UK, the stated policy of the BBC closely mirrors that of US news outlets, especially in privileging a conception of unnamed sources as whistle-blowers, a point described below (BBC, n.d.). However, the widespread use of source anonymity with top British officials has resulted in what Nicholas Jones has called "the state-sanctioned leaking of official information" (Jones, 2008). At the same time, journalistic confidentiality retains its unfixed status around the globe, sparking public debates, for example, in the Netherlands over the jailing of reporters for refusing to testify about a source (Reporters Without Borders, 2008). These examples point to the volatility of unnamed source use across nations as journalists, governments, and audiences struggle with how best to approach anonymity.

JUSTIFYING ANONYMITY

Access to elite sources has become a hallmark of being an elite news outlet, and anonymity displays a connectedness to influential sources that props up the authority and standing of the outlet without necessitating the identification of the source. A quote from a "senior White House official" denotes access to such authorities, but it also connotes the authority of the outlet itself. While news organizations flaunt their access to top sources, individual reporters also compete to demonstrate their close ties to people in power. Simultaneously, unnamed sources benefit from circulating messages in highly visible ways without being personally linked to them. All of this raises questions regarding the much more cloudy benefit to the public—if a benefit is to be had at all.

To cope with this ambiguity, journalism has honed a set of normative arguments propping up its defense of unnamed sources and the need for confidentiality privileges. These public arguments emerge from cultural assumptions about journalism that require unpacking. Journalists advocate for professionally based legal rights separate from the commonly held rights of citizens by situating such rights in the public interest rather than the limited interests of the journalism community. In one common iteration, a Minneapolis *Star-Tribune* editorial rallied public support for a federal shield law protecting journalistic confidentiality through an appeal to the public: "[confidentiality] should matter also to Americans generally, for the question at issue—the ability of journalists to protect confidential sources—bears directly on the ability of journalists to keep Americans informed" (*Star Tribune*, 2005). This rhetoric links the professional and public benefits of enhanced legal protections for journalists while warning of the public harm caused by the lack of such privileges. Another US newspaper, the *Seattle Times*, used its editorial voice to join journalists and the public as victims of an aggressive government: "It's open season on journalists—and by extension, information the government doesn't want people to know" (*Seattle Times*, 2005). The assertion of a common fate for journalists and citizens forms the meat of the normative justification for legitimating unseen news practices. On the surface, this argument is not without merit. However, several lurking assumptions need to be confronted.

First, defenses of journalistic confidentiality assert that journalists, through the authority of their professional standing, should have rights above other citizens. Yet such a notion finds doubters even within mainstream journalism. As *Chicago Tribune* columnist Steve Chapman wrote: "Journalists like nothing better than exposing self-seeking behavior by special interests who care nothing for the public good. In this case, they can find it by looking in the mirror" (Chapman, 2005, p. 9). The question should be asked whether empowering journalism to set itself apart from the rest of society truly benefits more than journalists (Carey, 1979).

A second assumption collapses the universe of unnamed sources into the idealized figure of the whistle-blower—a brave insider undertaking personal risk by coming forward with valuable and unattainable information on the condition of anonymity. This condensation into an ideal-type belies a whole array of unnamed sources who crave anonymity to offer unattributed opinions or information. In the examples from the *New York Times* above, this is especially apparent. Top administration officials coming forward to provide secret prewar intelligence findings were hardly whistle-blowers—many were officials abusing anonymity to echo public statements to sell the war. Additionally, the unnamed producer quoted for her opinion about Julia Roberts had nothing to do with exposing malfeasance. A third assumption holds that journalistic rights are transferable to sources granted anonymity. This results in certain sources having more rights than others.

The final assumption holds that journalists should be able to operate without transparency. To expose unseen practices at other institutions, journalists advocate for their own evasion of scrutiny. Yet, as with any institution, a lack of public oversight risks a loss of trust and legitimacy. This potential jeopardy is rarely plumbed in discussions of enhanced legal rights protecting the identities of unnamed sources.

Taken together, these assumptions underlying normative arguments for a confidentiality privilege show the vulnerability arising with source anonymity. Coupled with their checkered record in practice, unnamed sources have become a questionable component of news discourse. This complexity undermines attempts to reduce the practice to its ideal. What is needed is careful consideration of unnamed sources weighing their potential benefits with their actual use.

DIVINING THE FUTURE OF UNNAMED SOURCES

The turmoil surrounding unnamed sources provides a lens for examining the ongoing economic, technological, and cultural upheaval of journalistic forms in the first decade of the 21st century. With traditional journalism experiencing reductions in resources, shrinking audiences, and increased consolidation, new voices flowing forth in a range of traditional and developing media have taken issue with the workings of news. In particular, an elite segment of news outlets has drawn complaints for being too close to the powerful institutions it covers and too unresponsive to the needs of the populace (see McChesney, 2004). The whole apparatus of source anonymity epitomizes these charges. To negotiate anonymity with a source is to simultaneously dictate a relationship with the audience wherein it is told what is happening but not who is doing the telling. The audience is allowed only a glimpse of the unnamed source-journalist relationship with no option but to trust what it is being offered.

The inherent opacity of unnamed sources has allowed for increased scrutiny to arise not only around the facts reported in a controversial news story, but also how the reporting was carried out. Various voices challenge the blind trust that makes the withholding of names possible by imputing a range of possible motives for both the source and the journalist. This is often political, leading critics on the left to accuse anonymity of masking inappropriately close source-journalist ties—as was the case with the prewar reporting—while critics on the right portray anonymity as a tool to hide the political biases of reporters. The latter occurred following a controversy at *Newsweek* magazine over an unnamed source's incorrect allegations of a US military report detailing Koran abuse at the Guantanamo Bay detention facility (Seelye and Lewis, 2005). In the wake of the magazine's subsequent retraction, Jay Rosen commented on his blog: "it is imperative that journalists in the United States raise their standards for reliability, because the consequences of being wrong—for themselves, for their profession as a whole, and for others far removed— are graver" (Rosen, 2005). Graver because of the increase in scrutiny made possible by the combination of an increase in news outlets and the trend of attacking reporting practices to deflect from the underlying issues being reported (Carlson, 2009b). We will leave aside the question of how warranted much of this criticism is to instead acknowledge its volume and intensity.

Much of the doubt accruing to the use of unnamed sources stems from the broader ongoing transformation in which media audiences formerly confined to being only consumers are now able to become producers. In the midst of this cultural shift, such notions as "transparency" and "anonymity" are being rethought and reconceptualized. Many practitioners of user-generated material and alternative news forms balk at the hidden dynamics underlying source anonymity (see Singer, 2003). New media forms, and particularly blogs, have championed transparency as an openness of process (Perlmutter, 2008). Bloggers have worked to establish their authority through alternative means that distance them from traditional journalistic modes (Park, 2009). At the same time, many new media practitioners choose to publish pseudonymously with varying degrees of disclosure as to their identity. While a blogger may refrain from using an unnamed source, she may be unnamed herself.

Aside from the growing empowerment of media audiences through enhanced opportunities to create and distribute their own messages, another shift concerns the area of investigative journalism. This type of reporting goes hand-in-hand with the use of unnamed sources, often in the vein of whistle-blowers coming forward with hidden information. Traditionally, investigative journalism projects remained the domain of well-staffed large news outlets with the resources to conduct time-consuming projects. While staffing cuts have hindered investigative projects, new types of investigative journalism organizations promise a resurgence of this valuable work and possibly new ways to think about unnamed sources. New organizations such as ProPublica, the Center for Investigative Reporting, Huffington Post, and Talking Points Memo Muckraker have proven that investigative journalism does not need to come only from traditional journalistic outlets. As a corollary, such attempts at in-depth reporting have also shown that, contrary to detractors within traditional journalism, new media forms are not purely speculative opinion and banter.

The organization ProPublica exemplifies the promise shown by novel forms of investigative journalism. While deviating from the norm of US journalism with its non-profit status, ProPublica is headed by a former *Wall Street Journal* managing editor and employs over 30 investigative journalists—far more than any individual news outlet in the US. The group articulates its mission in public service terms, stating: "We uncover unsavory practices in order to stimulate reform" (ProPublica, n.d.). This particular definition points to a journalism of discovery involving the active agency of journalists to generate stories challenging their news sources rather than engaging them collaboratively in a mutually career-enhancing exchange.

This development deserves appreciation not merely for its impact on the quantity of investigative stories, but because it fundamentally alters the relationship between journalists and their sources. Unnamed source use has been plagued by the unknown motives not only of sources but of journalists as well. Detaching investigative reporting—and accompanying unnamed sources—from individual news outlets also detaches the status interests of both individual reporters and their news organizations. Instead of reporters and news outlets clamoring after exclusives for competitive purposes, stories get distributed across news outlets. Such a model shows promise for tackling problems posed by unnamed sources while preserving their utility. The transition from traditional news outlet-based investigative reporting to newer organizations received a boost in the summer of 2009 when the Associated Press agreed to begin distributing the work of several non-profit groups to its 1,500 member newspapers at no additional cost (Pérez-Peña, 2009).

A final developing model having an impact on unnamed sources is collaborative journalism that leverages the power of an active audience to conduct large scale reporting projects unrealizable by overly taxed traditional news outlets. The mythology of the lone reporter gives way to an open, collaborative undertaking in which many participants handle small segments of the overall project. This is an offshoot of crowdsourcing—utilizing the experiences of the audience—by putting the audience to work in doing research. A few projects have sprung up, including newassignment.net and the Huffington Post's Off the Bus project. The latter is a play on Timothy Crouse's seminal account of pack journalism in *The Boys on the Bus* (1973). Instead of a roving band of interlinked journalists, Off the Bus collected accounts of campaign coverage from numerous discrete citizens. As this style of journalistic alliance develops, it is bound to confront issues of source anonymity. It may even supplant the need for unnamed sources by using the collective knowledge of connected people to circumvent the insider control of knowledge by individuals.

CONCLUSION

The future use of unnamed sources in news discourse requires nego-tiation with a number of larger cultural, technological, and economic developments impacting on media. As traditional journalistic outlets confront the crisis of credibility that has befallen their industry, the trust needed to deploy source anonymity becomes more difficult to accumu-late. At the same time, new sites of media scrutiny raise issues regarding reporting in a more widespread and persistent fashion than has been possible before the advent of networked digital technologies with low barriers to entry. Another component of this shift has been the ongo-ing transformation of transparency in which hidden actions have come to seem untenable across institutions—including journalism. All of this adds up to a practice that will continually come under fire in the years to come.

The question is whether this is a good thing or a bad thing. Certainly, a shift away from kneejerk applications of anonymity seems beneficial. Journalism's closed practices are undesirable for much of the public, which remains wondering who is talking, why their identity is hidden, and, perhaps most crucially, what is being left out. At the same time, evacu-ating altogether the practice of granting sources anonymity in exchange for (ostensibly) vital information carries negative consequences. With so much criticism already, journalists should not lose a tool for holding power accountable. Nor should journalism allow scrutiny of its practices to deflect attention away from the issues it reports. Timidity should not be a virtue connected to journalism

Unnamed sources have an uncertain future, but one worthy of atten-tion and scholarly focus. There needs to be more voices entering into a conversation rethinking how unnamed sources are being used, how they are being impacted by the addition of new voices and new ideas of transparency, and how the practice could be improved in the future to do what it is supposed to do: to give journalists the teeth needed to bite on our behalf.

REFERENCES

BBC (n.d.) "Anonymous Sources." Available: http://www.bbc.co.uk/guidelines/editorialguidelines/edguide/accuracy/anonymoussource.shtml. Accessed June 26, 2009.

Boeyink, David (1990) "Anonymous sources in news stories: Justifying exceptions and limiting abuses," *Journal of Mass Media Ethics* 5(4): pp. 233–246.

Carey, James W. (1979) "A plea for the university tradition," *Journalism Quarterly* 55: pp. 846–855

Carlson, Matt (2009a) "Dueling, dancing or dominating? Journalists and their sources," *Sociology Compass* 3(4): pp. 525–542.

Carlson, Matt (2009b) "Media criticism as competitive discourse: Defining reportage of the Abu Ghraib ccandal," *Journal of Communication Inquiry* 33(3): pp. 258–277.

Carlson, Matt (2011) *On the Condition of Anonymity: Unnamed Sources and the Battle for Journalism*, Champaign, IL: University of Illinois Press.

Chapman, Steve (2005) "Special Privileges and Reporters," *Chicago Tribune*, July 3, 2005, p. 9.

Cieply, Michael (2009) "Julia Roberts Steps Back into a Starring Role," *New York Times*, February 11, 2008, p. C1.

Crouse, Timothy (1973) *The Boys on the Bus*, New York: Random House.

Editor & Publisher (2003) "The 'Times' Addiction to Anonymous Sources." Available: http://www.editorandpublisher.com/eandp/news/article_display.jsp?vnu_content_id=1892916. Accessed June 12, 2009.

Epstein, Edward (1973) *News from Nowhere*, New York: Random House.

Ettema, James and Glasser, Theodore (1998) *Custodians of Conscience*, New York: Columbia University Press.

Jones, Nicholas (2008) "Televised Lobby Briefings Would Bring Discipline and Accountability," *Spinwatch*. Available: http://www.spinwatch.org/blogs-main-menu-29/nicholas-jones-mainmenu-85/5146-televised-lobby-briefings-would-bring-discipline-and-accountability. Accessed June 26, 2009.

Keller, Bill (2004) "The Times and Iraq," *New York Times*, May 26, 2004, p. A10.

McChesney, Robert (2004) *The Problem of the Media: U.S. Communication Politics in the 21st Century*, New York: Monthly Review Press.

Mnookin, Seth (2005) *Hard News*, New York, Random House.

New York Times Company (n.d.) "Confidential News Sources Policy." Available: http://www.nytco.com/company/business_units/sources.html. Accessed June 12, 2009.

Park, David (2009) "Blogging with authority: Strategic positioning in political blogs," *International Journal of Communication* 3: pp. 250–273.

Perez-Pena, Richard (2009) "A.P. in Deal to Deliver Nonprofits' Journalism," *New York Times*, June 13, 2009, p. B3.

Perlmutter, David (2008) *Blogwars*, New York: Oxford University Press.

Propublica (n.d.) "About Us." Available: http://www.propublica.org/about/. Accessed June 26, 2009.

Reporters Without Borders (2008) "Release Welcomed of Two Telegraaf Journalists Amid Calls for Better Protection of Sources." Available: http://www.rsf.org/Release-welcomed-of-two-Telegraaf.html. Accessed June 26, 2009.

Risen, James and Lichtblau, Eric (2005) "Bush Lets U.S. Spy on Callers Without Courts," *New York Times*, December 16, 2009, p. A1.

Rosen, Jay (2005) "Newsweek's Take-Our-Word-For-It World," *PressThink*. Available: http://journalism.nyu.edu/pubzone/weblogs/pressthink/2005/05/17/nwsk_err.html. Accessed June 26, 2009.

Sang-Hun, Choe (2009) "North Korea Conducts Another Missile Test," *New York Times*, 30 May 2009. Available: http://query.nytimes.com/gst/fullpage.html?res=9A0CE7DD133EF933A05756C0A96F9C8B63. Accessed September 13, 2010.

Scheer, Robert (2000) "No Defense: How the 'New York Times' Convicted Wen Ho Lee," *The Nation*. Available: http://www.thenation.com/doc/20001023/scheer. Accessed June 12, 2009.

Seattle Times (2005) "Prosecuting the Messenger," July 1, 2005, p. B6.

Seelye, Katharine and Lewis, Neil (2005) "Newsweek Says it is Retracting Koran Report," *New York Times*, May 17, p. A1.

Singer, Jane (2003) "Who are these Guys? The online challenge to the notion of journalistic professionalism," *Journalism*, 4(2): pp. 139–163.

Star-Tribune (2005) "Secret Sources: Courts, Reporters are Both Right," June 29, 2005, p. A12.
Tuchman, Gaye (1972) "Objectivity as strategic ritual: An examination of newsmen's notions of objectivity," *American Journal of Sociology* 77: pp. 660–679.
Wheeler, Marcy (2007) *Anatomy of Deceit*. Berkeley, CA: Varster.

3 Journalists as Unwilling 'Sources'
Transparency and the New Ethics of Journalism

Angela Phillips

INTRODUCTION

Professional journalists rate investigating, fact checking, and standards of accuracy, high, among the qualities that set them apart from amateurs and bloggers (Kovach and Rosenstiel, 2001; Fenton and Witschge, 2010). Paradoxically, however, borrowing material from other journalists, un-attributed, and usually un-verified, is common practice. A 'cuttings job' may be a simple re-hash of old material with a new introduction, or it may be an elaborate patchwork of quotes from a variety of sources. In either case, the originators are rarely credited. Often the excuse given is that there is no room for elaborate referencing or that such referencing is a turn-off for readers.

The internet could have provided new opportunities for greater transparency. Linking need take up no space at all nor need it be obtrusive to readers, but, instead of providing an opportunity for increasing transparency, the net seems to have added booster rockets for the practice of lifting without attribution. Exclusive material, such as quotes and case histories, can often be found on another site within minutes of publication. What might once have been a marginal activity, accepted on the understanding that nobody complains because nobody is entirely innocent, has arguably, become a threat to the practice and even the economic future of journalism.

This chapter addresses the spread and the implications of news 'cannibalization', (taking material from other news organizations, without attribution). It asks how the loss of exclusivity is impacting on practices of reporting and on standards of "accuracy" and "sincerity" (Williams, 2002) and suggests that establishing new standards of transparency could help protect professional reporting in the new, networked era, as well as improving ethical standards in journalism.

VANILLA NEWS

Organizations seeking publicity have always looked for ways to simplify the circulation of information to the public and news organizations are happy to share sources of routine news. Both sides have made use of the telegraph, news agencies, news conferences, press releases, news pools and, more recently, the internet, in order to do so. Much of the material used by news organizations is pushed out to news desks by public relations professionals who are trained to catch the attention of journalists (Fenton, 2010). Most information circulating is doing so precisely because those responsible for it want people to know about it. This serves the function of alerting the public to information that they need to know and it is part of the mix of all news (McNair, 2009).

Research by scholars at Cardiff University suggested that 54% of news is derived from, makes use of, or has some connection with PR sources (Davies, 2008, p. 84; see also Petley Chapter 5 and Franklin Chapter 6). Indeed this figure may be low. Virtually all news reports make some use of public relations sources because journalists are expected to follow up rumors and allegations by approaching the organizations concerned for comment. Most of that comment will be organized by PR professionals. This information is fed into news-rooms directly via press release and email, and indirectly, via news agencies. News agency copy was found by the Cardiff reporters to figure in 70% of stories surveyed (Davies, 2008, p. 74) and in German research (Carsten, 2004) 90% of political journalists said that news agencies were an important source of stories. This is not surprising: news agencies were established by newspapers in order to reduce the considerable cost of news-gathering (Silberstein-Loeb, 2009).

Original reporting should add value to 'vanilla news'. It questions, or follows up information provided by official sources, or is derived from unofficial sources that have been cross-checked and verified. This is the type of reporting that holds power to account rather than merely reporting on the powerful. It is only via questioning and investigating that journalists challenge the information that is sliced, diced and packaged for their consumption. Investigation is often singled out as a special category of news but in a reasonably well resourced news-room, original reporting is both a means of unearthing new stories and also of questioning the information that is presented via the various news feeds. An experienced reporter, on a specialist beat, should have the knowledge to recognize inconsistencies and contradictions in information received via 'vanilla' news-feeds and press releases.

The balance of investigative and 'vanilla' news is as important to the future of news (and democracy) as worms and soil are to the future of agriculture. If routine reporting was abandoned and public relations professionals ignored, citizens would undoubtedly be deprived of a great deal of the information they need to stay informed about the operations of government and business. On the other hand, if information is not questioned, and politicians and officials are not held to account, information too easily becomes propaganda. The job of public relations is to present the story in a way that is most favorable to the organization it represents, and which pays it to do so. The job of journalism is to dig behind the facade. If a lively, plural media is to survive, the diggers need to represent a variety of view-points, all of which will have different questions to ask and different secrets they want to uncover.

The question under examination here then is not whether routine news should be disseminated by journalists, but rather how is it used and inter-rogated? Is the routine pushing out the original, or making more space for it? Is the flow of information from one medium to another, via news aggregators and blogs, a straightforward benefit to democracy, or is it mud-dying the news pool and making it harder for citizens to verify and follow up information? Should there be a greater commitment to transparency so that citizens are more easily able to trace information to its source? Would greater transparency improve the quality of the news that is produced as well as the health of those organizations in the news production business? These last questions are important because original reporting may not only serve the immediate requirements of democracy and the audiences. It may also have an important role in maintaining the diversity of news outlets in the longer term.

Bourdieu (2005), discussing field theory in relation both to individual journalists and also to news organizations, describes the paradox at the centre of the journalism field:

> To exist in a field . . . is to differentiate oneself. It can be said of an in-tellectual that he or she functions like a phoneme in a language: he or she exists by virtue of difference from other intellectuals. Falling into undifferentiatedness . . . means losing existence. (39–40)

In the news industry, Bourdieu suggests that the fierce competition for differentiation is: "usually judged by access to news, the 'scoop', exclusive information and also distinctive rarity, 'big names' and so on." However, he suggests, commercial competition functions, paradoxically, to under-mine the very differentiation it seeks, as competitive pressures force orga-nizations to copy one another in order to monopolize the greatest number of readers who are assumed to occupy the middle ground (2005, p. 44). The results can readily be seen: as new technologies lower the cost of entry into news production, far from an increase in the number of different news outlets, competition has led to greater consolidation. (Herman and McChesney, 1997; House of Lords, 2008a, p. 41) There may be more out-lets but they tend to be servicing the same people and largely with the same information.

This pressure intensifies as news organizations are increasingly forced to look to advertisers for funding rather than to the audience itself. Pressure has been particularly intense since the move to online news delivery. In May 2009, the *Economist* suggested that 70 news organizations had closed in that time (*Economist*, 2009). As small to medium sized news organiza-tions continue to be squeezed out of the business, the news agencies, which depend on subscriptions for their own survival, are also coming under pressure. Associated Press (in the US) and Press Association (in the UK) are owned by the newspapers and as they contract, so do the subscriptions they pay to the agencies.

Journalists who remain are expected to work faster and to fill more space, as Nick Davies argued in his study of *Flat Earth News*, (Davies, 2008, p. 60). Davies dubbed this form of journalism "churnalism" and "churnalism" was also described by Deirdre O'Neill and Catherine O'Connor (2008) when they examined 2,994 stories from four daily newspapers: the *Halifax Courier*, the *Huddersfield Examiner*, the *Yorkshire Evening Post* and the Bradford *Telegraph & Argus* and found that 76% of stories relied on just a single source. Relying on press releases without any follow-up calls may disseminate information but it cannot interrogate it.

NEWS CANNIBALISM

At least as worrying is the practice of taking material from other news outlets without follow up or attribution. Before convergence, newspapers were inhibited from simply taking copy from another paper by the strictures of the technology. They would have to wait for the early editions of rival newspapers before they were able to take any material, and then they were limited by the sheer inconvenience of re-placing large swathes of text and possible pictures at the last minute. A big newspaper scoop would give that publication a day to pick up new readers who were unable to get the same news elsewhere. Today news can be immediately 'scraped' off the site of a rival and re-organized a little. The intensity of competition on the internet, coupled with the lack of technical or temporal barriers to making use of information lifted from elsewhere, means that it is difficult for any news organization to retain exclusivity for more than a few minutes. In one interview, a journalist working at the *Daily Telegraph* remarked:

> I'd imagine people are really pissed off with me because I'm quite often told to take things. I put my by-line on there and it just looks as though I'm just stealing stuff all the time. (Research interview with author, 2008)

In the qualitative research undertaken to investigate changing relationships between journalists and their sources (Phillips, 2010), it was journalists on the *Daily Telegraph* who most often described using stories and material, un-attributed, taken directly from other newspapers. A small but representative sample of reporters from *The Times*, *Guardian* and *Telegraph* were interviewed in-depth. Interviews were face-to-face, semi structured and transcribed verbatim. Each reporter was asked to describe, in detail, where each of a random selection of recent news items had originated, and where follow-up information had been obtained. The intention was not to compare practices across news organizations but to look for changes in the ways in which journalists are currently using news sources. However the practices at the *Telegraph*, the only national newspaper with a 'Web first' approach at that time (early 2008), were starkly different. A third of the *Daily Telegraph* stories discussed had been lifted directly from another news organization. *Telegraph* reporters also made fewer follow-up calls when covering a story. One junior reporter explained the routine:

> They go: "Can you do 400 words on this," and it's something from the *Daily Mail* or something. I'd read it through, find out who the people are, try and move it forward a bit. So I was doing that one day . . ., and the news editor came over and goes, "You haven't filed that thing . . .," and I was like , "I'm just speaking to the mother now to get some quotes," and he was like, "don't bother with that, it's been in the *Daily Mail* just rewrite it." (Phillips, 2008)

On another story:

> I got that [indicates story selected by interviewer] this morning when I came in. It's Page 5 in The *Sun* I think. That bit wasn't in it. . .I added that in yeah, but all the quotes are from The *Sun*. (Phillips, 2008)

A specialist reporter on the *Guardian* (Phillips, 2008) remarked that her exclusive stories were routinely picked up by the *Daily Telegraph* within minutes of appearing on-line. They were slightly re-organized but never attributed. The attitude in the UK seems to be that taking copy from other news organizations is normal and accepted behavior, part-and-parcel of the rough and tumble of journalism as it is practiced. Janine Gibson editor of Guardian.co.uk, explained their view: "When other newspapers take our stories and use them without attribution we have drawn it to their attention. There isn't much more you can do if you don't want to start a war" (Interview with author, February 2010).

The *Guardian* may not want to start a war but audiences deserve some clarity. The merging of platforms has speeded up the flow of news so radically that it is impossible (as the Media Standards Trust [2009] has pointed out) for any casual observer to know where a story originated, or how to verify the information. Editors can simply copy original stories at will without mentioning the journalist who put all the hard work into unearthing them and the algorithms which organize the story ranking do nothing to reward the originator of information. The rewards always go to the last person to add to a story. This practice means that the journalist no longer gets the credit for an exclusive and the newspaper can no longer count on the added value of a scoop. Why buy the *Guardian* for an exclusive story when you can just go online and read the same thing in *The Times*?

MAINTAINING THE NEWS POOL

It is hard to see why news organizations should continue to invest in original reporting if all they do is give it away. It is a great deal cheaper to take material from another source and then spend money on coloring it. The difficulty is that if news organizations do go further down this route, they will be contributing to a diminution of the news pool that will in turn, impoverish all news organizations. This journalist was explaining why he had not attempted to follow up a story by going to the place where it happened and knocking on doors:

> I mean it's all to do with money. The agencies don't do things because they can't afford it because we don't pay them enough and we don't go out because there's not enough of us to fill all the holes in the website and the paper so it just becomes a sort of vicious circle I think. The sources become ever fewer sources and more and more outlets for them. (*Telegraph* reporter, Leverhulme research, 2008)

If there are no commercial reasons for pursuing exclusives, then there is little reason for a purely commercial media to maintain the considerable cost of pursuing investigations and scoops. However, without an investment in producing exclusive content, the main force for differentiation between news outlets will disappear. This would lead to increasing homogenization of news delivery, and to a collapse of the major means by which journalists and news organizations derive the cultural capital that sets them apart from rivals within the journalism field. If the job of a journalist is simply to re-write material which has been generated by public relations professionals, it is hard to see how high caliber entrants to journalism will find the means to "differentiate themselves" within the field (Bourdieu, 2005, 39–40). They are likely to look elsewhere for rewarding work and news journalism will be even further impoverished.

Ironically perhaps, the best recent example of the power of a real 'scoop' in the UK is the *Daily Telegraph's* revelations of the MPs expenses scandal. According to reports in the *Guardian* newspaper (Wilby, 2009) the exclusive led directly to an increase in sales of 50,000 or more per day which is a rise in paid-for print circulation of some 14%. By buying a disc of material taken from the House of Commons fees office, the *Telegraph* invested in a source of data which it then went on to mine and exploit on a drip-feed basis. Initially six journalists were devoted to the task, twelve hours a day, increasing to a dozen journalists as the enormity of the task, and its commercial value, became clearer (Bell, 2009). The information proved to be so explosive that within two weeks it had forced the resignation of the Speaker of the House of Commons—the first time this had happened in 300 years—and over time a number of MPs also resigned or decided to stand down at the next elections.

For a twenty-four hour a day, Web first, newspaper, it is instructive to note that the revelations were first published, not online, but in print. This provided the paper with a twenty-four hour lead on the other print media and ensured that it would be difficult for other news media simply to scrape the information off their website and re-use it un-attributed. The rival news media, led by the BBC, were scrupulous about attributing the *Telegraph* throughout the considerable length of the story's run. This generosity might have been due, at least partly, to initial fears that the *Telegraph* might be prosecuted for receiving stolen goods (Brook and Gillan, 2009) but the result was a massive publicity campaign for the *Telegraph* newspaper and its website.

This investigation (which relied heavily on the use of computers for data mining) is a good example of what could be lost if big, independent, news organizations are further undermined by the fragmentation occurring online. No single blogger, alone in a bedroom, would have had the means to buy the material in the first place, or the staff to spend time analyzing it. It might have been possible to have just put the whole lot on line and allow 'citizens' to do the analysis but would lone individuals have seen the necessary connections and, without the power of 'big media', would it have had the impact? It is not likely either that a single, dominant or state supported, media organization would have taken the risk of prosecution. The *Telegraph* took that risk for competitive, commercial reasons (Bell, 2009) as much as for any concern about 'the public interest'. Indeed this scoop demonstrates rather effectively why newspapers neglect at their peril, the need to invest in research and investigation. Without any means of differentiating their product, the process of consolidation, homogenization and monopoly building, noted by numerous researchers (Herman and McChesney, 1997; Witschge, Fenton, and Freedman, 2010) will rapidly accelerate as smaller organizations fail to compete for advertising and news sources merge both vertically and horizontally.

There is little sign yet that the reporting functions of either newspapers or agencies will be replaced by new-Web native- brands. Most of those currently gathering readers on-line have done so entirely through the practice of 'cannibalizing' information from existing news organizations (Kovach and Rosenstiel, 2001; Messner and Distaso, 2008, p. 458). True the Huffington Post has announced a small fund which will be made available to investigative journalists (Bauder, 2009) but this cannot replace a system in which trained professionals are paid to gather, interrogate and disseminate, news which then circulates through local, to national and international hubs, and back again.

ACCURACY, SINCERITY, AND TRANSPARENCY IN THE INTERNET AGE

If the news-pool is to be retained (even in its current much reduced form) then news organizations need to have some incentive to interrogate and investigate at every level of society (not just when there is a big story to cover) and journalists need to feel some kind of investment in standards which set them apart from casual users of the internet. Fact checking, following up sources, verifying information are the core skills which journalists believe set them apart from what they consider to be an inferior product produced online by bloggers (Fenton and Witschge, 2010).

If this professionalism is what divides 'real' journalists from amateurs then the differences are in places paper thin and desperately in need of strengthening. If journalists are using material without checking it, or attributing its source, readers are in no position to know who wrote the original story, where the information originated, or how the source could be checked. Attribution of sources is standard practice in academic circles, and to re-use someone's work without doing so would be an act of plagiarism. A journalist on the *Daily Telegraph* explained that similar rules obtain when handling journalism from the US: "You have to attribute American newspapers because they get annoyed," he explained (Phillips, 2008). Yet a casual attitude towards attribution goes largely un-questioned in UK news-rooms.

The coverage of the Maureen Dowd plagiarism affair in May 2009 goes someway to show the difference in approach between the UK and the USA in relation to attribution but more pertinently between newspapers and 'Web native' publications. Maureen Dowd was found to have lifted a line from a blog (TalkingPointsMemo). The line was of no particular importance and, as plagiarism goes it was of minimal significance, but it was clear that she had used someone else's formulation in writing her sentence and bloggers were very quick to point it out.

> Now, I'm all for cutting & pasting. As a blogger I do it all the time, but I always give credit. . . . (Joshua, 2009)

Another blogger commented:

> If I was e-mailed a 40-plus-word block of text for this blog, and I used it, I'd include some sort of attribution—whether "a reader writes in," "media insider points out" or whatever the case may be. (Calderone, 2009)

British newspapers were quick to jump on the discussion. *Daily Telegraph* US editor, Toby Harnden, even entered the fray. None of course pointed out that this sort of behavior is utterly commonplace on their own pages and rarely, if ever, is a correction or apology offered, even when they are caught in the act. Brian Attwood, editor of *The Stage*, wrote to the UK's *Press Gazette* complaining that the *Daily Telegraph* had lifted material without attribution and had not responded to a complaint (Attwood, 2008).

According to cross-national research comparing major newspapers with a significant online presence it would appear that, old media, as they have moved online, have not taken on the obligation of transparency, indeed it seems to be moving in the opposite direction (Quandt, 2008, p. 729). As the Cardiff study underlines, the use of agency copy is commonplace and as the Leverhulme study indicates, use of copy from other news organizations is also common and yet Quandt found that (with exception of *Le Monde*, in France and *USA Today*) the standard approach, internationally, was to credit only one author for news items.

Research by Redden and Witschge (2010) confirmed that mainstream British news websites rarely link to other outside sources. Where there are links in news items they are almost always to other parts of their own website or previous stories they have generated themselves. (The BBC and the *Independent* were cited as exceptions to this rule. The BBC consistently provided links to outside source material. The *Independent* provided links to *Wikipedia*.) Quandt (2008, p. 732) found a similar reluctance to link to outside organizations in all but two of the news organizations examined. One exception was the BBC the other was Russian site Lenta.ru.

TRANSPARENCY: A NEW ETHIC

Journalism, if it is to contribute anything beyond entertainment to the life of the community, must be rooted in truth telling. This does not mean an adherence to some non-negotiable essential version of events, but it does mean that journalists, in telling their version of events, should be able to say, with sincerity, that they believe their version of events to be correct. "Accuracy is the disposition to take the necessary care to ensure so far as possible that what one says is not false, sincerity the disposition to make sure that what one says is what one actually believes" (Phillips, Couldry, and Freedman, 2010).

Online, where speed is considered to be more important than painstaking fact checking, accuracy and sincerity reside in transparency (Blood, 2002; Singer, 2007). Bloggers see truth as a work in progress. They will publish rumors and wait for readers to react to them believing that the interactivity of the Web will provide its own corrective. That is the reason why attribution on the Web is one of the few ethical norms agreed by bloggers: "What truth is to journalists, transparency is to bloggers" (Singer, 2007, p. 86). If the 'public' is to act as a corrective it needs to be aware of where the information originated.

This should not be difficult for mainstream news organizations to do. The Media Standards Trust is currently working to produce the metadata that would allow every piece of news to be tagged with information about where it originated as well as information about the news principles of the organization that produced it. The data would not be intrusive; it is visible only to those who want to access it. The Associated Press (Smith, 2009) has shown an interest (for commercial reasons as it will allow them to keep tabs on their own material) but so far no other significant sized news organization has signed up.

Attribution is not only a means of allowing people to trace a story back and check it. It is also a means of giving credit to the originators of information. If professional journalism was to fully embrace the blogger's code and attribute story sources routinely it would help to produce a different form of competition for cultural capital and differentiation.

Clearly there must be some limits to this. The obligation not to reveal a confidential source should still trump the obligation to be transparent, if journalists are to be able to investigate behind the scenes. However, protection of confidentiality is not an issue with the vast majority of material routinely handled by journalists. And there is absolutely no reason (beyond a distorted concern for commercial and brand protection) why journalists should not credit fellow professionals from other news organizations when the occasion demands that a real scoop should be recognized. Routine use of attribution and linking would also make it rather more difficult for journalists to quote selectively and in so doing completely distort the facts.

There would be other benefits too. If journalists could no longer pretend that the material they have lifted from another source is written by them there would be little point in spending a great deal of time re-angling it. Press Association copy could be used and attributed and journalists could spend their time following up angles and investigating original stories. The expansion of the news pool would be of value to readers and clear attribution would help those searching for stories because search engines would not be clogged up with endless repetitions of exactly the same story with the lead paragraph re-written. The value of original investigation would start to rise again and, with it, the cultural capital of journalists who produce it. If every time an original story is produced it is properly credited and points traffic back to the source, then it will also, albeit at the margins, help to stimulate greater differentiation of content.

In a time-pressured world in which few people really have the time to source their own news, journalists and news organizations must continue to have a role. It seems unarguable that a well-resourced news-room is better able than an individual blogger to afford the cost of employing journalists who can spend time verifying information and following up sources. If the news base is to be broadened it has to be possible for a mixture of large and small organizations to co-exist because, without companies sufficiently well funded to put 12 journalists onto a single story in order to find out what really happened, all news organizations, and the public, will be the poorer.

Time and budgetary pressures are pushing news organizations in the wrong direction—towards an increasing reliance on re-purposing the same material and a decreasing amount of time spent on the kind of investigation that allows for differentiation. The inevitable result of this increasing homogenization of news will be a decrease in the diversity of news organizations and a narrowing of the number of views available. While it is clear that there was no golden age in which every journalist did his or her own reporting without recourse to PR or agency copy, it is equally clear that good, solid, regular reporting, alongside the use of PR and agency copy, is necessary for a functioning democracy. PR people will tell journalists what they want them to know—not what they would rather cover-up, and investigative journalism has never been the responsibility of the agencies. If governments and business are to be held accountable, as more than ever they need to be, then democracy requires a functioning, independent news media. A move towards greater transparency in sourcing might be a step in that direction.

REFERENCES

Attwood, Brian (2008) "Letters to the Editor", *Press Gazette,* August 2008, p. 14.

Bauder, David (2009) "Huffington Post Launches Investigative Journalism Venture," March 29, 2009. Available: http://www.huffingtonpost.com/2009/03/29/huffington-post-launches-_0_n_180498.html. Accessed July 9, 2010.

Bell, Matthew (2009) "One Disk, Six Reporters: The Story Behind the Expenses Story," *The Independent*, June 21, 2009. Available: http://www.independent.co.uk/news/media/press/one-disk-six-reporters-the-story-behind-the-expenses-story-1711261.html. Accessed June 26, 2009.

Blood, Rebecca (2002) *The Weblog Handbook,* New York: Perseus.

Bourdieu, Pierre (2008) "The political field, the social science field and the journalistic field," in Rodney Benson and Eric Neveu (Eds) *Bourdieu and the Journalistic Field*, Cambridge: Polity.

Brook, Stephen and Gillan, Audrey (2009) "The Ex-Army Major, the City PR and Sneak Peaks", *Guardian*, May 18, 2009, p. 3.

Calderone, Michael (2009) "NYT Defends Down in TPM Flap," *Politico*, May 18, 2009. Available: http://www.politico.com/blogs/michaelcalderone/0509/NYT_defends_Dowd_in_TPM_flap.html. Accessed September 7, 2009.

Carsten, Reinemann (2004) "'Everyone in Journalism Steals from Everyone Else'. Routine Reliance on Other Media in Different Stages of News Production," Conference paper, International Communication Association, June 2, 2009. Available: http://www.allacademic.com/meta/p112639_index.html. Accessed September 7, 2010.

Davies, Nick (2008) *Flat Earth News,* London: Chatto and Windus.

Economist (2009) "Tossed by a Gale," May 14, 2009. Available: http://www.economist.com/displaystory.cfm?story_id=13642689. Accessed July 20, 2009.

Fenton, Natalie (2010) "NGOs, new media and the mainstream news: News from everywhere" in Natalie Fenton (Ed) *New Media Old News*, London: Sage.

Fenton, Natalie and Witschge, Tamara (2010) "Comment is free, facts are sacred: Journalistic ethics in a changing mediascape," in Graham Miekle and Guy Redden (Eds) *OnLine News and Journalism*, London: Palgrave Macmillan.

Guardian (2009) "Name of Article," May 18, 2009, p. 3.

Herman, Ed and McChesney, Robert (1997) *The Global Media, The New Missionaries of Corporate Capitalism*, London: Cassel.

House of Lords Select Committee on Communications (2008) 'The Ownership of the News. Vol I: Report." Norwich: The Stationery Office Limited. Available : http://www.publications.parliament.uk/pa/ld200708/ldselect/ldcomuni/122/122i.pdf. Accessed September 7, 2010.

Joshua (2009) "NY Times' Maureen Dowd Plagiarizes TPM's Josh Marshall," *TPM*, May 17, 2009. Available: http://tpmcafe.talkingpointsmemo.com/talk/

blogs/thejoshuablog/2009/05/ny-times-maureen-dowd-plagiari.php. Accessed September 7, 2009.

Kovach, Bill and Rosenstiel Tom (2001) *The Elements of Journalism: What Newspeople Should Know and the Public Should Expect*, New York: Crown.

Letter Press Gazette (2008) "Name of Article," August X, 2008, p. 14.

McNair, Brian (2009) News and Journalism in the UK, 5th edition, New York: Routledge.

Media Standards Trust (2009) http://www.mediastandardstrust.org/home.aspx

Messner, Marcus and Distaso, Marcia Watson (2008)"The source cycle," *Journalism Studies* 9(3): 447–463.

O'Neill, Deirdre and O'Connor, Catherine (2008) "The passive journalist: How sources dominate local news," *Journalism Practice* 2(3): pp. 487–500.

Perez-Pena, Richard (2009) "A.P. Seeks to Rein in Sites Using Its Content," *New York Times*, July 17, 2009. Available: http://www.nytimes.com/2009/04/07/business/media/07paper.html.

Phillips, Angela (2008) Research interviews for the Spaces of the News research, Goldsmiths College, London: Leverhulme Trust.

Phillips, Angela (2010) "Old sources: New bottles" in Natalie Fenton (Ed) *New Media Old News,* pp. 87–101, London: Sage.

Phillips, Angela, Couldry, Nick, and Freedman, Des (2010) "An ethical deficit: Accountability, norms and the material conditions of contemporary journalism," in Natalie Fenton (Ed) *New Media Old News*, pp. 51–68, London: Sage.

Quandt, Thorsten (2008) "News on the world wide web," *Journalism Studies* 9(5): pp. 717–738.

Redden, Joanna and Witschge, Tamara (2010) "A New News Order? Online News Content Examined", in Natalie Fenton (Ed) *New Media, Old News: Journalism and Democracy in the Digital Age*, London: Sage, pp. 171–186.

Silberstein-Loeb, Jonathon (2009) "Free Trade in News, 1850–1945," Paper prepared for Cambridge Economic History Seminar, February 19, 2009, Cambridge, UK.

Singer, Jane (2007) "Contested autonomy: Professional and popular claims on journalistic norms," *Journalism Studies* 8(1): pp. 79–95.

Smith, Patrick (2009) "AP, Media Standards Trust Propose News Microformat," *paidContent UK*, July 10, 2009. Available: http://paidcontent.co.uk/article/419-ap-media-standards-trust-propose-news-microformat/. Accessed September 7, 2009.

Wilby, Peter (2009) "Return of the Old Fashioned Scoop," *Media Guardian*, June 1, 2009. Available: http://www.guardian.co.uk/media/2009/jun/01/daily-telegraph-mps-expenses. Accessed September 1, 2009.

Williams, Bernard (2002) *Truth and Truthfulness: An Essay in Genealogy.* Princeton, NJ: Princeton University Press.

Witschge, Tamara, Fenton, Tamara, and Freedman, Des (2010) *Carnegie UK Inquiry into Civil Society and the Media UK and Ireland: Media Ownership,* London: Carnegie Foundation.

4 Activist Media as Mainstream Model
What Can Professional Journalists Learn from Indymedia?

Chris Atton

INTRODUCTION

The activist media of the global online network of Independent Media Centres (Indymedia) presents challenges to ways of doing journalism (Atton, 2004). Research into Indymedia has tended to focus on three aspects of the network: the nature of its organization (Kidd, 2003; Pickard, 2006); its methods of journalism and its journalistic content (Atton, 2003; Jankowski and Jensen, 2003; Platon and Deuze, 2003); and its contribution to political activism in civil society (Downing, 2003; Pickard, 2006). The network's practice of grassroots, eyewitness reporting by activists (rather than by professional journalists) enables a strategy of self-representation that offers "a different cast of voices" (Harcup, 2003, p. 360) from those that tend to populate mainstream journalism. Moreover, the use of open publishing software, coupled with avowedly non-hierarchical and collective methods of organization, enables (in principle at least) a large number of contributors to report on an equally large number of topics. Consequently, news reporting across the Indymedia network provides multiple accounts of stories viewed from multiple perspectives. The Indymedia network becomes a space for the implicit critique of more conventional practices of news gathering and presentation, emphasising as they do professional detachment ('objectivity'), the pursuit of a single version of the 'truth' and the construction of that truth through a largely exclusive compact between the expert culture of journalism and the expert cultures of other professional groups as sources.

By contrast, the amateur and inclusive nature of Indymedia's practices function as an exemplary critique of the dominant practices and philosophy of professional journalism. This critique might be seen as an attempt to re-imagine the structures, sourcing routines and representational strategies of journalism that deals with civil society issues. What might the profession of journalism learn from the practices of Indymedia? It would be quite unrealistic to expect any commercial media organization to adopt Indymedia's approach *in toto*, yet there might be opportunities to be seized from within the network's practices, not least the opportunity for self-reflexivity (Platon and Deuze, 2003). This is a necessary opportunity in the light of the perceived vulnerabilities of contemporary mainstream journalism (Lowrey, 2006).

TRANSFORMING PROFESSIONAL JOURNALISM

Lowrey (2006) identifies a number of features of professional journalism that make it vulnerable to "jurisdictional encroachment" by non-professionals. Among these, three are particularly important. First, the need to serve "every client" (p. 492) in the interests of maximizing circulation or audiences tends to restrict the range of stories and the degree of specialist content available in the commercial media. Second, the powerful and institutionalized relationships between media organizations and source institutions (such as governments, corporations and public relations agencies) encourage a reliance on a narrow range of official and elite sources. Third, the practice of journalism is not difficult to learn: the process of news reporting is based on a simple sequence of investigation (data collection), making sense (analysing and organizing data) and treatment (presentation of data). Lowrey calls this the "inference process" (p. 492) and argues that its routinization in professional journalism makes it easily recognizable and available to anyone wishing to work journalistically. More generally, the occupational boundaries of journalism and its jurisdiction are far from clear (Carlson, 2007; Gerlis, 2008; Knight, 2008). There is no obligatory licensure or membership of a professional organization; despite the growth of journalism schools many journalists are hired without professional qualifications. Given the "porous'" nature of the occupation (Lowrey, 2006, p. 485), it is no surprise that "anyone and everyone can be a journalist" (Gerlis, 2008, p. 126). When we turn from the production of news to the generation of comment and opinion, the potential for democratizing journalism is even greater.

Lowrey argues that the adoption of blogging—a practice that began as a form of alternative journalism—by professional journalists has gone some way to regaining the trust of a disaffected public through its explicit construction of an individual in the social world. This is confirmed by Matheson and Allan (2007), whose study of professional journalists who maintained blogs during the last Gulf War found that readers tended to trust their blogs precisely because the journalists' methods were transparently subjective. Readers did not consider the blogs as absolute truth; instead they understood them as a set of accounts told from different perspectives. Journalists did not appear to present their eyewitness reports as "fact," nor use their professional authority to present a definitive version of events (though they did, of course use their professional status to gain access to the locations from which they were blogging). Instead, they used an alternative form of representation in a reflexive manner, developing their own practice as a result.

What if professional journalists were to draw further on alternative practices of journalism to include Harcup's different cast of voices in their sourcing and representational routines? This would have particular implications for representations in terms of agenda setting and the discursive representation of civil society.

AGENDA SETTING

There is suggestive evidence that on occasion alternative journalism has proved to be "in both timeliness and content. . . a more dependable information resource" (Kettering, 1982, p. 7). Brief case studies by Kettering (1982) and Schuman (1982) show how in the US, female rape was given more extensive and serious coverage by the alternative press than it was by the mainstream. Shuman notes, for example, how the construction of rape as a "sex crime" first appeared in the alternative press, a full year before the *New York Times* identified it as such. However, there is little evidence for the agenda-setting function of alternative journalism.

Mathes and Pfetsch (1991) offer a rare example of agenda setting in their study of "spill-over" effects from alternative to mainstream media. In their examination of "counter-issues" from the mid-1980s in the former West Germany, they found a significant "inter-media" effect: the established West German liberal press tended to adopt both the topic of the issue from the alternative press as well as its frame of reference. Key to this process was *Die Tageszeitung* (or *taz)*, a large-circulation and nationally distributed, alternative daily newspaper, founded in 1978. By the mid-1980s, *taz*'s reach went far beyond any alternative public sphere: it was read by prominent intellectuals and numerous mainstream journalists. It explicitly sought to "initiate a multiplier effect" (Mathes and Pfetsch, 1991, p. 37) by highlighting counter-issues to the mainstream media and actively moving these issues into wider public fora than those of the activist left.

This is encouraging, yet the apparent rarity of similar examples suggests that this is far from everyday practice. Moreover, Mathes and Pfetsch's study highlights the mainstream media's emphasis on the content of a single paper, with its suggestion of the persistent reliance on what is considered an authoritative source (after all, *taz* enjoyed wide circulation and included professional journalists amongst its readership. (An analogous relationship in the UK is that between the satirical magazine *Private Eye* and British journalists, though in this case the relationship is complicated by the use of those journalists as sources for many of the magazine's stories; Lockyer, 2006.) This is somewhat removed from Harcup's "different cast of voices." It does not address the diversity of voices and approaches that are emblematic of alternative media practices and that might function as mainstream sources. Perhaps the most notable example in recent years of attempts to diversify sources for professional journalism has been the use of user-generated content and what has become known as citizen journalism.

USER-GENERATED CONTENT AND "DIVERSITY"

The rise of user-created content and citizen journalism presents a current challenge to professional news organizations, and one that is likely to persist. The challenge has been dealt with by the incorporation of this content (and implicitly its techniques) into the routines of professional journalism (See the chapters in Part III of this collection for a variety of views on this). Incorporation is particularly frequent in breaking television news, where news organizations find it impossible to obtain images from anything but amateur sources. However, such a strategy has little to do with the principles of alternative journalism. Indeed, the use of 'consumer content' is closer to the routines of vox pops than it is to that of the de-professionalized, politically engaged and reflexive alternative reporter. It is only the content that is being incorporated, not the philosophy or point of view of the citizen (except in the most banal way). In general, mainstream journalism appears to treat citizen journalism as user-generated content to add occasional color to professional news reports. There are occasions, of course, where user-generated content has proved invaluable to the mainstream media, where amateur photographers have captured images on mobile phones and camcorders in the absence of the professional camera crew (Thurman, 2008). The value of these contributions is inevitably circumscribed by the dominant news values of the mainstream. (In some cases they are literally circumscribed: news bulletins broadcast by the UK's Channel 5 have displayed user-generated video content in a frame to distinguish it from professional footage.) Such contributions do not present the 'citizen' as active participant in democratic discourse; the citizen is merely the amateur 'advance guard' of the camera crew.

We might see the mainstreaming of citizen journalism as a cynical attempt to recuperate radical forms of representation for the purposes of marketing, taking emerging forms of alternative journalism and reworking them in order to add a contemporary sheen to dominant practices. Audiences might not even recognize these forms as having any radical origins. Given that public knowledge of media practices seems to be largely derived from the knowledge of dominant media practices (Livingstone, Van Couvering, and Thumin, 2005), then what *passes for* citizen journalism (that is, crudely speaking, amateur video of events deemed newsworthy by professional journalists) might well *become* citizen journalism, discursively speaking. As a consequence, audiences might not be exposed to citizen journalism beyond its attenuated form. Media literacy becomes important here. To a degree, though, the use of citizen journalism demonstrates that established news organizations are at least sensitive to popular cultural change. Sensitivity to cultural change is also found in recent representations of civil society protests. These too attempted to cope with the contributions of citizens, but perhaps in a more productive manner, to the degree that they presented possibilities of representation beyond the expected.

REPRESENTATION: SOURCES AND DISCOURSES

Professional news media have tended to portray social movement activists as marginal to wider political processes, often trivializing their methods and constructing them as deviant. These representations present participants as troublemakers and emphasize violence, incoherence and criminality (Ashley and Olson, 1998; Gitlin, 1980; Halloran, Elliot, and Murdock, 1970; Van Zoonen, 1992). By contrast, a study of the media representation of the mass protests against the invasion of Iraq in 2003 found that the mainstream media acknowledged the "new complexity" of the protests, which drew on a heterogeneous coalition of trade unionists, church members, NGOs, non-aligned activists and members of political parties. Hitherto there had been evidence of a shift towards portrayals that approached this complexity, for example in liberal newspapers such as the *Guardian* (Atton, 2002). Here, though, the representation was filtered through a reliance on the classic primary definers (representatives of elite groups), at times supplemented by 'expert' eyewitness testimony from journalists themselves.

Rojecki's (2002) study of the protests in Seattle against the World Trade Organisation meeting in 1999 found that mass media coverage of the demonstrations took into account the diversity amongst protesters. Rojecki shows that "the range of views in the news and the commentaries was as wide as that expressed by the protesters themselves" (p. 166). Under these conditions normative representations of protest appear to shift from the standard frames of deviance and conflict towards frames that emphasize consensus and normalization. An important factor in this shift is that protest is no longer considered the province of the young radical: we see "the emergence of a class of ordinary citizens who increasingly see the sites of their political action as ranging from local to global" (Bennett, 2003, p. 27).

As protest activities become more populous with a heterogeneous membership, so the likelihood grows that protesters will be drawn from mass media audiences. Editorial accounts therefore need to take account of their audience's attitude towards key issues, even where these might conflict with the editorial stance of the media. Coverage of the 2003 protests against the Gulf War was far from the generally negative representations identified by previous social movement studies (Atton, 2007). The coverage of the 2003 protests highlighted the heterogeneous nature of the protesters and their 'ordinariness'—protest became normalized as a public practice and not merely the preserve of 'activists'. Nevertheless, an important omission in the coverage was any substantive presentation of the issues underlying the protests. This suggests that, as Robinson et al. (2006) have shown, press coverage remained driven by the remarkable nature of the events and not by the significance of their underlying rationale.

ASSESSING THE OPPORTUNITIES

We have seen how mainstream journalism has responded to practices and ideologies that have their origins in alternative journalism. Any transformations in professional practice seem circumscribed by abiding "ideological and ideal-typical journalistic principles" (Platon and Deuze, 2003, p. 351). The use of blogging remains located in the authority of the professional, eyewitness reporter, where matters of trust and 'truth' are placed in the hands of the experienced foreign correspondent, for example. The use of alternative news as a source for its mainstream counterpart also appears to be determined by authority. Mathes and Pfetsch's study of *taz* strongly suggests that the paper's influence amongst professional journalists was as much the result of what is for most alternative publications a high circulation, as well as its currency amongst professional journalists. The apparent shift towards the normalization of anti-war protest and recognition of the heterogeneous nature of political activism seems to result more from an unwillingness to alienate the readership than from any deep transformation in the ideology of media representation. Nevertheless, however superficial or limited these responses might be, they do at least suggest that the vulnerabilities found by Lowrey are indeed open to repair.

Platon and Deuze (2003) believe that it is unlikely that mainstream news media will adopt the methods of Indymedia's journalism in any detailed way; the abiding principles of professional journalism are too robust for that. Not least among these principles is the definitiveness of news reporting that is founded on the professional authority of the journalist. To replace that with the contingency and provisionality of the multiple storytelling that characterizes so much of Indymedia's news output would be to cede that authority, and with it the risk of commercial failure in an already fragile market—any risk of failure would surely lie in the uncertain impact of radical experimentation on audiences.

Must the use of the principles and practices of alternative journalism be reduced either to the recuperation of radical models for short-term gain, or to an incoherent babble of voices that destroys journalistic norms rather than critiquing them? In a study of Indymedia's Athens center, Milioni (2009) argues that three key functions of Indymedia point to the value of alternative media in broader contexts of journalism and democracy. First, it has an exemplary function that places it in "direct opposition to the dominant model of mainstream media" (p. 419). Its oppositional character derives from 1.) its "explicitly political character"; 2.) its autonomy from '"state control and political institutions"; 3.) its "non-hierarchical, non-professional and collective handling of information"; 4.) the diversity of its sources; and 5.) its participatory nature (ibid.). Second, Indymedia has a competitive function towards the mainstream media, setting its own agenda through the use of activist reporters that, according to Milioni, enables the "building of an autonomous channel of unmediated communication with the lifeworld" (ibid.). Third, it has a supplementary function, by which Milioni means that Indymedia practices enable its readers to develop skills of critical media literacy. This development is possible because the news stories produced by Indymedia construct reality differently from those of the mainstream. In addition, the technique of posting mainstream news stories on Indymedia sites and subjecting them to an activist critique provides demonstrations of how media literacy might be practiced. For Milioni, to work supplementarily is to signal a powerful reflexivity in media production by Indymedia groups; it encapsulates the processes of "actively monitoring media content, checking on media processes and criticizing their own logic" (p. 426).

Defined in this way, supplementarity resembles what Axel Bruns (2005) has termed "gatewatching," where tactical media (broadly speaking, media set by social movement activists for short-term gain, such as to organize protests) observe and critique the news content of established, mainstream media organizations. This is a valuable function but, as Bruns points out, for long-term success tactical media need to "grow beyond their beginnings . . . linked to specific causes and temporary actions, and . . . establish themselves as a permanent force in the news landscape" (Bruns, 2008, p. 249). Indymedia might appear far from temporary; after all, it was established in 1999 and is now a global network. Yet, as Bruns points out, recent years have seen a "comparative absence of discussion and debate" on Indymedia sites, in favor of content that often resembles "press releases for the latest cause" (p. 250). With reduced opportunities for supplementary practices of media critique, the autonomous and oppositional function of Indymedia (what Milioni terms the '"exemplary" function) might be limited to contributing to "a mere shouting match between mainstream and alternative Web sites" (Bruns, 2008, p. 250). The value of building a news agenda that simply seeks to confront, rather than explain, becomes of questionable value. Moreover, is it ever possible to conceive of such an agenda as being "unmediated," simply because its origins lie in the work of non-professional, activist reporters, rather than in the output of professional journalists?

Seen in this light, the promise of supplementarity—that it avoids the separatist and marginalising arguments that have too often come to define alternative journalism as a practice apart from other, more dominant forms of journalism—seems unattainable. Such pessimism is only appropriate, however, if we are to place all our hope in a single media organization. It is noteworthy that Indymedia has been the focus of a remarkable amount of scholarly interest, but this does not mean that it is the only space from which supplementarity might emerge. Neither must we necessarily always expect alternative media organizations to set news agendas that are radically different from those of the mainstream. Current TV typically uses mainstream "news texts to fuel discussion" alongside readers' responses, which themselves might well include links to other mainstream news coverage (Redden and Witschge, 2010, p. 180). The level of engagement between journalist and reader has also been found to be significant on some alternative media sites. Redden and Witschge cite the example of an editorial writer for OpenDemocracy who, by replying to readers' critical posts, achieved a "level of communication [that] transcends that found on mainstream news sites" (ibid.).

There is a risk, of course, that the potential of alternative journalism to set agendas is seriously weakened by the adoption of the news priorities of the mainstream. Alternative journalists—like political bloggers—may simply "reproduce rather than challenge the work of the mainstream media, and they may adopt similar practices [and, we might add, similar values and priorities] to . . . a narrow range of elite traditional media" (Lowery and Latta, 2008, p. 187). This is not to say that the mainstream and the alternative might not productively share other aspects of their journalistic work. South Korea's *OhmyNews* has successfully brought together amateur citizen reporters with a team of professional editors to set news agendas very different from those of the dominant news organizations. Nevertheless, in other respects *OhmyNews* is classically neoliberal, for example in its dependence on advertising (Kim and Hamilton, 2006). It is in a "pro-am approach" to partnerships rather than through confrontation that Bruns (2008, p. 265) is hopeful for the future of journalism, where professional writing and reporting skills are put in the service of participatory sourcing practices and grassroots agenda-setting. Conceptually this is a profitable move too, in that it moves away from the binary opposition between two sets of media practices, and warns against the assumption that "alternative media are essentially separate, distinct, or different from the mainstream" (Hamilton, 2008, p. 19). Moreover, collaborative media practices can demonstrate how media literacy need not simply be a critical response, but a productive one. Hamilton (2008) draws on Raymond Williams's notion of "direct autonomous composition" to explain this as a

> critical-modernist critique of professionalization (a critique that, importantly, has nothing to do with attained levels of skill—only with the degree of social restriction of the practice) . . . [that] emphasizes formulating and making rather than solely interpreting and demystifying. (p. 237)

Supplementarity, complementarity, collaboration: together they might enable a move away from separatism and conflictual models of journalism towards a productive engagement that emphasizes a multiperspectival approach of news production.

CONCLUSION

As noted at the beginning of this paper, *Indymedia's* practices involve the critique of mainstream media's ideologies and practices; they also, as Milioni points out, involve auto-critique. Perhaps here we find the most profitable avenue for the use of *Indymedia* practices by the mainstream. Rather than expecting professional journalism to transform itself by adopting radical and contingent practices, or being satisfied with the adoption of alternative practices for reasons of commercial expediency, we can envision and encourage a professionalized journalism that takes more account of the self-reflexive lessons to be learned from alternative journalism. Contemporary media economies are becoming increasingly competitive as audiences become fragmented and less loyal to the classic forms of mass media.

We should not be over-optimistic, however. As we have seen, some alternative media sites prefer to reproduce the dominant news agendas, though in doing so the value they add is that of critical communication between readers, and between readers and journalists. This is a significant activity in itself, part of what Livingstone et al. (2005, p. 39) term the "literacy task." Graham Meikle reminds us that "news that anyone can write demands active, questioning readers—but then so does professional news" (Meikle, 2009, p. 193). This requires audiences to be able to compare and contrast different sources; when the range of sources narrows to a small number of institutionalized "big brands," the task becomes one of "locating and evaluating alternative news sources" (p. 39). A key factor is the ability of audiences to find alternative sources: "interested people must commit considerable time to actively seek out such sites" (Redden and Witschge, 2010, p. 181). The uneven awareness of alternative news sources is likely to lead to further fragmentation of audiences than we are already experiencing. There is a role here for the mainstream organizations that still dominate online news production. Signposting, increasingly the province of professional online content aggregators (Chalaby, 2000), could become integral to enabling media literacy. Currently there is limited signposting and aggregating of alternative news sources by mainstream media organizations. What exists tends to be either event-based and transient (used to enhance a specific news story) or more like consumer guides ("this week's top ten blogs").

Alternative news sources might be more regularly incorporated into the signposting and aggregating practices of mainstream news organizations, not merely as bare hyperlinks, but supplemented by prefatory and contextual material intended to encourage audiences to become literate users of the media beyond the dominant forms. By suggesting the epistemological limits of professional norms of objectivity and 'balance', such a development might also lead to critical media literacy practices within and between journalists and their audiences. This would not only demonstrate a commitment to citizen journalism beyond its superficial use by professional journalists, it would also suggest—without too much ontological risk to the profession—a multi-perspectival approach to constructing reality through partnership. We are already seeing experiments in partnership, albeit in rather attenuated forms. In April 2009, for example, the UK's *Daily Telegraph* began linking to the citizen journalism provider Demotix on its world news page. There is, however, little explanatory material on the site to explain the significance of the link to readers.

Professional media producers need take reflexive account of their and others' practices. Might this not be the moment for professional journalism to learn from its amateur counterparts? Not to emulate or exploit them, but to engage in a praxis of journalism that takes account of provisionality and contingency, that works not adversarially but supplementarily with alternative journalism, and that is more sensitive to multiple perspectives and storytelling rather than pursuing the inflated narrative of journalism as "the first draft of history."

REFERENCES

Ashley, Laura and Olson, Beth (1998) "Constructing reality: Print media's framing of the women's movement, 1966–1986," *Journalism and Mass Communication Quarterly* 75(2): pp. 263–277.
Atton, Chris (2002) "News cultures and new social movements: radical journalism and the mainstream media," *Journalism Studies* 3(4): pp. 491–505.
Atton, Chris (2003) "Indymedia and 'enduring freedom': An exploration of sources, perspectives and news in an alternative internet project," in Naren Chitty, Ramona R. Rush, and Mehdi Semati (Eds) *Studies in Terrorism: Media Scholarship and the Enigma of Terror*, Penang: Southbound Press, pp. 147–164.
Atton, Chris (2004) *An Alternative Internet: Radical Media, Politics and Creativity*, New York: Columbia University Press.
Atton, Chris (2007) "Keeping the peace: Media representations of the anti-Gulf War movement in the British press," in Sarah Maltby and Richard Keeble (Eds) *Communicating War: Memory, Military and Media*, Bury St. Edmunds: Arima, pp. 117–128.
Bennett, W. Lance (2003) "New media power: The internet and global activism," in Nick Couldry and James Curran (Eds) *Contesting Media Power: Alternative Media in a Networked World*, Lanham, MD: Rowman and Littlefield, pp. 17–37.
Bruns, Axel (2005) *Gatewatching: Collaborative Online News Production*, New York: Peter Lang.
Bruns, Axel (2008) "Gatewatching, gatecrashing: Futures for tactical news media," in Megan Boler (Ed) *Digital Media and Democracy: Tactics in Hard Times*, Cambridge, MA.: MIT Press, pp. 247–270.
Carlson, Matt (2007) "Blogs and journalistic authority: The role of blogs in US election day 2004 coverage," *Journalism Studies* 8(2): pp. 264–279.
Chalaby, Jean K. (2000) "Journalism studies in an era of transition in public communications," *Journalism: Theory, Practice and Criticism* 1(1): pp. 33–39.
Downing, John (2003) "The independent media center movement and the anarchist socialist tradition," in Nick Couldry and James Curran (Eds) *Contesting Media Power: Alternative Media in a Networked World*, Lanham, MD: Rowman and Littlefield, pp. 243–257.

Gerlis, Alex (2008) "Who is a journalist?," *Journalism Studies* 9(1): pp. 125–128.
Gitlin, Todd (1980) *The Whole World is Watching: Mass Media in the Making and Unmaking of the New Left*, Los Angeles and London: University of California Press.
Halloran, James, Elliott, Philip and Murdock, Graham (1970) *Demonstrations and Communication: A Case Study*, London: Penguin.
Hamilton, James F. (2008) *Democratic Communications: Formations, Projects, Possibilities*, Lanham: Lexington Books.
Harcup, Tony (2003) "'The unspoken—said': The journalism of alternative media," *Journalism: Theory, Practice and Criticism* 4(3): pp. 356–376.
Jankowski, Nicholas W. and Jensen Marieke (2003) "Indymedia: Exploration of an Alternative Internet-based Source of Movement News," Paper presented at Digital News, Social Change and Globalisation Conference, December 11–12 2003, Hong Kong Baptist University.
Kettering, Terri A. (1982) "The alternative press and the mass media: Two case studies," in James P. Danky and Elliott Shore (Eds) *Alternative Materials in Libraries*, Metuchen, NJ: Scarecrow Press, pp. 6–11.
Kidd, Dorothy (2003) "Indymedia.org: A new communication commons," in Martha McCaughey and Michael D. Ayers (Eds) *Cyberactivism: Online Activism in Theory and Practice*, New York: Routledge, pp. 47–69.
Kim, Eun-Gyoo and James F. Hamilton (2006) "Capitulation to capital? *OhmyNews* as alternative media," *Media, Culture and Society* 28(4): pp. 541–560.
Knight, Alan (2008) "Journalism in the age of blogging," *Journalism Studies* 9(1): pp. 117–124.
Livingstone, Sonia, Van Couvering, Elizabeth and Thumin, Nancy (2005) *Adult Media Literacy: A Review of the Research Literature*, London: Ofcom.
Lockyer, Sharon (2006) "A two-pronged attack? Exploring *Private Eye*'s satirical humour and investigative reporting," *Journalism Studies* 7(5): pp. 765–781.
Lowrey, Wilson (2006) "Mapping the journalism-blogging relationship," *Journalism: Theory, Practice, Criticism* 7(4): pp. 477–500.
Lowrey, Wilson and Latta, John (2008) "The routines of blogging," in Chris Paterson and David Domingo (Eds) *Making Online News: The Ethnography of New Media Production*, New York: Peter Lang, pp. 185–197.
Mathes, Rainer and Pfetsch, Barbara (1991) "The role of the alternative press in the agenda-building process: Spill-over effects and media opinion leadership," *European Journal of Communication* 6: pp. 33–62.
Matheson, Donald and Allan, Stuart (2007) "Truth in a war zone: The role of war-blogs in Iraq," in Sarah Maltby and Richard Keeble (Eds) *Communicating War: Memory, Media and Military*, Bury St. Edmunds: Arima, pp. 75–89.
Meikle, Graham (2009) *Interpreting News*, Basingstoke: Palgrave Macmillan.
Milioni, Dimitra L. (2009) "Probing the online counterpublic sphere: The case of Indymedia Athens," *Media, Culture and Society* 31(3): pp. 409–431.
Pickard, Victor W. (2006) "United yet autonomous: Indymedia and the struggle to sustain a radical democratic network," *Media, Culture and Society* 28(3): pp. 315–336.
Platon, Sara and Mark Deuze (2003) "Indymedia journalism: A radical way of making, selecting and sharing news?," *Journalism: Theory, Practice and Criticism* 4(3): pp. 336–355.
Redden, Joanna and Tamara Witschge (2010) "A new news order? Online news content examined," in Natalie Fenton (Ed) *New Media, Old News: Journalism and Democracy in the Digital Age*, London: Sage, pp. 171–186.
Robinson, Piers et al. (2006) "Media Wars: News Media Performance and Media Management during the 2003 Iraq War," ESRC Research Report No. RES-000–23–0551, Swindon: Economic and Social Research Council.

Rojecki, Andrew (2002) "Modernism, state sovereignty and dissent: Media and the new post-cold war movements," *Critical Studies in Media Communication* 19(2): pp. 152–171.

Schuman, Patricia Glass (1982) "Libraries and alternatives," in James P. Danky and Elliott Shore (Eds) *Alternative Materials in Libraries,* Metuchen, NJ: Scarecrow Press, pp. 1–5.

Thuman, Neil (2008) "Forums for citizen journalists? Adoption of user generated content initiatives by online news media," *New Media and Society* 10(1): pp. 39–157.

Van Zoonen, Elisabeth A. (1992) "The women's movement and the media: Constructing a public identity," *European Journal of Communication* 7: pp. 453–476.

Part II

Entrenched Practices, Entrenched Sources

5 Rules, Recycling, Filters and Conspiracies
Nick Davies and the Propaganda Model

Julian Petley

THE FLAT EARTH RULES

In *Flat Earth News*, his scathing critique of the standards of contemporary British journalism, Nick Davies argues that, for the most part, news stories are now selected according to embedded and largely unacknowledged rules, "a kind of quality control system which instantly rejects any raw material which does not meet the factory's requirements" (2008, p. 113). Davies enunciates ten such rules, which, it will be noted, overlap somewhat:

- *Run cheap stories.* This rule simply requires the selection of stories which are quick to cover and safe to publish. Consequently, journalists typically eschew complex, long-running and thus expensive journalistic inquiries while foregrounding stories which are simple, uncontentious and easy to obtain.
- *Select safe facts.* Reporters go with the official line because it is safe and means they are less likely to be attacked by the subjects of their stories.
- *Avoid the electric fence.* As well as reporting only safe facts, journalists favor official sources and adopt deferential attitudes to any organization or individual with the power to hurt them or the news organization to which they belong.
- *Select safe ideas.* The safe facts are then embedded within frameworks of safe moral and political values. These values are not expressed overtly in the story but are the undeclared assumptions on which it is built. They are also all the more covert in that they seamlessly reflect the surrounding consensus. In Davies' view, the effect of this approach is to "rip the rudder off journalism and leave it to be swept along by the current of prevailing prejudice. Moral and political judgements are allowed, but only if they are rendered invisible by reflecting popular belief" (ibid., p. 129).
- *Always give both sides of the story.* Davies calls this 'the safety net' approach because "it suggests that, if all else fails and you end up having to publish something that is not 'safe', you bang in some quotes

from the other side to 'balance' the story" (ibid., p. 131). Thus "the honourable convention aimed at unearthing the facts has become a coward's compromise aimed at despatching quick copy with which nobody will quarrel" (ibid., p. 133).

- *Give them what they want.* This is the mantra of market-driven journalism in which audience-maximization is all: "if we can sell it, we'll tell it" (ibid., p. 133).
- *The bias against truth.* This rule extends the commercial imperative of the preceding rule beyond the mere selection of stories and into a series of prejudices about the way in which the stories themselves are actually told. Davies argues that the effect of this rule is to rob stories of their context and to institutionalize "a preference for human interest over issue; for the concrete over the historic; for simplicity rather than complexity; for certainty rather than doubt" (2008, p. 139). As stories become shorter and shorter, so the events at their heart become ever more drained of meaning and significance, generating distortions so severe that they amount to a "bias against truth."
- *Give them what they want to believe in.* Not only facts, but also ideas should be selected with profit in mind.
- *Go with the moral panic.* This applies particularly in times of perceived crisis and "combines the recycling of readers' values with the bias against truth, by attempting to sell the nation a heightened version of its own emotional state in the crudest possible form" (ibid., p. 142).
- *Ninja Turtle syndrome.* This might also be called the rat pack syndrome, and requires a media organization to run the same stories which are being widely published elsewhere, even if they clearly lack any journalistic credibility.

In Davies' view, these unwritten but all-pervasive rules have their origins in the fact that newspapers and broadcasters across the developed world have been taken over by a new generation of corporate owners who have both cut staffing and increased output in the pursuit of profit. In such a situation, journalists who are denied the time to work effectively survive by taking the easy stories which everybody else is running. Journalists are required above all to produce stories which will sell, and this means that media outlets, far from trying to distinguish themselves by producing different kinds of stories from their competitors, obsessively circle like vultures over a smaller and smaller selection of the same kinds of stories, all of which have one thing in common—their revenue-generating properties.

THE PR BOOM

Meanwhile, as Davies points out, as the journalistic workforce is slashed and the workloads of the survivors increase exponentially, the public and corporate PR ranks swell daily. According to Davies, there are now 47,800 PR people, as opposed to 45,000 journalists, employed in Britain. PR and news agencies thus become ever more dominant sources of news for journalists (See Franklin, Chapter 6, this volume; and Strahan, Chapter 8, this volume). One of the most striking revelations in his book is the extent to which British newspapers are routinely recycling unchecked second-hand material from PR companies and from wire agencies such as the Press Association, passively processing material which is designed to serve the political or commercial interests of those providing it. Thus news gathering and news reporting becomes increasingly "outsourced" in a process which Davies calls "churnalism." His revelations are based on research which he commissioned from the School of Journalism, Media and Cultural Studies at the University of Cardiff, Wales and which examined the sources of all domestic stories published over a two week period in *The Times, Guardian, Independent, Telegraph* and *Mail*. (A detailed account of this research can be found in Lewis, Williams and Franklin 2008; and in Chapter 6, this volume.) As Davies explains:

> They found that a massive 60% of these quality-print stories consisted wholly or mainly of wire copy and/or PR material, and a further 20% contained clear elements of wire copy and/or PR to which more or less other material had been added. With 8% of the stories, they were unable to be sure about their source. That left only 12% of stories where the researchers could say that all the material was generated by the reporters themselves. (Ibid, p. 52)

Furthermore, only 1% of wire stories carried by these papers made clear the source of the news, and in 70% of the stories which relied on a specific statement of fact, the alleged fact had passed into print without any independent corroboration or checking. Davies reports that the Cardiff researchers concluded that their data

> Portray a picture of journalism in which any meaningful independent journalistic activity by the press is the exception rather than the rule. We are not talking about investigative journalism here, but the everyday practices of news judgement, fact-checking, balance, criticising and interrogating sources, etc, that are, in theory, central to routine, day-to-day journalism. (Ibid., p. 53)

The situation is all too clearly summed up by Nigel Hawkes, the health editor at *The Times*, who notes that:

> There is much more PR these days. I get hundreds of press releases in my mailbox every day, and I get lots of calls from drug companies offering to pay for me to go to this international conference or that

convention . . . It's become a lot easier to use PR because of the technology. It's very easy and convenient, and as we're producing so many more stories, we use it . . . If you're not feeling too energetic it's almost as if you could surf this great tidal wave of PR all the way to the shore and not come up with any original material all day. (Quoted in Lewis, Williams and Franklin 2008, p. 41)

According to Davies, the effect of the unwritten and unstated rules of journalism combined with journalists' massive over-reliance on uncorroborated copy is to generate an account of the world which

> generally suffers from three weaknesses which are fatal to truth-telling: an arbitrary selection of subjects, which fundamentally distorts reality by systemic omission; routine use of a host of factual claims which are frequently unreliable and sometimes false; and the steady imprint of a political and moral consensus which tends to reflect the values only of the most powerful groups in the surrounding society. (Ibid. pp. 113–14)

Thus is produced, albeit not necessarily consciously or deliberately, a form of journalism which heavily favors the status quo and generates what Davies calls the "mass production of ignorance" (ibid., p. 108). Ideology is there in every sentence but this being a democracy, "it lies down and hides beneath the surface. There is no need for a totalitarian regime when the censorship of commerce runs its blue pencil through every story" (ibid. p. 152).

THE PROPAGANDA MODEL

The last two quotations suggest there may be certain parallels between Davies' account of contemporary journalistic practices and Edward S. Herman and Noam Chomsky's 'propaganda model' of the media. Herman and Chomsky argue that within the media, five filters act to squeeze out certain kinds of news and actively encourage the production of others; this they do by fixing the "premises of discourse and interpretation, and the definition of what is newsworthy in the first place" (2008, p. 2). Their operation has become so much a 'natural' part of the taken-for-granted daily reality of news production that

> media news people, frequently operating with complete integrity and goodwill, are able to convince themselves that they choose and interpret the news "objectively" and on the basis of professional news values. Within the limits of the filter constraints they often are objective; the constraints are so powerful, and are built into the system in such a fundamental way, that alternative bases of news choices are hardly imaginable. (Ibid., p. 2)

Herman and Chomsky's filters consist of:

- The size, concentrated ownership and profit orientation of the dominant media companies.
- Advertising, to whose requirements more and more media content is now tailored in an increasingly liberalized and profit-driven media environment.
- The governmental and corporate sources on which news organisations are so heavily dependent. Such sources provide what Oscar Gandy called a form of "information subsidy" to the journalist, which is particularly helpful at a time journalistic retrenchment but such sources rapidly become routinized and thus less subject to critical scrutiny than they should be, either because journalists are under pressure of time or are simply insufficiently skeptical of information carrying the "official" imprimateur. This means that mainstream sources may be more trusted than they deserve to be but also that non-routine or alternative sources may find themselves at a considerable disadvantage by comparison (See Chapters 4 and 6, this volume).
- The 'flak' (such as threats of lawsuits, or of withdrawal of advertising and sponsorship) which powerful interests mobilize deliberately and systematically in order to discourage critical media coverage.
- Anti-Communism which, by mobilizing popular sentiment against an external enemy, helps to construct a comforting sense of 'us' in the face of the threat from 'them'. In today's post-Cold War world the anti-Communist filter has mutated into two more generalized ideological filters, one of which helps to shape the news in the interests of fighting the 'war on terror' while the other helps to propagate a neo-liberal world view in which there are no viable alternatives to the market, which, moreover, is assumed to be benevolent and even democratic.

Thus are created what Chomsky aptly describes in *Necessary Illusions* as "the bounds that are set on thinkable thought" (1989, p. 147).

Though originally elaborated in 1988, the propaganda model, Edward Herman argues, is even more relevant today than it was then:

> The dramatic changes in the economy, communications industries, and politics over the past decade have tended to enhance the applicability of the propaganda model: The first two filters—ownership and advertising—have become ever more important. The decline of public broadcasting, the increase in corporate power and global reach, and the mergers and centralization of the media, have made bottom line considerations more controlling. The competition for serving advertisers has become more intense. Newsrooms have been more thoroughly incorporated into transnational corporate empires, with shrunken

resources and even less management enthusiasm for investigative journalism that would challenge the structure of power. In short, the professional autonomy of journalists has been reduced. (1999, p. 268)

Meanwhile, far from breaking the corporate stranglehold on journalism, as was once predicted, the new communications technologies have exacerbated the problem by allowing media companies to reduce staff while simultaneously increasing their output. New technologies have also facilitated global production and distribution systems which have accelerated the process of media concentration on a global scale.

In broad terms, there are certainly parallels between the Davies and Herman/Chomsky theses, with both raising important concerns about the sourcing of news. More generally, both argue that an ever-increasing emphasis on the media as essentially *commercial* enterprises has had a negative effect on journalism: the relentless pursuit of profit has led both to staff cuts, which mean fewer staff doing more work, and to journalistic output being judged in primarily commercial terms rather than in terms of its contribution to the public sphere. Both regard the workings of the rules/filters as largely institutionalized and taken-for-granted, and as producing journalism which endorses the status quo and whose ideology is all the more effective for being largely implicit and thus invisible.

Particularly significant in the present context, Herman and Chomsky concur with Davies that the simultaneous decline in journalistic numbers and rise in PR numbers has had an extremely negative effect on journalism by enhancing the significance of public relations as a source of news stories for journalists (See Franklin, Chapter 6, this volume; and Van Hout, Chapter 7, this volume). Thus in their introduction to the 2002 edition of *Manufacturing Consent*, they note that:

> Media centralisation and the reduction in the resources devoted to journalism have made the media more dependent than ever on the primary definers who both make the news and subsidise the media by providing accessible and cheap copy. They now have greater leverage over the media, and the public relations firms working for these and other powerful interests also bulk larger as media sources . . . Studies of news sources reveal that a significant proportion of news originates in public relations releases. There are, by one count, 20,000 more public relations agents to doctor the news today than there are journalists writing it. (2008, p. xvii)

Similarly, drawing on the work of Aeron Davis (2002), Nick Davies points out that between 1979 and 1999, the major corporations in the UK increased their hiring of PR consultants eleven-fold. And throughout the 1980s, the number of PR consultants increased every year by between 25 and 30%. Meanwhile, local and national government public relations services were growing rapidly. From the beginning of the Thatcher era to the end of John Major's premiership, the number of Whitehall press officers rose from 628 to 1163. In the first two years of the Blair government, a further 310 were taken on, and the annual volume of press releases rose by 80% to some 20,000 per year.

'A SELLING MESSAGE'

However, once we move away from the influence of sources on news content, the similarities between Davies and Herman/Chomsky become rather less apparent. Take, for example, the influence of advertisers on journalism. Although Davies pins much of the blame for what he sees as the debased state of contemporary British journalism on the increased commercialization of the media environment in which journalism operates, it is rather curious that he largely exonerates the advertisers who, after all, are among the main drivers of the commercial media. This is a position that journalists (not to mention media owners) habitually, and usually self-defensively, adopt, but it does seem distinctly at odds with the rest of Davies' trenchant critique of the commercialization of news values. However, he clearly regards the idea that advertisers play a key role in shaping media content as a form of conspiracy theory:

> There is a popular theory that mass-media coverage is orchestrated or at least fundamentally restricted in order to win the favor of corporate advertisers. To an outsider's eye, this is very tempting: these advertisers have money, the media outlets need the money, so they must be vulnerable to some kind of pressure from the advertisers to describe the world in a way which suits their interests. It's a fine theory, particularly favored by left-wing radicals ... But when critics try to use this theory to explain the systemic flow of Flat Earth news through the global media with its heavy skew towards the interests of the status quo, the evidence simply evaporates. (2008, p. 14)

On the other hand, Herman and Chomsky argue that an advertising-based broadcasting system will gradually increase advertising time and marginalize or eliminate altogether programming that has significant public affairs content.

> Advertisers choose selectively among programmess on the basis of their own principles. With rare exceptions these are culturally and politically conservative. Large corporate advertisers on television will rarely sponsor programmes that engage in serious criticisms of corporate activities, such as the problem of environmental degradation, the workings of the military industrial complex, or corporate support of and benefits from Third World tyrannies ... Advertisers will want, more generally, to avoid programmes with serious complexities and

disturbing controversies that interfere with the "buying mood." They seek programmes that will lightly entertain and thus fit in with the spirit of the primary purpose of programme purchase—the dissemination of a selling message. (2008, pp. 16–17)

It could be argued that Davies and Herman/Chomsky's differences on the matter of advertiser influence stem from the fact that the American broadcast media are more heavily dependent on advertising and sponsorship than are their British counterparts. But it should be noted that Davies refers above to the *global* media, and thus his thesis is challenged by the very considerable evidence of advertiser influence on US media content marshalled by, amongst others, Erik Barnouw (1978) and Ben Bagdikian (2004). Admittedly there is a pressing need for more up-to-date research on the effects of advertising on the US media, but in the case of the UK, the evidence, *pace* Davies, far from evaporating, has simply never been gathered and interrogated in any detailed and systematic way. However, the thesis that the left-of-center British national press has been gradually decimated by lack of advertising has been convincingly demonstrated by James Curran (1978), who has also argued that advertising has played a key role in the shaping of the content of the modern British press. In particular, Curran noted a remarkable growth from 1946 onwards in advertising-related editorial features, defined as editorial items covering the same product or service as advertisements on the same or facing page. Furthermore, newspapers have been increasingly sectionalized in a way that "organises readers into market lots, packaged in suitable editorial material, for sale to advertisers" (p. 235). Thus, for example, the travel section exists in effect to deliver travel advertisements to readers interested in travel, the film section to deliver advertisements for the latest releases to film fans, and so on. This may sound unexceptionable enough, but the problem is that editors are all too aware that advertisers, not unnaturally, like their advertisements to appear within a sympathetic editorial ambience. This then encourages, at best, over-caution and, at worst, self-censorship. So, for example, is a feature on a Caribbean island, a feature which owes its very existence to the advertisements surrounding it, likely to report that it's a veritable hellhole—particularly if the feature writer's trip to the island was facilitated by a PR company working on the island's behalf? Similarly, is a local newspaper, which is heavily reliant on estate agency advertisements, likely to run features which suggest that house prices are grotesquely over-inflated and need to fall rapidly in order to help first-time buyers onto the first rung of the housing ladder? Are national newspapers which feature advertisements for the latest models of cars, and local papers full of advertisements for the garages which sell them, likely to focus on the contribution of road travel to global warming (a phenomenon towards which newspapers are anyway increasingly hostile, since combating it strikes at the very heart of the consumer culture on whose existence they largely depend)? And might it not be the case that one of the reasons why British newspapers failed so spectacularly to warn their readers of the unsustainability of the British economy was not simply their owners' and editors' infatuation with neo-liberal economics but also the papers' heavy reliance on advertising by banks, building societies, investment trusts and other financial institutions?

As Curran concludes:

> Advertising sponsorship raises a much wider and more important question than whether individual advertisers are shielded from criticism or receive preferential treatment. For advertising sponsorship distorts the news values of the press, and consequently the images of society mediated by the press. Not only does it influence what topics are covered and at what length, but it also indirectly influences the way in which these topics are covered. Sponsorship helps to set the editorial agenda of sponsored features and, perhaps more important, to define their intended audience. In this discreet and indirect way, rather than in the more obvious sense of overt pressure, advertising sponsorship has come to colour portrayals of reality in the press. (1978, p. 240)

This is a topic that urgently needs revisiting and further investigation rather than cavalier dismissal which it receives at Nick Davies' hands. Indeed, at the time of writing this chapter, the UK Advertising Standards Authority (ASA) issued a particularly stinging rebuke to the UK tabloid *Daily Express*, which is owned by Richard Desmond, for repeatedly publishing pages whose top half consisted of highly favorable editorial about a particular product while the bottom half featured an advertisement for that product. In its adjudications on three separate cases,

> The ASA noted that the articles were always and uniquely favorable to the product featured in the accompanying ad and contained claims that have been or would be likely to be prohibited in advertisements. We noted that the same or substantially similar articles had appeared on different dates; we considered that whilst it was normal for advertising copy to be repeated on different dates, it was unusual for genuine editorial pieces to appear in the same or similar form in the publication on different dates. We noted that the articles gave the company's website address for more information about the product featured in the ad. Although we accepted that, at first sight, the articles appeared distinct from the ads that featured below it, we considered the information presented in the articles complemented and added to the information provided in the ads. (*http:// www.asa.org.uk/asa/adjudications/Public/TF_ADJ_46734.htm*)

'ANTICIPATORY COMPLIANCE'

Davies also tends to play down media owners' role in the shaping of media content, stating that: "the other widespread conspiracy theory is that the problem lies with proprietors who lean down from on high and impose their demands on a compliant staff. And this is true. Owners can and do interfere in the editorial process of their outlets. But, again, it is not quite the way that outsiders imagine" (2008, p. 15). But what 'outsider' actually believes that the real problem is *direct* proprietorial intervention? Certainly not any academic analyst of journalism; and most certainly not Herman and Chomsky. In their model of the media, the propaganda function is achieved not by crude personal diktat but by the selection of right-thinking personnel (especially in the upper managerial and editorial echelons), by working journalists' internalization of the priorities and definitions of newsworthiness, and their largely unconscious adaptation to the constraints of ownership, organization, and market and political power. As they themselves put it:

> We are very clear that the Propaganda Model does not rest on any conspiracy assumption but is rooted mainly in market-oriented processes. But many critics have not been able to see how similar results could arise without conspiracy, hence there must be an underlying conspiracy assumption. But in fact what seems to be conspiratorial behavior is easily explained by natural market processes (e.g., use of common sources, laziness and copying others in the mainstream, common and built-in biases, fear of departure from a party line, etc.). (2009, p. 17)

Of course, this is not to deny that in Britain newspaper owners have indeed intervened directly on occasion in the editorial affairs of the papers which they own, *vide* Robert Maxwell, Tiny Rowland, Rupert Murdoch and Richard Desmond. Davies claims that the new breed of corporate owners "will impose a political framework on their outlets, but this is much looser than the political control of their propagandist predecessors" (2008, p. 20) but, without wishing to appear a "conspiracy theorist," it is surely important to point out that within five years of acquiring the Labour-supporting UK tabloid the *Sun* in 1969 and within two years of securing ownership of the then liberal UK paper, the *Sunday Times* in 1981, Murdoch had turned both into particularly vociferous cheerleaders for Thatcherism. Similarly, when he acquired the ailing tabloid *Today* in 1987, he transformed it from an SDP-supporting newspaper to a Conservative one (and immediately hitched it to his self-interested crusade against the terrestrial broadcasters). By the 1997 general election New Labour had shown itself to be sufficiently Thatcherite for Murdoch to consider the party worthy of the *Sun*'s support, but the paper was returned safely (and dramatically) to the Tory stable in September 2009 in readiness for the 2010 general election. Indeed when in 2007 Murdoch gave evidence to the House of Lords Select Committee on Communications enquiry into the ownership of news media, he was quite happy to admit that in the case of the *Sun* and the *News of the World*, "he is a 'traditional proprietor'. He exercises editorial control on major issues—like which party to back in a general election or policy in Europe" (2008, 120). Similarly, four years after buying the daily tabloid *Express* title in 2001, Desmond turned it back into the Conservative-supporting newspaper which it had been before he acquired it. If all this represents "much looser" political control it is difficult to imagine what form of bondage tight editorial control would feel like.

As journalist and academic Roy Greenslade expressed in the *Guardian*, July 27, 2009, at the close of the libel trial brought by Desmond against the author Tom Bower, a trial which revolved precisely around Bower's claim that Desmond interfered with the editorial content of the *Express*:

> In all sorts of ways, almost all newspaper owners exert control over editorial content. Most do it with subtlety. Some do it crudely. On very rare occasions, some do it overtly. Only one, the late Lord Beaverbrook, was candid enough to admit that he owned papers to make propaganda. In truth, the majority do the same. As even many journalists privately concede, what's the point of newspaper ownership if not to get one's own views across? (p. 1)

Bower had claimed in his book on the media tycoon Conrad Black that, after a row with Black over shared printing facilities, Desmond had ordered that the *Express* report that Black's company Hollinger was "facing its biggest crisis ever" after a "credit facility was cancelled by his bankers" (Bower 2007: 137–138). And indeed, in spite of the best efforts of the trial judge, Lord Justice Eady, to limit the nature of the evidence put forward by Bower's defence team, the trial produced ample proof that Desmond frequently used his newspapers to run negative stories about those who had crossed him in some way, and also spiked stories critical of his commercial allies. However, it is the subtle and long-term forms of control, not the occasional interventions in specific stories, which have the deepest and most far-reaching impact on journalism. As Greenslade, a former editor of the *Mirror* during Robert Maxwell's ownership of the paper (2009) argues:

> Owners act through proxies, usually senior management executives. Direct orders on specific stories are very rare. It is a matter of setting the tone, of ensuring that editors know what is required of them. Editors know what their proprietors think about economics and politics and, although they would deny it, they act accordingly. Given the vulnerability of their positions—especially at a time of declining sales—they are hardly going to set out to attract hostility from their employers. That's where second-guessing comes in, a form of self-censorship that can become so automatic that it is done unconsciously. The other key, the master key, to proprietorial control is turned at the moment of appointment. (p. 1)

One of the best accounts of how this process actually works is to be found in the memoirs of former *Sunday Times* editor Andrew Neil (1997).

Noting that Murdoch "has an uncanny knack of being there even when he is not" (p. 203), he admits that:

> Even when the Sun King has not expressed an interest or shown any desire to become involved, or you think his attention is absorbed in another part of his vast empire, such is his omnipresence that you strive to keep in mind whatever you think his wishes are. The knack of second-guessing the Sun King is essential for the successful courtier; anticipation of his attitudes is the court's biggest industry. (p. 198)

Similarly, Bruce Dover, a former lieutenant in Murdoch's Chinese operations, revealed that:

> The thing about Murdoch is that he very rarely issued directives or instructions to his senior executives or editors. Instead, by way of discussion he would make known his personal viewpoint on a certain matter. What was expected in return, at least from those seeking tenure of any length in the Murdoch Empire, was a sort of "anticipatory compliance." One didn't need to be instructed about what to do, one simply knew what was in one's long-term interests. (2008, p. 149)

When discussing the way in which Murdoch behaves towards the newspapers which he owns, Davies does concede that he uses them "as tools to secure political favours, and he uses those political favours to advance his business" (2008, p.18). And after examining a number of examples of such practices, he rightly concluded that "all this intervention is deeply damaging behavior—the truth being traded for political favor and commercial advantage. If honesty is the defining value of journalism, then this precisely qualifies as journalism which is entirely bad" (ibid. p. 22). But although Davies cites approvingly Bruce Page's magisterial *The Murdoch Archipelago*, he nonetheless understates the extent to which the multiple activities detailed in this book amount to a devastating critique of thoroughgoing, old fashioned proprietor power, except now operating on a global scale. In brief, Page's thesis is that Murdoch's activities need to be understood in terms of a "politico-business model" (2003, p. 406), and that Newscorp's core competence is "swapping approval with the controllers of the state" (ibid., p. 482). In this vision of things, the function of political journalism in the Murdoch media is not to act as a watchdog but, on the contrary, "consists of maintaining sympathetic relations with authority" (ibid., p. 372). Governments that support Murdoch's media interests are in turn supported by them, and those which are hostile or even merely critical have the flame-thrower turned upon them. The result is the publication of "pseudo-newspapers" (ibid., p. 414), and, at worst, as when the Murdoch press helped Thatcher to cover-up the Westland affair or amplified her government's attack on the Thames TV documentary *Death on the Rock*, a

pernicious form of "anti-journalism" (ibid., p. 382) and "privatised government propaganda" (ibid.: p.452) in which "official lies simply flow in, to be
parroted out" (ibid., 414).

PROFITS AND PROPAGANDA

One suspects that the reason why Davies underplays the role of Murdoch
and other modern media barons in the decline of modern journalism is
because, in his view,

> As with interference by advertisers, it is essential to recognise that in-
> terference by owners falls a long way short of explaining the consistent
> pattern of media failure across so many stories, big and small. Owners
> and advertisers are only part of the reason for the ideological problems
> in the mass media; and ideology is only part of the total problem of the
> retreat from truth-telling . . . The important point here is that, as the
> new owners of the mass media have shifted their priority from propa-
> ganda to commerce, that shift itself has introduced a whole new set of
> obstacles for truth-telling journalism. (2008, p. 22)

What Davies is arguing here is that it is commercial pressures that have
created a form of market-driven journalism that is inimical to the values
of the Fourth Estate. But whilst such an assertion is entirely valid, it rather
overlooks the fact that the modern British press has been immersed in commerce since its birth in the 19th century but has still, on occasion, managed
to produce journalism in the Fourth Estate mould. What has happened in
the post-Wapping era is that commercial pressures and imperatives have
massively intensified, making it much more difficult to produce such journalism; this, however, has been entirely at the behest of media owners–be
they prominent individuals or anonymous corporations—who have installed
macho managers and bullying editors-in-chief in the Paul Dacre mould to
ensure that their assets are sweated for the last drop of profit. Consequently
there has been a very significant increase in the commercial factors which
entail that stories are run which will sell, and those which don't, or which
are in some way inconvenient, are ignored or suppressed. The influence of
these factors has been greatly enhanced by the growth of PR, making a
depleted and overworked journalistic workforce more dependent than ever
on the very considerable 'information subsidy' which it receives from those
whose job it is to feed it information.

Furthermore, appealing to populist prejudices (for example, the *Express*
on asylum seekers, the *Sun* and *News of the World* on pedophiles, and
most of the press on Islam and Muslims) at one and the same time performs both the conservative ideological function—confirming people in
their already-existing beliefs—which has long been the hallmark of most

of the British press, and a profitable economic one, in that it sells more newspapers than does telling people what they don't want to hear. And it is the owners, as previously noted, who use their media to cozy up to governments or political parties which will help to advance their commercial interests (media or otherwise) and to excoriate those which wish to limit their power and wealth. The result is at worst manipulation and distortion of the news, at best self-censorship by compliant journalists. These are of course processes that involve deep-seated economic, political and ideological forces rather than personal daily diktats emanating from individual owners; indeed, it could be argued that these forces act through owners as much as they are enacted by them. Nonetheless, *pace* Davies, it is still possible to argue convincingly that these forces derive directly from the way in which the media are owned and from the manner in which, and the purposes for which, the owners run their media. In sum, and as Peter Cole and Tony Harcup put it, the media owner now "presides over a corporate structure rather than a baronial fiefdom" (2010, 85) but it would be extremely unwise to underestimate their very considerable powers, which have mutated rather than lessened.

For all the critical vigor and empirical detail of the grim picture of contemporary journalism which *Flat Earth News* paints, it would have been extremely valuable if the book could have shown how the forces which Davies rightly blames for today's debased journalistic standards have their ultimate, if not always immediately obvious, origins in both the corporate structures of the modern media and the wider political, economic and ideological system within which journalism is currently produced and of which the vast modern machinery of corporate and political PR is such a potent expression. Again, this is not to take a 'conspiratorial' view of the media. To quote Herman and Chomsky:

> An important factor in the charge of "conspiracy theory" (and general hostility to the Propaganda Model) is that many journalists find it difficult to accept the notion that institutions like those comprising the mainstream media can work to produce outcomes that run contrary to the self-understanding of the social actors who work for these institutions, and who contribute to these outcomes. Thus, harking back to something we asserted in the first edition of our book, whereas this type of critic appears to believe that the societal purpose of the media is to enlighten the public, and to enable "the public to assert meaningful control over the political process by providing them with the information needed for the intelligent discharge of political responsibilities," we believe, to the contrary, that the evidence shows that the societal purpose of the media is "to inculcate and defend the economic, social, and political agenda of privileged groups that dominate the domestic society and the state." This difference in view of the media's role is hard to bridge. (2009, p. 17)

Indeed. Thus for all the undoubted strengths of *Flat Earth News*—and they are considerable—it does, in the last instance, tend to suggest that the main problems with modern journalism are not enough time, too few resources, too many commercial pressures, over-reliance on and a lack of proper skepticism towards 'official' sources, and an excess of PR people and organizations. On the other hand, Herman and Chomsky make it abundantly clear that the basic problem is that in capitalist societies mainstream journalism is produced within a corporate media system which makes it a propagandist for the established order as opposed to a watchdog over it.

REFERENCES

Bagdikian, Ben H. (2004) *The New Media Monopoly*, Boston, MA: Beacon Press.

Barnouw, Erik (1978) *The Sponsor: Notes on a Modern Potentate*, Oxford: Oxford University Press.

Bower, Tom (2007) *Conrad and Lady Black*, London: Harper Perennial.

Chomsky, Noam (1989) *Necessary Illusions: Thought Control in Democratic Societies*, London: Pluto Press.

Cole, Peter and Harcup, Tony (2010) *Newspaper Journalism*, London: Sage.

Curran, James (1978) "Advertising and the press," in: James Curran (Ed) *The British Press: A Manifesto*, London: Macmillan, pp. 229–267

Davies, Nick (2008), *Flat Earth News*, London: Chatto and Windus.

Davis, Aeron (2002) *Public Relations Democracy: Public Relations, Politics and the Mass Media in Britain* Manchester: Manchester University Press.

Dover, Bruce (2008) *Rupert's Adventures in China: How Murdoch Lost a Fortune and Found a Wife*, Edinburgh: Mainstream Publishing Company.

Gleenslade, Roy (2009) "Controlling Interest", *Guardian*, July 27, p. 1.

Herman, Edward S. (1999) "The propaganda model revisited," in Edward S. Herman (Ed) *The Myth of the Liberal Media*, New York: Peter Lang, pp. 259–271.

Herman, Edward S. and Chomsky, Noam (2008) *Manufacturing Consent: The Political Economy of the Mass Media*, London: The Bodley Head.

Herman, Edward S. and Chomsky, Noam (2009) "The propaganda model after 20 years: An interview with Edward S. Herman and Noam Chomsky," *Westminster Papers in Communication and Culture*, 6 (2): pp. 12–22.

House of Lords Select Committee on Communications (2008) "The Ownership of the News: Volume 1," Report, London: TSO.

Lewis, Justin, Williams, Andrew, and Franklin, Bob (2008) 'Four rumours and an explanation: A political economic account of journalists' changing newsgathering and reporting practices', *Journalism Practice* 2(1): pp. 27–45.

Neil, Andrew (1997) *Full Disclosure*, London: Pan Books.

Page, Bruce (2003) *The Murdoch Archipelago*, London: Simon and Schuster.

6 Sources, Credibility and the Continuing Crisis of UK Journalism

Bob Franklin

This chapter argues that the crisis confronting UK journalism, which is undermining both the financial viability and editorial integrity of UK local and national newspapers, has a longer tap root into the history of UK journalism than many observers suggest. One aspect of the crisis that has received considerable emphasis has been journalists' increasing reliance on PR materials to fill their editorial columns in the context of a growing problem with profitability which has triggered job cuts and declining resources within the journalism industry (Franklin, 2008, 2009b; Phillips, 2010; Starr, 2009). Drawing on the findings of early studies conducted since the mid 1980s, this chapter illustrates that journalists in the local and national press have *always* relied heavily on sources in public relations not only to set their editorial agenda, but to actually deliver stories which directly shape their editorial copy. The financial recession since 2008 has undoubtedly exacerbated this relationship of dependence, but evidently and logically, has not created it. Distinguished Editor John Lloyd, current Director of Journalism at Oxford University, argues that journalism's alleged separation from PR has rested too often on little more than a "grossly self serving" myth which "glosses over the fact that much of current journalism . . . is public relations in the sense that stories, ideas, features and even interviews are either suggested, or in the extreme actually written by public relations people" (Lloyd, cited in Fletcher, 2006).

Many precursors illustrate that there is little exceptional in Lloyd's claim. More than 35 years ago, the distinguished public relations scholar Scott Cutlip (1976) claimed that 45% of newspaper stories had their origins in public relations sources while a later study suggested the figure for content derivative from PR might be as high as 80% (Cameron, Sallot, and Curtin, 1997); the Editor of *PR Week* estimated that a minimum 50% of broadsheet newspapers' copy and "more for tabloids" is now written and provided by PRs who now "do a lot of journalists thinking for them" (Franklin, 1997, p. 20). Bringing the story of the fourth-estate's reliance on the "fifth estate" of public relations (Baistow, 1985) up to date, Nick Davies' *Flat Earth News* described public relations as one of the two "primary conveyor belts" (the other being news agencies) feeding "the assembly line in the news factory with the 'raw materials' which journalists use to construct the news" (Davies, 2008, p. 74. See also Larsson, 2006; Maloney, 2006; Manning, 2008; Reich, 2009; White and Hobsbawm, 2007).

An understanding of the relationship between journalists and their sources is central to the scholarly field of journalism studies. As Simon Cottle acknowledged, "Who gets 'on' or 'in' the news is important—very important indeed" (Cottle, 2000, p. 427). This chapter examines and analyses the shifting pattern of journalists' relations with news sources in the UK local and national press across the last 25 years. This analysis is preceded by a brief outline of the current crisis in journalism, a discussion of expansion and decline in the public relations and journalism industries respectively, along with an overview of some of the ways that media scholars, as well as journalists, have formulated the key relationship of journalists and sources.

THE CRISIS IN JOURNALISM AND THE PROBLEM OF "CIVIC ADEQUACY"

Journalists, scholars and pundits of every stripe agree that journalism confronts a global crisis reflecting extensive and rapid developments in media technologies, changing business models, shifting organizational and regulatory structures and the transfer of advertising revenues to online sites. Additionally, the expansion of new media competitors such as Google News and Twitter, have impacted radically on journalism practice, stifled the flow of revenues to fund journalism and sent media companies on an increasingly desperate search for new revenue streams to fund and deliver journalism in the future. The closure of newspaper titles and the loss of journalists' jobs have been the inevitable consequence (Franklin, 2009b; Franklin, 2010; McChesney and Nichols, 2010; Rusbridger, 2010). Jeremy Dear, General Secretary of the National Union of Journalists (NUJ), claims that "almost one in four jobs in local newspapers have gone. Thousands of jobs have gone across national newspapers . . . Editions are cut, supplements axed, specialists ditched . . ." One media analyst predicts that "half the country's 1300 local newspapers will close between now and 2013 destroying a further 20,000 media jobs" (Dear, 2009).

Jay Blumler identifies two dimensions to the crisis (Blumler, 2010). The first is the crisis of financial viability mentioned above which is "threatening the existence and resources of mainstream journalistic organisations." But there is a second crisis which Blumler labels a crisis of "civic adequacy" which is "impoverishing the contributions of journalism to citizenship and democracy." Significantly Blumler argues that although these two dimensions of the crisis are "interrelated," it is important to remember "that they are also distinct," so that resolving the crisis of viability offers no automatic guarantee that the civic element of journalism's crisis will be restored to rude good health: indeed, this would be to "indulge in wishful thinking."

Blumler's analysis is supported by recent press history in the UK. During the past 25 years the five major regional and local newspaper groups which dominate the industry (Trinity Mirror, Johnston Press, Newsquest, Northcliffe and Associated Press) have delivered exceptional returns to investors, often as high as 38%, whereas research studies across the same period have revealed growing concerns about the civic or democratic vitality of newspapers measured by their reduced coverage of what might be termed political, public service or democratic issues (Engel, 2009, p. 55; Fenton, 2010; Franklin, 2009b; Williams, 2006, pp. 89–91).

But for the moment, the crisis of economic viability is exacerbating journalisms' democratic shortcomings. Cuts in resources and journalism jobs have reduced press attention to foreign news and cut coverage of national and local political affairs in Westminster, regional assemblies and local councils. These vital areas of journalism responsibility can be reported only with journalists' growing reliance on corporate and public sector public relations (Davies, 2008; Franklin, Lewis, and Williams, 2009). Such PR specialists offer the prospect of—at best—a third rate, unaccountable and partial journalistic service to replace the professionally trained, experienced, journalists working in independent newsrooms who draw on a wide range of sources and with a commitment to impartiality, in writing their stories (McChesney and Nichols, 2010, p. 81). Dear expresses the growing democratic crisis of the UK press in unequivocal terms:

> As a result [of job cuts and newspaper closures] local and national democracy is suffering—Councils, Courts and public bodies are no longer being scrutinised. Journalists are increasingly stuck in offices rewriting press releases relying ever more on corporate or celebrity PR, experienced journalists are being replaced by unpaid interns. (Dear, 2009)

UNDERSTANDING THE JOURNALIST-SOURCE RELATIONSHIP: THE FIFTH ESTATE SUBVERTS THE FOURTH?

Two classic formulations of the relationship between journalists and sources offer helpful starting points for contextualising the empirical data presented later. Gans' celebrated dance metaphor has been highly influential by highlighting the cooperative, although not equal, character of this relationship: "It takes two to tango" he claims, but adds significantly that "sources usually lead" (Gans, 1979). Developing this idea, Reich argues that journalist-source relations vary across distinctive stages of news production with sources proving influential in the 'discovery phase' but with journalists prominent in the 'gathering phase' (2006, p. 497). Larsson also envisages variable roles for sources and journalists and consequently their influence in the construction of news. Journalists and sources can each be "more active" or "less active" in their professional roles delivering a grid of four possible relationships between the groups. When journalists and sources are both "less active" the result is "documentary journalism," while active journalists deliver "watchdog journalism;" significantly for democratic outcomes and the editorial integrity of the resulting journalism, active sources but less active journalists results in what Larsson terms "promotional journalism" (Larsson 2002, p. 31).

Journalists typically object to these accountss arguing that they allocate sources too great an influence in news making while compromising a key tenet of journalists' professional culture that getting 'too close' to sources threatens their editorial independence, integrity and neutrality. This perhaps explains journalists' longstanding and strong dislike of PR professionals (L'Etang, 2004): the fourth estate must never risk getting into hock to the fifth estate of public relations. As journalist Christine Odone brusquely observed, "journalists should meet PR in a spirit of hostility—treating the information passed on as suspect . . . a link to a PR firm should spell professional suicide for a journalist" (Odone cited in Miller and Dinan, 2009, p. 253). But the belief that public relations is influential in shaping the editorial content of newspapers has become increasingly commonplace among academics (Maloney, 2006), journalists (Marr, 2004) and public relations professionals (White and Hobsbawm 2007).

A second theoretical contribution has been provided by Oscar Gandy's (1982) exploration of information subsidies, understood as "efforts by policy actors to increase the consumption of persuasive messages by reducing their costs" (1982 See also Chapter 7 this Volume). Gandy argues that PR practitioners subsidize news production via the distribution of press releases, the convening of press conferences and other professional routines. These subsidies allow news organizations to accommodate a corporate policy of cost cutting (by reducing journalists' wages and the numbers of journalists employed), while sustaining, if not increasing, news output (which has occurred in the context of UK newspapers), in order to maintain profitability in the highly competitive but, in recent years, declining market in which news media operate. But these subsidies exact their own demanding price and feed the democratic deficit identified by Blumler (Blumler, 2010).

Recent empirical research offers suggestive endorsement of Gandy's analysis. A study conducted at Cardiff University, for example, which focused specifically on the number of newspaper journalists employed between 1985–2004, illustrates unequivocally the relative decline in print journalists employed but also (and perhaps paradoxically) their proliferation of news output, across the same period; and this before the job losses noted by Dear above and triggered by recession. The study suggests this paradox might be resolved by exploring journalists' growing reliance on PR sources as well as their growing uses of agency copy since 1985 (Lewis, Williams, Franklin, Thomas, and Mosdell, 2006).

Analysis of the annual reports of the nine leading UK newspaper groups between 1985–2004, illustrated that throughout the 1990s, "the total number of employees . . . remained at a fairly stable average of 1000 employees per group with average editorial employees [journalists and editors] also being fairly constant at around 500 employees per group"[1] (Lewis et al. 2006, p. 7). The average number of journalists employed by each group was 786 in 1985 compared to 741 twenty years later in 2004, highlighting a remarkable stability of journalist employment. There was considerable variation, however, between newspaper groups with Express Newspapers reducing journalists from 968 to 532 between 1996 and 2004, while the total number of *Guardian* employees (editorial and other staffs) almost doubled from 725 to 1429 between 1991 and 2000 (Lewis, et al. 2006, pp. 7–8).

Significantly, while the number of working journalists remained fairly static, the study identified "a very substantial increase" in the pagination of national dailies with the average number of pages devoted to news and other editorial—not counting advertising and other non editorial materials—increasing virtually threefold from "a 14.6 page average in 1985 to 41 pages by 2006" (Lewis, et al. 2006, pp 10–11). The *Sun*, for example increased news pages from a 9.9 average in 1985 to 12.5 in 1995 and 27.3 in 2006, while *The Telegraph* similarly experienced a threefold increase in news pages moving from 19 pages in 1985 to 41.5 in 1995 and 45.4 in 2006 (ibid). This expansion in newspapers' news sections, moreover, occurred alongside a marked growth in the number and pagination of supplements as well as the substantial development of online editions. The study concludes that journalists' productivity increased significantly since the 1980s signalling a "relative decline" in editorial staffing across the period.

Contemporaneous with these developments, but in striking contrast, UK public relations has experienced explosive growth in the corporate private sector measured by the number of consultancies, their employees, revenues and profitability. During the 1980s and 1990s, "growth rates for the medium and large British consultancies typically reached 20–40% per annum" (Miller and Dinan, 2000, p. 5). By the late 1990s, the 3,318 practitioners employed in the top 114 PR consultancies had grown to 6,578, while the fee income of the 150 largest consultancies rose from £15 millions in 1979 to a remarkable £383 millions by 1998 (Miller and Dinan, 2000, pp. 11–12).

The public sector of PR has also enjoyed rapid expansion. The Institute of Public Relations (IPR) Local Government Group, for example, claimed that "a thousand public relations professionals work in local government, producing 60,000 items of publicity a year and spending £250 millions; they generate over a 100,000 news releases annually with coverage running into miles of print" (Harrison, 1995, p. 151). In the new millennium, a survey by the Local Government Association revealed that 85% of all authorities employ one or more PR officers with the larger authorities averaging 13

PR practitioners. PR budgets have grown apace and varied from £17,000 to £3,945,500 in a large London Borough in 2001 (Vasterman and Sykes, 2001; cited in Franklin, 2004, pp. 103–105).

Summarizing this growth in agencies, practitioners, income and profits in UK public relations, Davis argued that "there are 2,500 agencies and 47,800 people working in the public relations profession in the UK. This figure excludes the 125,000 people working in the associated advertising and marketing industries, those working in PR support industries (e.g., press cutting, media evaluation, news distribution services), and the many professionals who have had media training. The estimated total turnover of the industry in 2005, consultancy and in-house, was £6.6 billion" (Davis, 2008, p. 273). But how does this growth in PR help to influence and shape news media content?

PUBLIC RELATIONS AND LOCAL JOURNALISM: ACTIVE SOURCES AND 'PASSIVE' JOURNALISTS

The impact of public relations on local journalists' working practices and news production in the local press has been a focus of sustained scholarly attention since the mid 1980s (Davis, 2008; Davies, 2008; Franklin, 1986; Franklin, 1988; Franklin and VanSlyke Turk, 1988; Harrison, 2006; O'Connor and O'Neill, 2009). The conclusion of these studies is that the influence of public relations has been extensive, longstanding and expansive. Significantly, the findings of a recent study confirmed Larsson's concerns about active sources, passive journalists, the resulting promotional journalism and the consequences for a local and democratic journalism. Analysis of 2,979 stories in four large circulation regional dailies based in Yorkshire, revealed that 76% (2,264 stories) cited only a single source (O'Neill and O'Connor, 2009, pp. 363–377). The authors conclude that this new generation of "passive journalists" is becoming "mere processors of one-sided information or bland copy dictated by sources" (O'Neill and O'Connor, 2009).

This influence for public relations in shaping the agenda for local journalists, as well as the content of their eventual copy, is evident in newspaper coverage of both *national* and *local* political affairs; and for at least the last 25 years.

Setting the Agenda for Electoral News

An early study of this public relations impact on local news reports compared press releases issued by the Labour party during the 1992 general election with local newspapers' election coverage of a constituency campaign. The findings illustrate the considerable influence the party was able to exercise over newspaper representations of the party, its policy and candidate (Franklin, 2004, pp. 156–159).

The 29 press releases issued and distributed by the party across the three week campaign generated 28 stories in the local daily paper. Five news releases failed to trigger coverage but on each day of the campaign the newspaper carried at least one story originating from party information subsidies. Some PR initiatives—for example the release headed "NHS Goes to Top of the Agenda"—resulted in stories in the paper on three consecutive days. On three days (March 31, April 1, and April 8, 1992) *all* of the published articles discussing the Labour Party and its candidate, derived from party press and public relations officers.

The party information subsidies were not only successful in generating favorable press coverage of the party, its policies and candidates—and this in the context of a general election—but also established an agenda which opposing Conservative politicians were then obliged to address. A press release titled "Unfiddled Unemployment" for example, which suggested that levels of unemployment were higher than official government statistics suggested, raised many of the questions about local unemployment which the newspaper's journalists posed to the then Conservative Employment Secretary when he visited the Constituency (Franklin, 1994, p. 168).

Significantly, journalistic revision of the news releases was minimal. A third (31.4%) were published verbatim, while a further fifth (17.9%) generated published stories which included between 50% and 75% of the contents of the original news release. Local journalists typically disdained local politicians' public relations activities claiming they 'spiked' the majority of press releases, but one journalist confided that "the Labour Party was well geared up, they had some events, some good press releases, some good copy, so they got a decent share of the coverage." A more confident Labour Press Officer tended to take for granted the ease with which press releases fashioned news coverage; "We actually write the press releases out" he claimed, "so all they've got to do is retype it or just edit it" (Cited in Franklin, 1994, pp. 167–169).

Local Government as News Source: Feeding a News-Hungry Local Press

Turning to newspaper coverage of *local* politics, the role of public relations is similarly evident. A study based in the County of Northumberland, in the north east of the UK, which compared the text of news releases issued across a two months sample period with the local government and politics stories published in the local press, concluded that 96% of press releases issued by the local authority generated stories in the local press. Significantly, most releases triggered stories in three or four newspapers; only 25% of news releases made a single appearance. The content of one press release was published in 11 newspapers as local sister newspapers belonging to the same newspaper group, recycled the identical news around the county. While this initially seemed a very high strike rate for the press releases, a closer analysis of newspapers' contents revealed that many of the other local government stories originated from the PR departments in the neighboring local authorities of Tyne and Wear and Newcastle City.

Editing the press releases, including any additional information beyond that contained within the release, or telephoning the contact person named at the bottom of the release, was rare; occasionally a photograph was used to enliven the story. When there was evidence of "original" journalism, it was minimal involving little more than editing out the last paragraph, "re-nosing" the opening paragraph, or simply reordering paragraphs (Franklin, 1986, pp. 25–33). The great majority of these news releases were swallowed eagerly, wholesale and verbatim by a news-hungry local press. In a subsequent national study of local government public relations, 82% of responding press officers confirmed that "more than three-quarters of press releases" they issued generated stories in the local press (Franklin, 1988, p. 81). This ability of PROs to "place" stories in local and regional newspapers was less noticeable in a comparative study of similar state public relations practices in Louisiana (Franklin and VanSlyke Turk, 1988, pp. 2942).

The willingness of newspapers to accept these public relations 'subsidies' related directly to their size and resources but especially the number of journalists they employed. At daily papers with larger editorial staffs including a specialist municipal correspondent, press releases were extensively edited while at the weeklies with leaner editorial resources, press releases were typically reproduced verbatim or edited by changing the order of paragraphs; in weekly free papers, editing of releases was non-existent (Franklin, 1986). The two daily newspapers in the study above, *The Journal* and the *Newcastle Evening Chronicle*, conformed to this resource-led pattern and were much less reliant on press releases as news sources, but nonetheless, 50% of the locally produced and distributed information subsidies triggered stories in these local daily papers. In this way, newspapers' variable journalism staffs constitute a hierarchy of dependence on PR subsidies in local communication networks with 42% of press officers identifying free weekly papers as "most likely to use a press release," compared to 30% for paid weeklies, 22% evening and 5% for daily newspapers (Franklin, 1988, p. 82).

The value of the information subsidy which local government public relations offers to local newspapers is considerable with a press officer claiming, "I estimate at Westminster" that "we spend at least 30% of our time, equivalent to one and a half press officers costing £50,000 on servicing the local media . . . Many of the requests from local papers are . . . pleas for letters and press releases to fill the gaps in pages. In this sense media officers are simply filling the gaps in the newsroom staff" (cited in Harrison, 2006, p. 188). Twenty years earlier the PRO at Northumberland made a similar observation; "it's clear that many local newspapers rely heavily on handouts from the public services to fill editorial columns" (Heathcote, 1986, p. 9).

For their part, local journalists routinely complain about the pressures of time, staff cuts, and lack of investment which oblige them to resort to using the convenient, cost effective, pre-packaged sources of news which PR delivers. They are also aware of the changes to their working practices that PR imposes; not least that journalism has increasingly become a desk-based job. In *Flat Earth News*, Nick Davies asked a newly qualified journalist to keep a diary across a working week at a regional daily tabloid. The paper publishes three editions daily with 24 pages of local news supplemented by two pages addressing national stories. The paper employs seven senior reporters earning a maximum £21,500 a year and five trainees earning £15,500 (Davies, 2008, p. 56). The diary records that the journalist was required to produce between seven and thirteen stories during each daily shift, ranging from page leads via feature stories to "one hundred lines of nibs" (short 'news in brief' items), which included such diverse and specialist subjects as sport, local planning decisions, a mother with learning disabilities whose children had been taken into the care of the local authority, a local marathon runner and the opening of a new supermarket in the town. On three of the five working days, the journalist never left the office; on three days, he never met or spoke face-to-face with anyone involved in any of the stories he wrote for publication (Davies, 2008, pp. 56–59). Davies summarizes this young journalist's working week as follows:

> Number of stories: 48 (9.6 per day)
> People spoken to: 26
> People seen face to face: 4 out of 26
> Total hours out of office: 3 out of 45.5" (Davies, 2008, p. 59)

"This is life in the news factory" he concludes. "This is not journalism, but 'churnalism' . . . This is journalists who are no longer out gathering news but who are reduced instead to passive processors of whatever material comes their way, churning out stories whether real event or PR artifice, important or trivial, true or false . . . All local and regional media outlets in Britain . . . have been swamped by a tide of churnalism" (Davies, 2008, p. 59). Davies argues that "churnalism" is also prevalent in the "news factories" of the national press.

THE UK "QUALITY" PRESS AND PUBLIC RELATIONS: NEWS IN THE ROUND OR FLAT EARTH NEWS?

A study conducted by researchers at Cardiff University which analysed 2,207 domestic news reports in a structured sample of UK 'quality' (*The Guardian, The Times, The Independent* and *The Telegraph*) and mid-market (*Daily Mail*) newspapers, during March and April 2005, generated clear evidence confirming journalists' extensive use of information subsidies from public relations sources and wire services such as the Press Association (Lewis et al. 2006). Researchers analyzed each news story to establish and quantify any element of public relations materials used by journalists in the writing of the story. Researchers were also interested in trying to establish what might be termed the 'transformational process'— i.e., the extent to which materials deriving from a PR or agency source had been rewritten or elaborated by the journalist. Consequently, Internet searches were conducted to trace relevant press releases which were then compared directly with published newspaper text to establish the extent of journalists' reliance on and rewriting of, PR and agency sources; broadly the same research protocol used for the local press studies. This procedure necessarily delivered conservative estimates since news stories were coded as deriving from PR materials *only* when conclusive evidence, resulting from direct textual comparison of a press release with a published story, could be established.

Approximately three quarters (1,564—71%) of the 2,207 newspaper stories analyzed comprised main page articles of variable length, with 561 (25.5%) shorter news in brief items (Nibs), while the remaining items were 'picture only' stories (0.5%) or opinion pieces (3%) (Lewis et al., 2006, pp. 13–14). The majority (72%) of articles were attributed to a by-lined reporter with only 1% of stories attributed to the Press Association (PA) or another wire service, as well as a small proportion (2%) to a generalized identity such as an "Independent Reporter;" approximately a quarter (24.5%) carried no by-line but these were typically the shorter nibs.

By identifying journalists in this way newspapers suggested that articles represented the assiduous efforts of independent in-house reporters. But the appropriateness of such attribution is undoubtedly questionable when analysis revealed that almost one-fifth (19%) of the sample stories derived "wholly" (10%) or "mainly" (9%) from PR sources. A further quarter (22%) were either a "mix of PR with other materials" or "PR but mainly other information" (11%) while a further 13% of stories strongly suggested a PR source which could not be identified and were therefore discounted; there was no identifiable PR source in only 46% of reports. While these data may seem surprising because of the extensive and documented role they attribute to PR in news reporting, some observers believe they are "almost certainly too low [since] in the day-to-day world of journalism . . . every organization wishing to address journalists will use public relations techniques" (Phillips, 2010, p. 95). But significantly, these data illustrate that for the published stories in this research sample, the role of public relations subsidies is not merely to set the agenda, to alert journalists to particular and possible story lines, but to provide the greater part of the content of the finished story.

Some stories offered near verbatim replication of source materials; even in newspapers of record that are expected to provide a benchmark of journalism quality and standards of professional practice. *The Times* report, for example, "George Cross for Iraq War Hero" on March 24, 2006, which carried Michael Evans' by-line, reproduces almost exactly a Ministry of Defence press release. Similarly, a story in the *Telegraph* headlined "Just What Blair Needs: B'Stard is back and in his Cabinet" which carried Nigel Reynolds by-line on March 21, 2006, simply replicated a press release accompanying a publicity stunt involving comedy actor Rik Mayall (Lewis et al. 2006, p. 17). The development of news published online creates even further opportunities for journalists to use other journalists' published work to create their own stories—and very much faster than in hard copy editions; a process which Phillips dubs 'news cannibalism' (see Chapter 3, this volume). As *Guardian* Editor Alan Rusbridger noted, "most scoops have a life expectancy of about three minutes" (Rusbridger, 2010).

This reliance on public relations is not wholly negative, of course, since public relations professionals may generate factually well-informed and newsworthy stories which potentially enhance the plurality of sources of news from which journalists and editors can select and construct stories. But examination of the origins of PR materials reveals a very limited range of established and powerful elite groups and communities as sources. The corporate sector dominates with 38% of PR materials referenced in press coverage deriving from the 'business/corporate' world. Other contributors to press reports via public relations include "public bodies" (the police, NHS, Universities—23%), "Government and politicians" (21%), NGO/Charities (11%) and "professional associations" (5%). These sources of news reflect closely the primary sources which are actually cited and in the sampled news stories. Cottle's (2003) reminder of the significance of who "gets on" or "in" the media is timely here. Of the 4418 sources which are cited in the 2207 stories analyzed, 28% are from political parties or politicians, 23% from national government sources, a further 22% derived from 'law and order' with 17% of citations from the business and corporate world and 13% from NGOs and pressure groups (Lewis et al, 2006, pp. 24–25).

In this battle for access to media, the voices of ordinary citizens remain all but mute; the opinions of ordinary men and women informed only 2% of stories (ibid., pp. 21–23). One consequence of journalists' increased reliance on public relations subsidies is that corporate and governmental voices enjoy extensive and unrepresentative access to the public debating chamber that newspapers provide. In contrast, press articulations of the public interest, which journalists so frequently claim to champion, are increasingly rare. Worse, Angela Phillips' recent study presents the argument that increasing and widespread use of email and internet to contact and address journalists may result in the counter-intuitive consequence that it will consolidate existing journalist—source relations as besieged specialist reporters "trying to deal with a 'blizzard' of information . . . prioritise known organisations just in order to control the flow" (Phillips, 2010, p. 95).

The same sample of news items was also analyzed using similar techniques to establish the extent of journalists' reliance on pre-packaged stories from news agencies, especially the PA; the findings are perhaps even more striking. Approximately half (49%) the news stories published in the quality press were wholly (30%) or mainly (19%) dependent on materials produced and distribute by wire services with a further fifth (21%) of stories containing some element of agency copy (ibid., p. 15). Again, newspapers make little acknowledgement of this reliance on agency copy even when it is published virtually verbatim. On March 24, 2006, for example, the *Daily Telegraph* attributed its front-page story about the delays and problems with constructing the new Wembley football stadium to in-house reporter Richard Alleyne and headlined the story "Now Wembley has Broken Sewer Pipes." But the greater part of the contents and quotations derived from Press Association copy from the previous day; interestingly, other information featured in the report but not PA copy, was identical to information published in similar stories in the *Sun* and *Evening Standard* the previous day (Lewis et al. 2006, 35–38).

When newspapers uses of both public relations and agency copy are considered jointly, only 12% of published stories are without pre packaged news content sourced from outside the newsroom; 60% of published stories rely wholly or mainly on external news sources (see Table 6.1).

The significance of these high levels of journalistic dependency on both PR and news agency materials is that they exercise a mutually reinforcing effect on newspapers' editorial contents. Journalists use PR subsidies directly in their stories, but PR text is also encoded in the agency copy that journalists use so routinely in news production. 47% of press stories which were based "wholly" around PR materials closely replicated agency copy, suggesting the existence of a "multi-staged" process of news sourcing in which PR materials initially generate agency stories which in turn promote coverage in newspapers. Consequently, a ladder of news sourcing exists

Table 6.1 Stories with Content Derived from PR and Agencies

Sources of Editorial Content	%
All from PR/Wires	38
Mainly from PR/Wires	22
Mix of PR/Wires with other information	13
Mainly other information	7
All other information	12
Unclear	8

Source: Lewis et al., 2006, p. 25.

in news production protocols which elevate PR copy into published news stories via its incorporation initially into agency copy.

A number of journalists (42) working on national newspapers at the Press Association and in PR companies were canvassed via emailed surveys and follow up interviews with respondents confirming this growing editorial role for public relations subsidies and suggesting that it is increasing reflecting their spiraling workload. The majority (28 of 42) of respondents claimed that PR informs their stories 'sometimes' with the remainder suggesting they use it 'often'. The substantive majority (38 of 42) suggested that the use of PR for editorial purpose had increased over the last decade (Lewis et al. 2006, p. 17). A seasoned and long serving journalist working on a national paper observed:

> The volume of stories we produce in a day has increased a lot. When I started out, in the days before the electronic revolution, I was producing one or two stories a day. Today it is not uncommon to be knocking out 5 or 6 in a day—and when you're doing that, you rely more on the wires and on PR than you did before. (Lewis et al. 2006, p. 49)

These sentiments were echoed in many interview and survey responses and particularly by journalists working news agencies who stressed the growth in their workload. "I'm definitely busier and write more stories these days. I average about 10 a day" one agency journalist announced. "When I first joined PA 25 years ago I used to write no more than three a day . . . there's no peace for an agency journalist . . . . I don't usually spend more than an hour on a story otherwise I wouldn't be able to write so many" (Lewis et al. 2006, p. 49). Given these pressures to deliver increasing numbers of stories, journalistic protocols designed to protect the integrity, quality and the sheer necessity for accuracy of the reported news, begin to break down.

The study discovered—anticipating O'Neill and O'Connor's work on passive journalists—that the great majority of the stories analyzed (87%) were based on a single source but only a half (50%) of these made an attempt to contextualize the published information; in less than a fifth of cases (19%) was this done meaningfully. Moreover, when stories were based on specific factual claims the study illustrated that on 70% of occasions these claims were entirely uncorroborated and in only 12% of cases were they corroborated completely. Two-thirds of surveyed journalists confirmed that the number of checks on source material had declined and many reported that Editors trusted the integrity and accuracy of PA copy and insisted it could be used in stories without the usual checks. A correspondent on a national paper confided, "Checking info has decreased and what is worse it is not expected by the . . . news desk . . . I can't tell you the number of times I'm told 'take it off the wires and knock it into shape' which is just terrible" (Lewis et al. 2006, p. 50).

These radical changes to the processes of journalistic verification (or their absence) have recently been highlighted by an extensive ethnographic study of 235 journalists' working practices across newspaper, radio, television and online media platforms in Germany. The study revealed that across each working shift journalists "only spend about eleven minutes per day checking sources and information in terms of plausibility or correctness" (Machill and Beiler, 2009).

CONCLUSIONS—A "DOG EAT DOG" CULTURE

UK local, regional and national newspapers, like their counterparts in Northern and Central Europe, Australia and the USA are confronting a crisis which has two dimensions; financial and democratic. The financial crisis is relatively recent reflecting the emergence of the Internet which has reduced newspapers' revenues from cover sales and advertising. The financial and industrial recession since 2008 has exacerbated these economic difficulties and radically reduced the resources available to fund current and future journalism.

The democratic crisis has a considerably longer pedigree which—perhaps counter-intuitively—has not reflected circumstances of financial stringency but, on the contrary has coincided with a period of substantial economic success at least if success is measured by the high rate of profitable return on investments enjoyed by the industry. The business model which has informed corporate thinking since the mid 1980s has foregrounded high profits above investment in "quality" journalism; newspapers have increasingly become a business success but a civic or democratic failure. Profitability has been sustained by reducing labour costs and editorial jobs requiring journalists to produce more news with less resources and encouraging journalists' growing reliance on news subsidies from public relations sources and news agencies to fill the gaping news hole. Across the last 25 years, the fourth estate has become increasingly in hock to the fifth estate of public relations.

Local newspapers' coverage of local politics and even the local constituency battle in the general election is routinely derived from news subsidies emanating from local government press offices or even the campaign headquarters of the local party. At the national level, even the most well regarded newspapers—the quality quartet of *The Times, Guardian, Telegraph* and *The Independent*, as well as the highly regarded mid market *Daily Mail*—attribute stories to their journalists which research reveals originate wholly or mainly from PR and agency sources in 60% of cases. Only one in five stories is properly contextualized and only 12% of stories' factual claims are thoroughly checked. The routine professional protocols necessary to produce original, verified and factually accurate news stories have been abandoned under pressures of time and resources with information subsidies from PR sources used as surrogates. The democratic crisis of the UK press is deep but also expansive.

The development of online media, moreover, has delivered no obvious resolution of the crisis and may indeed be exacerbating certain aspects of the problem. Digital technology in news-rooms may lead to the spread of the 'cut and paste' culture in which journalists not only use PR to inform their stories, but increasingly 'gobble up' stories written and published online by fellow journalists working on competitor papers, as the basis for their own stories; a process which Phillips calls "news Cannibalism" (see Chapter 3, this volume). If this widespread practice continues to develop, the journalistic culture of the digital age may well come to be described as a 'Dog eat Dog' world in which journalists (literally) ingest each others' stories and spew them out in their own publications. Any thought that Web 2.0 technology might create a more pluralistic environment via an increasingly participative journalism culture built on user-generated content (see Bruns, Chapter 12, this volume) seems unlikely, even to the extent envisaged in less optimistic assessments of its use (Williams et al., Chapter 10, this volume)—and despite the fact that UGC constitutes a classic form of information subsidy. As news sources proliferate their credibility will be harder for journalists to establish, tempting them to consolidate their existing reliance on the 'tried and tested' sources in news agencies and public relations. This dog eat dog world seems likely to increase the flow of "flat earth news" rather than producing a more balanced and rounded diet of news.

NOTES

1. The study included the following newspaper groups: (1) Express Newspapers Ltd; (2) The Financial Times Ltd; (3) MGN Ltd; (4) News Group Newspapers Ltd; (5) the Telegraph Group Ltd; (6) Guardian Newspapers Ltd; (7) Independent News and Media Ltd; (8) Times Newspapers Ltd; (9) Associated Newspapers Ltd.

REFERENCES

Baistow, Tom (1985) *Fourth Rate Estate*, London: Macmillan.
Blumler, Jay G. (2010) "Foreword: The two legged crisis of journalism" in *Journalism Studies* 11 (4): pp. 439–441.
Cameron, Glenn T., Sallot, Lynne, and Curtin, Patricia (1997) "Public relations and the production of news: A critical review of theoretical frameworks" in Burleson, Brant R. (Ed) *Communication Yearbook 20*, Thousand Oaks, CA: Sage, pp. 111–155.
Cottle, Simon (2000) "Rethinking news access," *Journalism Studies* 1 (3): pp, 427–448.
Cutlip, Scott M. (1976) "Public relations in the government" *Public Relations Review* 2 (2): pp. 19–21.
Davies, Nick (2008) *Flat Earth News; An Award-Winning Reporter Exposes Falsehood, Distortion and Propaganda in the Global Media*, London: Chatto and Windus.
Davis, Aeron (2008) "Public relations in the news" in Franklin, Bob. (Ed) *Pulling Newspapers Apart; Analysing Print Journalism*, London: Routledge, pp. 272–281.

Dear, Jeremy (2009) "The Media are Failing Democracy—The Politicians are Failing the Media," Paper presented to the Media For All Conference organized by the Campaign for Press and Broadcasting Freedom, October 30–31, London. Available: http://www.cpbf.org.uk/page2/page2.html. Accessed May 7, 2010.

Engel, Matthew (2009) "Local papers: An obituary," *British Journalism Review* 20(2), pp. 55–59.

Fletcher, Kim (2006) "The Web trail," *Media Guardian* 12 (June): p. 7.

Franklin, Bob (1986) "Public relations, the local press and the coverage of local government," *Local Government Studies*, 12(4): pp. 25–33.

Franklin, Bob (1988) *Public Relations Activities In Local* Government, London: Charles Knight.

Franklin, Bob (2004) *Packaging Politics; Political Communications In Britain's Media Democracy*, London: Arnold.

Franklin, Bob (2006) *Local Journalism and Local Media; Making the Local News*, London: Routledge.

Franklin, Bob (2009a) *The Future of Newspapers*, London: Routledge.

Franklin, Bob (2009b) "A Viable Future for Local and regional Newspapers? Economic, Organisational and Democratic Considerations," Paper presented to the Campaign for Press and Broadcasting Freedom Conference Media for All? October 30–31 2009, London, UK. Available: http://www.cpbf.org.uk/page2/page2.html. Accessed February 21, 2010.

Franklin, Bob (2010) "Introduction—The Future of Journalism," *Journalism Studies* 11(4).

Franklin, Bob (2011) *The Future of Journalism*, London: Routledge.

Franklin, Bob, Lewis, Justin, and Williams Andrew (2009) "Journalism, news sources and public relations" in Allan, Stuart (Ed) *The Routledge News and Journalism Studies Companion*, London: Routledge, pp. 202–211.

Franklin, Bob and VanSlyke, Judy (1988) "Information subsidies: Agenda setting traditions," *Public Relations Review*, Spring: pp. 29–41.

Gandy, Oscar (1982) *Beyond Agenda Setting: Information subsidies and public policy*, New York: Ablex.

Gans, Herbert (1979) *Deciding What's News*, New York: Pantheon.

Harrison, Shirley (1995) *Public Relations: An introduction*, London: Routledge.

Harrison, Shirley (2006) "Local Government Public Relations and the Local Press" in Bob Franklin *Local Journalism and Local Media: Making the Local News*, London: Routledge, pp. 175–188.

Heathcote, Colin (1986) "The Disappearing Council Reporter," *Newstime* September: pp. 9–11.

Larsson, Larsake (2002) "Journalists and politicians: A relationship requiring manoeuvring space," *Journalism Studies* 3(1): pp. 21–33.

L'Etang, Jacquie (2004) *Public Relations in Britain: A history of professional practice in the twentieth century*, Mahwah, NJ: Lawrence Erlbaum Associates.

Lewis, Justin, Williams, Andrew, and Franklin, Bob (2008) "A compromised fourth estate? UK news journalism, public relations and news sources," *Journalism Studies* 9(1): pp. 1–20.

Lewis, Justin, Williams, Andrew, and Franklin, Bob (2008a) "Four rumours and an explanation: A political economic account of journalists' changing news gathering and reporting practices," *Journalism Practice* 2(1): pp. 27–45.

Lewis, Justin Williams, Andrew Franklin, Bob, Thomas, James, and Mosdell, Nick (2006) "The Quality and Independence of British Journalism," commissioned report for the Joseph Rowntree Charitable Trust. Cardiff: Cardiff University.

Machill, Marcel and Beiler, Markus (2009) "The importance of the Internet for journalistic research," *Journalism Studies* 10(2) April: pp. 178–203.

Maloney, Kevin (2006) *Rethinking Public Relations: PR, Propaganda and Democracy*, Routledge: New York.

Manning, Paul (2008) "The press association and news agency sources," in Franklin Bob (Ed) *Pulling Newspapers Apart; Analysing Print Journalism*, London: Routledge, pp. 262–271.

Marr, Andrew (2004) *My Trade: A short history of British journalism*, Basingstoke: Macmillan.

McChesney, Robert, W. and Nichols, John (2010) *The Death and Life of American Journalism: The media revolution that will begin the world again*, Philadelphia: Nation Books.

Miller, David and Dinan, William (2000) "The rise of the PR industry in Britain, 1979–1998," *European Journal of Communication* 15(1): pp. 5–35.

Miller, David and Dinan, William (2008) "Journalism, public relations and spin" in Wahl-Jorgensen, Karin and Thomas Hanitzsche (Eds) *The Handbook of Journalism Studies*, New York and London: Routledge, pp. 250–264.

O'Neill, Deirdre and O'Connor, Catherine (2009) "The passive journalist: How sources dominate local news," *Journalism Practice* 2(1): pp. 487–500.

Phillips, Angela (2010) "New sources and old bottles" in N. Fenton (Ed) *New Media, Old News: Journalism and democracy in the digital age*, London: Sage, pp. 87–101.

Reich, Zvi (2006) "The process model of news initiative: Sources lead first, reporters thereafter," *Journalism Studies* 7(4), pp. 497–514.

Reich, Zvi (2009) *Sourcing The News; Key Issues in Journalism—An Innovative Study of the Israeli Press*, Cresskill, NJ: Hampton Press.

Rusbridger, Alan (2010) "Does Journalism Exist?" The Annual Hugh Cudlipp Lecture, January 25, 2010. Available: http://www.guardian.co.uk/media/2010/jan/25/cudlipp-lecture-alan-rusbridger. Accessed January 26, 2010.

Starr, Paul (2009) "The end of the press: Democracy loses its best friend," *The New Republic*, March 4, pp. 28–35.

Tunstall, Jeremy (1971) *Journalists At Work*, London: Constable.

White, Jon and Hobsbawm, Julia (2007) "Public relations and journalism: The unquiet relationship—a view from the United Kingdom," *Journalism Practice* 1 (2): pp. 283–292.

Williams, Granville (2006) "Profits before product? Ownership and economic of the local press." in Bob Franklin (Ed) *Local Journalism and Local Media: Making the local news*, London: Routledge, pp. 83–92.

7 Sourcing Business News
A Case Study of Public Relations Uptake

Tom Van Hout

INTRODUCTION

Scene 1. Senior business reporter Rutger receives a morning telephone call from a spokesperson for the Flemish Minister of Science. He informs Rutger that new management agreements between the Flemish Government and two Flemish research institutes have been signed. Rutger makes note of this information on a notepad. The spokesperson also announces that a press release will be issued later that day and that the PowerPoint slides used during the press conference are available upon request.

Scene 2. Halfway through the 2:00 p.m. story meeting a few hours later, Rutger mentions the newly signed agreements, adding that the research institutes in question will be receiving a 20% budget increase. Following a brief exchange, the desk chief assigns Rutger a 60-line story on p. 4 of the business section.

Scene 3. At 4:20 p.m., Rutger retrieves an email received at 2:59 p.m. from the Flemish Ministry of Science, opens the attached press release, skims, prints, and closes it. He then opens the second attachment and scans the six slides and their notes of a PowerPoint presentation. Next, Rutger opens a text-editing window and starts writing the lead. Exactly 24 minutes and 40 seconds later, he forwards his story to the copy editors.

This brief analytical vignette, drawn from my field notes, describes journalism practice as a form of *literacy*. The current proliferation of literacy studies (Barton, Hamilton, and Ivanic, 2000; Coiro et al., 2008; Collins and Blot, 2003; Gee, 2007; Kress, 2003; Lankshear and Knobel, 2003, p. 425; 2006) draws on a social theory of literacy (as articulated in Heath, 1983; Scribner and Cole, 1981; Street, 1985—three seminal texts in this tradition) that understands literacy as a textually-mediated interpretive process, rather than just the ability to read and write. In this approach, language use is seen as a contextually embedded *social achievement*. Acts of literacy then become domain specific, highly variable (hence the ubiquity of *literacies* in the literature), historically located, goal oriented and socially structured. Two analytical units are central to the field of literacy studies: *literacy events* and *literacy practices*.

Literacy events are observable episodes of textual mediation. Cooking from a recipe, writing a blog post, listening to a museum audio-guide, using visual aids during a presentation are all examples of activities that revolve around texts—they usually feature talk *around* and/or *about* texts. Coined by Anderson, Teale, and Estrada (1980), the term 'literacy event' was used by Heath (1983, p. 93) to analyze the role of spoken and written language in particular communicative acts, namely "any occasion in which a piece of writing is integral to the nature of participants' interactions and their interpretive processes."

Literacy practices are the things people do with literacy. They refer to the particular uses texts have in social life and how these relate to higher order phenomena such as the workings of power and authority in particular social fields. In each of the three scenes described above, Rutger engages in specific literacy practices: he writes down the information received, introduces the newly signed agreements during the story meeting, reads a press release and a PowerPoint presentation on his computer screen and writes a news article based on this information. The empirical challenge lies in linking these socially situated practices (the micro) to models of doing journalism (the macro) which provide "the normative frame of interpretation for a given act of reading or writing" (Collins and Slembrouck, 2007, p. 38).

This chapter analyzes one such literacy event in detail: the technological, social and discursive practices a senior business reporter engages in as he discovers, negotiates and writes a short news article from two institutional news sources: a press release and a PowerPoint presentation. I will use the three scenes above to analyze *journalism as a literacy event*, focusing in particular on the literacy practices that underpin Rutger's reanimation of the telephone conversation during the story meeting in Scene 2 and his subsequent use of PR materials during the writing process in Scene 3. From there, I link up Rutger's literacy practices with broader conceptions of journalism.

FOLLOWING THE STORY

The news story (henceforth: the VIB story) is concerned with increased government funding of biotechnology and nanotechnology research. Two Flemish research institutes, the *Flanders Interuniversity Institute for Biotechnology* (VIB) and the *Interuniversity Microelectronics Centre* (IMEC) were awarded 5-year research contracts by the Flemish government. This news was not listed in the story budget; it was an unplanned story that was brought to Rutger's attention by a spokesperson for the Flemish Minister of Science. The spokesperson had telephoned Rutger to ask if he was planning on attending the press conference. On hearing that he was not, the spokesperson informed Rutger that a press release would be distributed and that the slides used during the press conference were also available. Rutger inquired about the increased funding, made a few handwritten notes, and said he would have a look at the documents.

The data presented below were collected during fieldwork between October 2006 and March 2007 at the business news-desk of *De Standaard*, a quality newspaper serving the Dutch-speaking population in Belgium. My interest in Rutger as an agent in the field was sparked by his newsroom status: he was promoted to adjunct desk chief and won a professional award for journalistic excellence during my fieldwork. He was also one of the first reporters to participate in my research project. Rutger occupied the workspace directly next to me and so I was able to observe him throughout the entire production process: I overheard him taking the call, I sat next to him at the story meeting (which I audio-recorded), I was able to record his writing process, conduct and record an interview with him shortly afterwards and collect the source material that was emailed to him. I did not gain direct access to his telephone notes.

To record Rutger's writing process in real time, I used two software applications with his informed consent: Inputlog and Camtasia. Inputlog (Leijten and Van Waes, 2006) is a Microsoft Windows based keystroke logging tool that records keyboard strokes and mouse movements. Camtasia Studio is an online screen registration tool which records computer screen action (Degenhardt, 2006). Both applications run in the background and do not interfere with normal computer operations. The software recorded the writing process from the moment Rutger started writing until he filed the story for copy-editing.

Analytically, the writing process data are combined with observational, textual and interview data in an attempt to follow the story from the moment it enters the newsroom until it is filed for copy-editing. This is an approach that studies how news production unfolds through time and space (Van Hout and Jacobs, 2008; Van Hout and Macgilchrist, 2010). Close attention is paid to Rutger's situated language use: (i) how he talks the story into being at the story meeting and how this talk finds its way onto his computer screen and into his news article; and (ii) how his literacy practices speak to wider (and contested) journalistic issues such as authorship, authority, and source reliance.

THE UPTAKE OF AN 'INFORMATION SUBSIDY'

Every day around 2:00 p.m., the economics news-desk convenes for a story meeting: informal editorial gatherings where decisions on story selection and play are made (cf. Clayman and Reisner, 1998; Cotter, 2010). These meetings are literacy events *par excellence*: ritualized (and hence discursively stable, repeated and observable) episodes of textual mediation that feature two dominant literacy practices:

(i) to talk about and around planned or spot news events; and
(ii) the inscription of mutually established decisions about story play and authorship

Extract 1 below is based on an audio recording of the story meeting during which Rutger introduces the VIB story. Relevant lines are indicated in bold. The story meeting was attended by nine members of staff (Frank, Jack, Koen, William, Rutger, Jef, Mitch, Kate, and Ann) and myself.

Extract 1

DS_W16_D4_eco. Rutger introduces the VIB story 10 minutes into the story meeting

```
1  William:  kheb Pieterke Pieter dan al voor z'n tekenfilms gezet
             "I've got lil' Pieter Pieter in front of his cartoons"

2            ( ) om ( ) (gelach)
             "by then ( ) to ( )" (laughter)

3  Rutger:   er is ook nog euh- (gelach)
             "there's also ehm-" (laughter)

4  Jef:      goh, gij begint daar nu al mee?
             "jeez, are you already doing that now?"

5  Koen:     ja, da's onge[loofelijk dat wordt een ramp die opvoeding
             "yeah, that's incredible that's some education"

6            zoiets
             "something"

7  Rutger:   de ondertekening van het nieuwe beheersovereenkomst
             "the signing of the new management agreement"

8            tussen de Vlaamse Overheid en euh het VIB en IMEC
             "between the Flemish government and erm the VIB and
             IMEC"

9            die krijgen 20% meer geld
             "they're getting 20% more money"

10 Koen:     wat? twee maand?
             "what? two months?"

11 William:  drie
             "three"

12 Koen:     drie maand en hij zet hem al voor tv (laughter)
             "three months and he's already watching tv" (laughter)

13 Rutger:   moet daar aandacht aan geschonken worden?
             "should attention be paid to this?"

14 Mitch:    60 lijn- op 60 lijntjes op eco 4, nee?
             "60 lin- 60 lines on eco 4, no?"
```

```
15                      als ze meer geld krijgen
                        "if they get more money"

16   Rutger:           ja 20 procent (  )
                        "yeah 20 percent (  )"
```

The extract begins as William, a new father, engages in a byplay (Goffman, 1981) about his parenting practices. This byplay crosscuts Rutger's attempt at introducing the VIB story (line 3). Of particular interest is the way in which Rutger formulates his story pitch. Shifting into a formal, nominalized register typically associated with written language, Rutger's lines 7 through 9 introduce the VIB story by referring to 'the signing' of the contract, the institutional partners involved and the budget increase. I would argue that Rutger is performing a social identity of professional *authority*: the reporter as fact finder, a reliable 'detached voice' who uncovers newsworthy events so he can report them objectively. Crucially, Rutger performs this identity by adopting an authorial voice of neutrality. This non-evaluative stance is known in the literature as *reporter voice* (Martin and White, 2005) and "involves a substantial curtailment of the author's use of explicitly attitudinal meanings" (Thomson, White, and Kitley et al., 2008, p. 221). Rutger animates just the facts of the VIB story, that is "the signing of the new management agreement between the Flemish government and erm the VIB and IMEC." This pitch draws on the interview notes Rutger made during the preceding telephone conversation with the government spokesperson. The theoretical upshot of this literacy practice is that it illustrates the *social uptake* of PR discourse.

Previously, the notion of *preformulation* (Jacobs, 1999) was seen as a textual property of press releases: the form and function of press releases mirrors that of newspaper articles in an attempt to facilitate their reproduction by reporters (Catenaccio, 2008; Lassen, 2006; McLaren and Gurău, 2005; Pander Maat, 2008). However, this extract illustrates a *performative function of preformulation*. Rutger's reanimation of the interview notes made during the telephone conversation with the government spokesperson exemplifies Freadman's (1994) notion of uptake: a tennis metaphor that captures how texts in a particular genre (e.g., a press release) can be seen as 'serves' that elicit 'returns', namely a responding text in another genre (e.g., a newspaper article). That Rutger's story pitch appeals to news values (i.e., prominence ['the Flemish Government'] and [future] impact ["a 20% budget increase"]) and constrains attitudinal language is neither revealing nor unusual; it is squarely within the calcified journalistic ethos of objectivity (see for instance Hampton, 2008; Muñoz-Torres, 2007; Schudson, 2001; Soffer, 2009; Thorsen, 2008; Tuchman, 1972). However, that he reanimates interview notes during a story pitch does break new ground. Moreover, this particular literacy practice offers empirical support for Lewis et al.'s (2008, p. 31) claim that "much news is recycled from other sources without acknowledgement," even during story meetings (See Chapters 5, 6, and 8, this volume).

What is more, Rutger's literacy practice during the story meeting illustrates how source-media interaction and source status impinge on the news production process, and, ultimately, how "source power is 'in play' in the process of producing business news" (Kjær and Langer, 2003, p. 3). That a spokesperson for the Flemish Government initiates the contact lends authority and credibility to the news story and supports Zvi Reich's (2006, p. 597) understanding of source-media interaction as neither unilateral nor reciprocal but as a combination of the two: "a two-phase process, in which the dominant initiator changes according to the phase, sources dominating in the discovery phase, reporters in the gathering phase" (see Chapter 1, this volume).

In the discovery phase of the VIB story, the spokesperson clearly has the advantage: he decides on the interactional context (in this case, a telephone conversation followed by email communication), initiates the contact and can "influence access, but within certain limitations so as not to alienate reporters" (Kjær and Langer, 2003, p. 7). While I can only rely on an impressionistic reconstruction of the telephone conversation (as encoded in my field notes and briefly discussed during the retrospective interview), it is clear that the spokesperson did not 'alienate' Rutger. On the contrary, by simply placing a call to Rutger, whom he knew professionally, the spokesperson gains newspaper access. In essence, the interaction constitutes a *market transaction*: Rutger is provided with (unsolicited) information from a presumably knowledgeable, elite news source which saves him valuable time. The spokesperson meanwhile gains public attention for the increased government funding through Rutger's press coverage. Basically, this is a game of 'tit for tat' (Fengler and Russ-Mohl, 2008, p. 677): a mutually beneficial source-media collaboration that is neither adversarial nor lopsided.

Conversely, during the story meeting, Rutger has the upper hand: as a member of staff, only Rutger has the agentive power to consult the desk chief whether or not to run an unplanned story. The passive voice construction in line 13 functions as a sort of authorship hedge: Rutger mitigates responsibility for writing this story. He is not asking whether *he* should write the story, he is asking whether it *should* be run or not. Mitch immediately assigns Rutger 60 lines on p. 4 of the business section but asks him for confirmation of the budget increase, which Rutger gives in line 16.

Before moving on to Scene 3 (story inscription), it is perhaps helpful to rephrase the gist of my argument. I see journalism as a socially situated practice—a news literacy event—that is built around at least three observable episodes of textual mediation: story inception (Scene 1), story negotiation (Scene 2) and story inscription (Scene 3). In my impressionistic reconstruction of Scene 1, we saw that Rutger engaged in a number of literacy practices: he received a phone call from a government spokesperson announcing new research contracts, he asked about the increased budget and made a few notes on a notepad. I then turned to the story meeting in Scene 2 to analyze how Rutger introduces the VIB story amid subordinate communication. It was shown that Rutger performs a social identity of professional authority ('the reporter as fact finder') that (i) reveals the social uptake of PR discourse; and (ii) constitutes a 'tit for tat' market transaction in which the spokesperson and Rutger rely on various degrees of authorial power: the spokesperson takes the lead in Scene 1 while Rutger does so in Scene 2. In what follows, I turn to Rutger's literacy practices as he writes the VIB story from source texts.

WRITING FROM SOURCE MATERIALS

Perrin (2003) distinguishes two "meso level" actions in the "writing progression" of journalists: the production of new text and the revision of text produced so far (Leijten, 2007). A similar approach is adopted here. Figure 7.1 graphically represents Rutger's writing process by plotting temporal data (in absolute time) against process data, namely number of keyboard strokes (in 1 minute intervals), and mouse commands (movement and clicks).

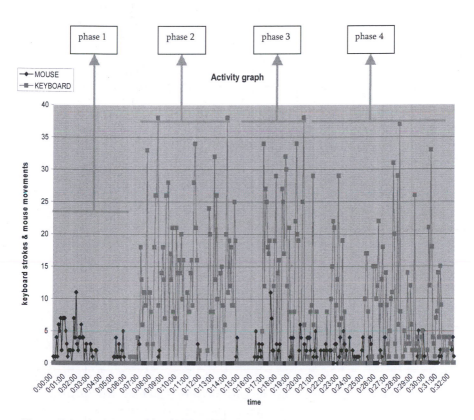

Figure 7.1   Activity graph of VIB writing process.

Figure 7.1 shows four distinct phases in Rutger's writing process, marked by patterns of mouse movements (bulleted line graphs) and keyboard strokes (squared line graphs): a preparatory phase (0'00"–7'00"), two text construction phases (7'00"–15'00" and 15'00"– 20'00") and a revision phase (20'00"– 32'00"). In what follows, I describe these four phases with interview, observational, keystroke logging and screen video data in an attempt to connect Rutger's literacy practices with wider journalistic norms.

Phase 1: Reading Source Texts

The preparatory phase consists of primarily mouse movements that correspond with the following computer literacies:

- checking email: Rutger opens a forwarded email message from the desk chief, a response from a reader to an article Rutger wrote and an email from a press officer at the Flemish Ministry of Science, received at 2:59 p.m.;
- reading email attachments: the 2:59 p.m. email contains two attachments: the PowerPoint presentation used during the press conference and the press release announcing the research contracts. I know this because the email (as later forwarded to me by Rutger) reads:

> Beste, In bijlage vindt u, zoals afgesproken met [naam woordvoerder], de slides en de persmededeling van vanmorgen. Met vriendelijke groeten, [naam medewerker persdienst en handtekening]

> *Dear sir, as agreed with [name of the spokesperson], please find attached the slides and press release from this morning. Kind regards, [press officer name and signature].*

Rutger first opens the press release, scrolls through it and sends it to the printer. Next, he opens the PowerPoint presentation and starts browsing the first two slides, including the text in the comments section. He pauses to walk to the printer, returns and goes through the remaining four slides of the PowerPoint presentation. Asked if he knows how he is going to write the story in advance or that he first makes notes, Rutger said:

> ik heb eerst die persmedeling gelezen en die slides goed bekeken tja en dan haal je eruit wat het nieuws is namelijk dat ze meer geld krijgen. Maar euh ik heb af en toe wel euh teruggekeken in die slides om dat laatste stuk te schrijven.

> *I first read the press release and took a close look at the slides and then well you pull out what the news is namely that they are getting more money. But ehm every now and then I ehm looked back at the slides to write that last piece.*

Having read the source documents, let us now look at exactly how Rutger extracts "what the news is" from the press release before turning to "that last piece."

Phase 2: Writing From the Government Press Release

With the PowerPoint presentation opened on screen and a printout of the press release in front of him, Rutger navigates to the control window in the editorial platform, opens the assigned editing window, writes the lead, the byline and the first sentence of the second paragraph and previews the article. These six operations take 1 minute and 35 seconds. Note the remarkable similarity in lexicogrammatical uptake between:

(i) Rutger's story pitch in Extract 1: "there's also ehm the signing of the new management agreement between the Flemish government and erm the VIB and IMEC they're getting 20% more money."

(ii) the "text produced so far":
[lead] The Flemish research centers VIB and Imec are getting more money from the Flemish Government.
[byline] Policy Brussels.
[body] The subsidy raise is included in the new management agreements that were signed yesterday in Ghent.

(iii) the opening lines of the Ministry of Science press release in Figure 7.2:

Press Release from Fientje Moerman, Vice-Minister-President of the Flemish Government and Flemish Minister for Economy, Enterprise, Science, Innovation and Foreign Trade

08-03-2007

<u>More than 400 million euro for biotech and nanotech</u>

Today Flemish Minister for Science and Innovation Fientje Moerman has signed the new management agreements (2007 – 2011) for VIB and IMEC. The Flemish government reserves more than 400 million euro in the coming five years for research in these two top institutes. The budget of operation of both institutes increases with 20%.

Figure 7.2 Opening paragraph of the ministry of science press release (official translation).

In each of these three texts, the signing of the contract, the institutional partners involved (the Flemish government, VIB and IMEC) and the contracted decision (a subsidy raise) are explicitly mentioned. These elements respectively account for the 'how?' 'the who?' and the 'what?' of this story. The 'when?' and the 'where?' are covered in Rutger's text produced so far ('yesterday', 'Ghent') and in the press release ('Today', 'UZ Gent'). That Rutger changes the temporal referent from 'today' to 'yesterday' is logical: this article was published on March 9, 2007, one day after the signing.

There is an interesting interactional dynamic at work here. Returning to the tennis metaphor that Anne Freadman (1994) employs in her work on genre, we see that the Ministry of Science spokesperson initiates a soft underhand serve that Rutger plays back—playbacks is perhaps more accurate here—at the 2:00 p.m. story meeting. By deduction, Rutger's return volley ("there's also ehm . . .") can only have been based on the information he received (and wrote down) from the spokesperson. Rutger received the press release electronically at 2:59 p.m., some 45 minutes after the story meeting had ended. Rutger's backhand slice ("should attention be paid to this?") is met with a drop shot from Mitch ("if they get more money") which Rutger lobs back ("yeah 20 percent"). Judging from the screen video, the press release that Rutger has in front of him as he writes functions as a ball machine that feeds him ready-made (preformulated) news discourse, namely a lead sentence and the opening sentence of his second paragraph. In other words, what we have here is a genre that travels remarkably well across semiotic spaces—the equivalent of a tennis player who performs equally well on carpet, clay, grass, and hard court. Indeed, the "information subsidy" (Gandy, 1982; Vanslyke-Turk, 1985) relayed by the spokesperson makes the leap from a fleeting telephone conversation to notes scribbled on a notepad, survives the 2:00 p.m. story unscathed and re-emerges as an email attachment that finds its way onto Rutger's editing window and into his news article.

That Rutger draws quite heavily on the press release is supported by the writing process data. As can be seen in the activity graph in Figure 7.1, there is a high count of keyboard strokes and a low count of mouse movements during the phase starting at the 7'00" mark and ending at the 15'00" mark. During this eight minute interval, Rutger composes five (out of seven) paragraphs: the lead and paragraphs two through five. Figure 7.3 represents this visually.

While I lack eye tracking data, this pattern of keyboard activity/mouse inactivity suggests that Rutger is switching back and forth between his computer screen and the press release that is on his desk; and that he writes 'what the news is' from the press release. Consider for instance Rutger's pausing behavior as he writes:

Meer geld voor techno-onderzoek

BELEID

De Vlaamse onderzoekscentra VIB en Imec krijgen meer geld van de Vlaamse regering.

BRUSSEL. De subsidieverhoging is opgenomen in de nieuwe beheersovereenkomsten die gisteren in Gent werden ondertekend door minister van Wetenschap en Innovatie Fientje Moerman (Open VLD). Ze zijn vijf jaar geldig. In die periode trekt de Vlaamse overheid meer dan 400 miljoen euro uit voor beide instellingen. Voor het Vlaams Interuniversitair Centrum voor Biotechnologie

(VIB) in Gent gaan de werkingsmiddelen voor de periode van 2007 tot 2011 naar meer dan 190 miljoen euro, 43 miljoen euro meer dan in de vorige periode.

Het Interuniversitair Microelectronicacentrum (Imec) in Leuven krijgt de komende vijf jaar meer dan 210 miljoen euro. Dat is een stijging met ruim 40 miljoen euro.

Het VIB heeft meer dan duizend onderzoekers in dienst, verdeeld over 65 onderzoeksgroepen. Bij het Imec werken zo'n 1.500 mensen. Beide instellingen zijn belangrijk voor de ontwikkeling van de Vlaamse nanotechnologie- en biotechnologiesector.

Tegenover de extra middelen

staan wel nieuwe eisen. Zo worden de instellingen verplicht een individuele code voor deugdelijk bedrijfsbeleid (corporate governance) te ontwikkelen. Er is ook een nieuwe verzameling prestatie-indicatoren, zoals de inkomsten uit onderzoek, het aantal samenwerkingsverbanden en het aantal spin-offs.

De nieuwe beheersovereenkomsten zijn opgesteld aan de hand van een soort typecontract dat voor alle Vlaamse toponderzoekscentra geldt. Dat contract zal ook gelden voor de Vlaamse Instelling voor Technologisch Onderzoek (Vito) en het Interdisciplinair Instituut voor Breedbandtechnologie (IBBT). (rmg)

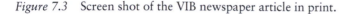

> Paragraphs one through five as composed during phase 2 of Rutger's writing process

Figure 7.3   Screen shot of the VIB newspaper article in print.

Ze zijn vijf jaar geldig. In die periode trekt de Vlaamse overheid meer dan 400 miljoen euro uit voor beide instellingen.

They are valid for five years. In this period the Flemish government reserves upwards of 400 million euro for both institutes.

In Inputlog notation, this becomes:

Having closed the preview pane, Rutger pauses for 12 seconds before writing that the new management agreements are "valid for five years." This sequence of pausing followed by text production is repeated three

Table 7.1   Linear Log Extract (5-second intervals, 2-second pause threshold)

0:08:36	[Left Button] [Movement] {12.2}
0:08:41	
0:08:46	Ze · zijn · viujf ·
0:08:51	jBS BS BS BS f · jaar · geldig.
0:08:56	· In · die · peroi
0:09:01	BS BS iode · {4.8}
0:09:06	trekt · de · Vlaamse · overheid · {2.1}
0:09:11	meer · dan · 400 · miljoen · euro ·
0:09:16	uit · voor · beide · instellingen. · {7.3}

times in this extract. I would argue that Rutger's pausing behavior here is the direct result of his reproductive labor. Every time he pauses, he shifts his gaze away from his computer screen, onto the press release and back to this screen. In other words, Rutger lifts information from the press release and inserts it in his news article. The two pieces of information that Rutger encodes in Table 7.1 can be found almost verbatim in the press release. That the contract runs for five years is mentioned twice in the press release, first in parenthesized numbers '(2007–2011)' and second as a nominal clause 'de komende vijf jaar' (Eng. *the coming five years*). The financial scale is mentioned in the first paragraph of the Dutch version press release:

De Vlaamse overheid trekt de komende vijf jaar in totaal meer dan 400 miljoen uit voor onderzoek aan beide topinstellingen.

The Flemish government reserves more than 400 million euro in the coming five years for research in these two top institutes.

Rutger copies this sentence almost verbatim, bar the "top" qualifier in "both institutes." Corpus linguistic research has found that such toning down or neutralizing of press copy is a common journalistic rewriting practice (Pander Maat, 2008).

It is not difficult to trace back Rutger's first five paragraphs to the press release. Indeed, there is a striking textual overlap between the press release and Rutger's article with respect to the budget increase specifications for both institutes and the VIB and IMEC boilerplates. Methodologically, this textual overlap can just as well be gleaned from a content analysis of both texts (see Table 7.2). However, the same cannot be said of Rutger's final two paragraphs.

Phase 3: Writing from the PowerPoint Presentation

So far, I have argued that

(i) Rutger draws primarily on a hard copy of the government press release to write the first five paragraphs of his news article; and
(ii) this literacy practice has a transparent intertextual history: its traces are easily revealed in a comparative analysis of source materials and newspaper articles.

In other words, Lewis et al.'s (2008, p. 43) method of establishing "textual precedents to an article" would likely arrive at the same conclusion: Rutger's first five paragraphs are wholly or largely derivative of press release copy (See Chapters 6 and 8, this volume). However, given that the PowerPoint presentation was not made publicly available (it was emailed to Rutger), a content analysis would find no "verifiable textual evidence" for Rutger's final two paragraphs. In this section, I present empirical evidence that shows how Rutger writes from the PowerPoint presentation.

Table 7.2   Textual Overlap between the Press Release and Rutger's News Article

	Press Release	News Article
Dutch	[2nd paragraph, 1st sentence] De werkingsmiddelen voor het VIB stijgen met meer dan 43 miljoen euro, van circa 147 miljoen euro in de vorige beheersovereenkomst naar meer dan 190 miljoen euro. Dit bedrag wordt gespreid over de komende vijf jaar.	[3rd paragraph, 2nd sentence] Voor het Vlaams Interuniversitair Centrum voor Biotechnologie (VIB) in Gent gaan de werkingsmiddelen voor de periode van 2007 tot 2011 naar meer dan 190 miljoen euro, 43 miljoen euro meer dan in de vorige periode.
English	VIB's budget increases with 43,320,000 euro, from 147,200,000 euro in the last management agreement to 190,520,000 euro now. This amount will be spread over the coming five years.	The Flemish Interuniversity Centre for Biotechnology in Ghent sees its 2007–2011 budget rise to more than 190 million euro, 43 million more than during the last period.
Dutch	[3rd paragraph, 1st sentence] IMEC ontvangt de komende vijf jaar meer dan 210 miljoen euro van de Vlaamse overheid, wat een stijging van ruim 40 miljoen euro betekent.	[4th paragraph, 1st sentence] Het Interuniversitair Micro-electronicacentrum (Imec) in Leuven krijgt de komende vijf jaar meer dan 210 miljoen euro. Dat is een stijging met ruim 40 miljoen euro.
English	IMEC receives over the next five years 212,045,000 euro from the Flemish government, which means an increase of 39,245,000 euro.	The Interuniversity Microelectronics Centre in Louvain receives over the next five more than 210 million euro. That is an increase of more than 40 million euro.
Dutch	[4th paragraph] Het VIB in Zwijnaarde heeft een wereldwijde reputatie op het vlak van onderzoek naar biotechnologie. Het is een autonoom onderzoeks-centrum met meer dan 1000 onderzoekers, verdeeld over 65 onderzoeksgroepen. Zij doen onderzoek in onder meer de moleculaire biologie, de ont-wikkelingsbiologie en de genetica.	[5th paragraph, 1st sentence] Het VIB heeft meer dan duizend onderzoekers in dienst, verdeeld over 65 onderzoeksgroepen.
English	VIB in Ghent has a worldwide reputation in the field of bio-tech research. This autonomous research center has more than 1000 researchers in 65 research groups. They perform research amongst others in molecular biology, developmental biology and genetics.	VIB employs more than one thousand researchers, divided over 65 research groups.

When he is 14 minutes and 26 seconds into his writing process, Rutger opens paragraph six with 'Tegenover de extra middelen staan wel nieuwe eisen' [*The extra funds do come with new demands*). This text insertion is followed by more than two minutes of keyboard inactivity during which Rutger navigates to the PowerPoint presentation, reading (interpreted as keyboard inactivity and mouse scrolling) the notes of the second slide in detail. A different material setup emerges here. Rutger navigates between his editing window and the PowerPoint file, recycling the notes from the latter in the former. Logically, this literacy practice results in mouse movements that minimize, move or maximize windows. The activity graph in Figure 7.1 above visualizes this dynamic. Note the increase in mouse activity in phase 3 as compared to phase 2.

Paragraph six in Rutger's news article details the performance demands of the new management agreements. These demands are outlined in the notes to slide 2 and comprise three elements: the development of a corporate governance code, the realization of a number of strategic goals and an annual evaluation based on a list of performance indicators. Rutger copies all three demands. Figure 7.4 shows a screenshot illustrating Rutger's onscreen window layout in combination with the corresponding linear log extract as he copies the first performance demand.

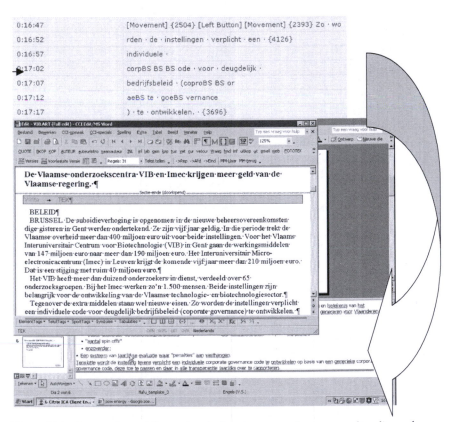

Figure 7.4   Screen shot of Rutger's window layout and corresponding linear log.

In this particular sequence, Rutger rewrites the bottom sentence under-
lined in green in Figure 7.4.

This sentence is hidden in the notes to slide 2 and reads:

> Tenslotte (sic) wordt de instelling tevens verplicht een individuele cor-
> porate governance code te ontwikkelen op basis van een generieke cor-
> porate governance code, deze toe te passen en daar in alle transparantie
> jaarlijks over te rapporteren.
>
> *Finally the institution is required to develop an individual corporate*
> *governance code based on a generic corporate governance code, apply*
> *this code and annually report on it in all transparency.*

Rutger rewrites this sentence as:

> Zo worden de instellingen verplicht een individuele code voor deugdelijk
> bedrijfsbeleid (coporate governance) te ontwikkelen.
>
> *The institutions are required to develop an individual code of proper*
> *company management (coporate governance).*

The linear log shows Rutger correcting himself four letters into
'corp'(orate) governance, hitting backspace three times and typing the somewhat more extensive Dutch alternative 'code voor deugdelijk bedrijfsbeleid'
[*code of proper company management*] and parenthesizing 'coporate governance' (but not correcting the typo), thereby explaining the term.

Next, Rutger turns to the other two performance demands of the new
agreement. In order to visualize these elements on his screen, Rutger has to
resize his editing window. The three performance indicators (research-gen-
erated revenue, the number of joint ventures and the number of spin-offs
realized) he lists in paragraph six and he details the model contract in paragraph seven, adding that this model contract also applies to two other Flemish
research institutes: Vito and IBBT. Rutger then previews the article.

If we compare Rutger's literacy practices in phases 2 and 3, we see that
they differ in their material setup: the dominant source text in phase 2 is
a hard copy of the press release. In phase 3, the dominant source text is a
PowerPoint presentation. In both cases, Rutger engages in what I would call
reading-to-write, a reproductive news literacy practice. In phase 2, Rutger
goes back and forth between his editing window and the press release he
has in front of him to write the first five paragraphs. In phase 3, Rutger
navigates between computer windows (his editing window and the presentation window) to write paragraphs six and seven.

Phase 4: Revising and Filling Out the Text Box

Seeing that he has some whitespace to fill (the editorial platform requires
authors to fill the text boxes they have been assigned), Rutger navigates to

the Vito and IBBT homepages, verifies what the acronyms stand for and writes them in full. Then, he googles 'vlaams instituut voor technologisch onderzoek' and finds that 'i' in Vito stands for 'instelling' [*Establishment*] and not 'instituut' [*institute*]. He corrects this in his article. Next, he navigates to the IMEC and VIB homepages, verifies what the acronyms stand for by means of a google search and writes them out. In this phase then, Rutger is no longer *reading-to-write*, he is *reading-to-revise*. Commenting on this literacy practice, Rutger says matter-of-factly:

> wel ik heb die dozen toegestuurd gekregen en ik moet die vullen.
>
> *well I was assigned these boxes and I have to fill them.*

However, Rutger is doing more than merely 'filling the box'; by double-checking what the acronyms stand for, Rutger is taking authorial responsibility for "the accuracy of the mimetic reproduction" (Peterson, 2001, p. 202) of the names listed in the PowerPoint presentation.

In what follows, Rutger adds the VIB and IMEC URLs at the bottom of his article, marks up the byline and writes the headline, something he usually does last he later told me. He then starts revising the article, adding for instance that the management agreements were signed by 'the Minister of Science and Innovation Fientje Moerman (Open VLD)'. Finally, Rutger adds his initials, previews the text and files it for copy-editing. The entire production process takes 33 minutes and 23 seconds.

WRITING NEWS AT SPEED

This chapter tracked the newsroom trajectory of an unplanned news story about increased government funding of biotechnology and nano-technology research from its point of entry until the moment it was filed for copy-editing. I argued that journalism can be productively described as a social practice, a *literacy event* comprising three distinct episodes of textual mediation: story inception, negotiation and inscription. These episodes were briefly contextualized in analytical vignettes that documented the various news literacies reporter Rutger engaged in: taking notes during a telephone conversation, reanimating those notes during a story meeting, writing from source documents (reading-to-write) and filling out the assigned text box (reading-to-revise). Table 7.3 summarizes these observed literacy practices.

By combining observational, textual, screen video, keystroke logging and interview data, I was able to document not only the mediating labor of the reporter as he reproduces a press release at speed but also the extent to which PR discourse shapes routine flows of business news. What started as a proactive telephone inquiry, resulted in a few quick notes on a piece of paper and a subsequent story pitch. Having been assigned 60 lines, the

Table 7.3   Journalism as Literacy: The Case of the VIB News Story

VIB news as a **literacy event**	
Three episodes of textual mediation	consisting of a range of **literacy practices**
Scene 1: Story inception	• Rutger takes a phone call; • he enquires about the new contract; • he makes a few notes on a notepad
Scene 2: Story negotiation	• Rutger introduces the VIB story during the story meeting by: • reanimating PR discourse; • appealing to the news values of prominence; and • constraining attitudinal language
Scene 3: Story inscription	• Rutger reads two source text; • he writes from the source texts; • and fills out the assigned text box

reporter drew quite heavily on email attachments from the ministry to source the story but he did not attribute the source in his news text.

During the retrospective interview, the reporter commented that overt source attributions such as *according to an official statement* are "rather useless" and that he makes a point of not mentioning them. However, in his news article, Rutger refers to the "new management agreements which were signed yesterday. . . ." Commenting on why he refers explicitly to this pseudo-event (but not to the press release), Rutger said "well, there was a press conference, so it would be weird not to write that." Rutger's journalistic authority is thus built on his concealment of the two preformulated news sources—which happened to fall on his lap—without having had to attend the press conference. This provides empirical evidence for what Zelizer (2007, p. 425) observes: "The combination of technology and nonconventional journalists [i.c. PR officers] has allowed the news media to claim that they 'have been there' as witnesses of events that they have not witnessed."

CONCLUSIONS

What implications can be drawn that extend beyond the analysis of a unique case? I would argue that the close analysis of journalists at work can provide fine-grained insights into the professional routines and mediating labor of journalists. Such knowledge has the potential to retrodict assumptions made by less close—but more comprehensive—studies of journalism. As I hope to have shown, writing news from sources is more complex than simply 'churning' ready-made materials into news. It crucially involves the curation of news texts (PR copy, interview notes), domain knowledge and professional experience into a single narrative, framed as an authoritative account of a pseudo-event. The work Rutger does bears some of the marks traditionally associated with journalism, namely the collection, processing and presentation of newsworthy information. A major difference is that internet technologies allow the reporter to source news quickly and efficiently *from his workstation*. By incorporating information from the PowerPoint presentation, Rutger is able to balance the story and neutralize its institutional slant. While not exactly hard-hitting, investigative journalism, the case study presented here shows how a senior business reporter accomplishes a routine task within the institutional and technical constraints that contextualize contemporary journalism.

REFERENCES

Anderson, Alonzo B., Teale, William H. and Estrada, Elette (1980) "Low-income children's preschool literacy experiences: Some naturalistic observations" *Quarterly Newsletter of the Laboratory of Comparative Human Cognition* 2: 59–65.

Barton, David, Hamilton, Mary, and Ivanic, Roz (Eds) (2000) *Situated Literacies: Reading and writing in context,* London: Routledge.

Catenaccio, Paola (2008) "Press releases as a hybrid genre: Addressing the informative/promotional conundrum," *Pragmatics* 18: 9–31.

Clayman, Steven E. and Reisner, Ann (1998) "Gatekeeping in action: Editorial conferences and assessments of newsworthiness, *American Sociological Review* 63: 178–199.

Coiro, Julie, Knobel, Michelle, Lankshear, Colin and Leu, Donald J. (Eds) (2008) *Handbook of Research on New Literacies,* Mahwah, NJ: Lawrence Erlbaum Associates.

Collins, James and Blot, Richard K. (2003) *Literacy and Literacies: Texts, power, and identity,* Cambridge: Cambridge University Press.

Collins, James and Slembrouck, Stef (2007) "Reading shop windows in globalized neighborhoods: Multilingual literacy practices and indexicality," *Journal of Literacy Research* 39: 335–356.

Cotter, Colleen (2010) *News Talk: Investigating the Language of Journalism,* Cambridge: Cambridge University Press.

Degenhardt, Marion (2006) CAMTASIA and CATMOVIE: Two digital tools for observing, documenting and analysing writing processes of university students, in L. Van Waes, M.Leijten, and C. M. Neuwirth (Eds) *Writing and Digital Media,* Amsterdam: Elsevier.

Fengler, Susanne and Russ-Mohl, Stephan (2008) "Journalists and the information-attention markets: Towards an economic theory of journalism," *Journalism* 9: 667–690.

Freadman, Anne (1994) Anyone for tennis? in A. Freedman and P. Medway (Eds) *Genre and the New Rhetoric,* London: Taylor & Francis.

Gandy, Oscar H. (1982) *Beyond Agenda Setting: Information Subsidies and Public Policy.* Norwood, NJ: Ablex Publishing.

Gee, James Paul (2007) *Social Linguistics and Literacies: Ideology in discourses,* London: Routledge.

Goffman, Erving (1981) *Forms of Talk,* Oxford: Blackwell.

Hampton, Mark (2008) "The 'objectivity' ideal and its limitations in 20th-century British journalism," *Journalism Studies* 9: 477–493.

Heath, Shirley Brice (1983) *Ways with Words: Language, life, and work in communities and classrooms,* Oxford: Oxford University Press.

Jacobs, Geert (1999) *Preformulating the News: An Analysis of the Metapragmatics of Press Releases,* Amsterdam: John Benjamins.

Kjaer, Peter and Langer, Roy (2003) "The Negotiation of Business News: A Study of Journalist-Source Interaction," Paper presented at the 19th EGOS Conference, Subtheme 14: "Organizing power and authority in a fluid society." July 3–5, 2003, Copenhagen.

Kress, Gunther R. (2003) *Literacy in the New Media Age,* London: Routledge.

Lankshear, Colin and Knobel, Michele (2006) *New Literacies: Everyday practices and classroom learning (2nd edition),* Maidenhead: Open University Press.

Lassen, Inger (2006) "Is the press release a genre? A study of form and content," *Discourse Studies* 8: 503–530.

Leijten, Marielle (2007) *Writing and Speech Recognition: Observing error correction strategies of professional writers,* Utrecht: LOT Publications.

Leijten, Marielle and Van Waes, Luuk (2006) Inputlog: New perspectives on the logging of on-line writing processes in a windows environment, in K. Sullivan and E. Lindgren (Eds) *Studies in Writing, Vol. 18: Computer key-stroke logging and writing, methods and applications,* Oxford: Elsevier.

Lewis, Justin, Williams, Andrew and Franklin, Bob (2008) "Four rumours and an explanation. A political economic account of journalists' changing newsgathering and reporting practices," *Journalism Practice* 2: 27–45.

Martin, James R. and White, Peter R. R. (2005) *The Language of Evaluation: Appraisal in English,* London: Palgrave Macmillan.

McLaren, Yvonne and Gurau, Calin (2005) "Characterising the genre of the corporate press release, *LSP & Professional Communication*" 5: 10–29.

Munoz-Torres, Juan Ramon (2007) "Underlying epistemological conceptions in journalism," *Journalism Studies* 8: 224–247.

Pander Maat, Henk (2008) "Editing and genre conflict: How newspaper journalists clarify and neutralize press release copy," *Pragmatics* 18: 87–113.

Perrin, Daniel (2003) "Progression analysis (PA): Investigating writing strategies at the workplace," *Journal of Pragmatics* 35: 907–921.

Peterson, Mark Allen (2001) "Getting to the story: Unwriteable discourse and interpretive practice in American journalism: *Anthropological Quarterly* 74: 201–211.

Reich, Zvi (2006) "The process model of news initiative. Sources lead first, reporters thereafter," *Journalism Studies* 7: 497–514.

Schudson, Michael (2001) "The objectivity norm in American journalism," *Journalism* 2: 149–170.

Scribner, Sylvia and Cole, Michael (1981) *The Psychology of Literacy,* Cambridge, MA: Harvard University Press.

Soffer, Oren (2009) "The competing ideals of objectivity and dialogue in American journalism," *Journalism* 10: 473–491.

Street, Brian (1985) *Literacy in Theory and Practice,* Cambridge: Cambridge University Press.

Street, Brian (2003) "What's 'new' in new literacy studies? Critical approaches to literacy in theory and practice," *Current Issues in Comparative Education* 5: 77–91.

Thomson, Elizabeth A., White, Peter R. R. and Kitley, Philip (2008) "'Objectivity'" and 'hard news' reporting across cultures," *Journalism Studies* 9: 212–228.

Thorsen, Einar (2008) "Journalistic objectivity redefined? Wikinews and the neutral point of view," *New Media and Society* 10: 935–954.

Tuchman, Gaye (1972) "Objectivity as strategic ritual: An examination of newsmen's notions of objectivity," *American Journal of Sociology* 77: 660–679.

Van Hout, Tom and Jacobs, Geert (2008) "News production theory and practice: Fieldwork notes on power, interaction and agency," *Pragmatics* 18: 59–84.

Van Hout, Tom and Macgilchrist, Felicitas (2010) "Framing the news: An ethnographic view of financial newswriting," *Text & Talk* 30: 147–169.

Vanslyke-Turk, Judy (1985) "Information subsidies and influence," *Public Relations Review* 11: 10–25.

Zelizer, Barbie (2007) "On 'Having been there': 'Eyewitnessing' as a journalistic key word," *Critical Studies in Media Communication* 24: 408–428.

8 Sources of Arts Journalism
Who's Writing the Arts Pages?

Lucinda Strahan

INTRODUCTION

This chapter presents the findings of a content analysis that explores the level of "public relations activity" (Zawawi, 1994) in a week's sample of arts journalism in two Australian daily newspapers based in Melbourne, *The Age* broadsheet and the *Herald Sun* news pictorial. The findings suggest that public relations activity has been used in the production of the published items in 97% of the combined sample of journalism reporting of the arts Further analysis to identify the role of PR in each of the newspapers' arts coverage revealed little difference between the two newspapers with 97% PR activity evident in *The Age* and 98% in the *Herald Sun*. Similar to the analysis presented by Turner, Bonner, and Marshall (2000) this chapter suggests that this very high level of public relations activity points to an embedded collaboration between arts public relations and arts journalism in Melbourne, to the extent where arts public relations professionals are now viewed as central to the news making process, such that basic arts publicity now assumes the value of arts news.

Questions are raised about shifting arts news values and the function of arts journalism at Melbourne's newspapers. Moreover, drawing on Hartley's (1999) idea of DIY-citizenship, the chapter discusses issues about further research concerning arts journalism's role in the construction of creative identities, both for the city itself and the arts-going inner city Melburnian. The chapter constitutes an important addition to the very slim body of research published in the specialist field of arts journalism and, following Harries and Wahl-Jorgensen (2007) and Forde (2001), emphasises arts journalism's notable differences from traditional news journalism.

ARTS PUBLICITY AND THE RISE OF 'ART-BITES'

A great deal of empirical evidence shows that the use of public relations material is rife in all kinds of journalism as Macnamara (2009, p. 8) notes: "a preponderance of data from quantitative studies conducted over more than 80 years shows that somewhere between 30 and 80% of media content is sourced from or significantly influenced by public relations practitioners, with estimates of 40–75% common." A recent study of quality journalism in four of Britain's 'broadsheet' newspapers which identified and traced the use of PR and wire copy in generating published content, found that independent journalistic activity was so rare it could be considered "the exception rather than the rule" (Lewis et al., 2009, p. 28; Chapter 6, this volume). But little of this research has focused on the relationship between arts journalism and public relations which, paradoxically, is often assumed to be so close, that the assumption has mostly been left unexamined and unpacked.

The extensive use of public relations material in the production of journalism in general is a phenomenon that is widely acknowledged (Schultz, 1998: Franklin, 2008; Turner, 2000; Macnamara, 2009; Davis, 2008; Zawawi, 1994)—not least by journalists themselves (see Chapter 6, this volume; Chapter 3, this volume)—but this usage is understood in different ways going, as it does, to the heart of fundamental ideas about the role of journalists and how they fulfill it. Public relations practice, for example, compromises the concept of journalism as an independent and impartial activity by the strategic practice of providing information in the interests of paying clients. In this way, it is argued that its pervasiveness is triggering a "crisis of journalistic integrity" (Franklin, 2008, p. 22) as key day-to-day journalistic practices such as the validation of information and verification of sources (Schultz, 1998, p. 56) are less frequently conducted in response to the routine feed of public relations materials and journalists' growing reliance on them, amid increased commercial pressures, technological changes, staff cuts and faster news cycles.

But some researchers make a different point. In a study of Australian print journalism that illustrated that more than 90% of business news was sourced from public relations activity, Zawawi (1994, p. 71) concluded that the question this raised was "not one of media or journalistic integrity," but rather whether the "generally accepted model of the journalist's role as the central one in the news-making process" remained valid. Such a suggestion requires a radical rethink of accepted journalistic practices and principles.

In a wide-ranging study of the production of celebrity in Australia, Turner et al. (2000, pp. 1–5) follow up this idea, arguing that "the media's function and its mode of operation have undergone a major redefinition" that includes "a professional articulation between the news and entertainment media and the sources of publicity and promotion." In this model of journalism, the relationship to public relations sources goes beyond the metaphorical "tango" (Gans, 1979; cited in Franklin, 2008, p. 17) or the "tug of war" (Davis, 2008, p. 273), to the point where they are now considered to be structurally embedded in media production practices. That is, journalism and public relations are thought to be one and the same.

When thinking about the relationship between arts journalism and public relations, the particular and "exceptional" (Harries and Wahl-Jorgensen,

2007, p.622) characteristics of arts journalism need to be taken into account. The slim body of research focused on arts journalism concurs that it must be considered as "qualitatively different" (Harries and Wahl-Jorgensen, 2007, p. 619) and "culturally and professionally distinct" (Forde, 2001, p. 113) from traditional news journalism. Key in this distinction is arts journalism's "complicated relationship to the strategic ritual of objectivity" (Harries and Wahl-Jorgensen, 2007, p. 635).

It is subjective "crusading" advocacy that is considered proper practice in coverage of the arts, a practice that flies in the face of the cool, impartiality of the fourth estate where "getting too close to sources is judged highly dangerous" (Franklin, 2008, p. 17). For arts journalists, a "lack of professional distance from sources and subjects" is not only commonly practiced, but sometimes seen "as essential to their job" (Forde, 2001, p. 114). In a sociological survey of the professional self-perception of 20 UK arts journalists, Harries and Wahl-Jorgensen (2008, p. 634) identified a revelatory underlying belief amongst respondents, about a differentiated public to the political entity that informs conventional journalism: "instead, interviewees imagined a cultural public, enlightened by the therapeutic powers of the arts communicated through passionate and involved journalism." What these insights indicate is that when it comes to thinking about arts journalism, key ideas such as journalistic independence, objectivity and the watchdog role of the fourth estate cannot be taken *prima facie*. Arts journalists are, as Forde (ibid., p. 113) expresses it, "journalists with a difference."

But just as characteristic as these exceptional and distinctive practices and principles, is arts journalism's "instability" as a category of news (Harries and Wahl Jorgensen, 2007, p. 630) that witnesses arts journalism run the gamut between high art to celebrity coverage and consumer lifestyle content. They might be passionate and involved, but arts journalists also "have difficulty . . . defining exactly what constitutes the arts, and, therefore, their area of professional expertise and responsibility" (ibid., p. 628). In Melbourne newspapers, arts coverage over the past decade has become increasingly 'lifestyle' and consumer-oriented with much space dedicated to colorful double-page spreads of 'editorial picks' and large color images giving the 'top ten' of what's on every day and weekend. The arts pages are now mostly taken up with snippets of news and other 'art-bites', quick Q&A profiles and clumps of 'capsule' reviews and articles under 100 or even 50 words.

A wide-ranging content analysis of US arts-journalism conducted between 1998 and 2003 (Szanto, Levi, and Tydall, 2004) reported similar trends in America suggesting that while arts features in the content sample had dropped by 5% over five years, the space given to bite-sized formats such as arts listings had risen by 7% across the same period (Szanto et al., 2004, p. 26). One of the most striking features of this style of arts journalism is its similarity to arts publicity in its key messages: 'this is what is on, this is where, this is how much'. The predominance of this kind of arts coverage prompts reflection and consideration of the question: how much of the arts journalism in Melbourne's two daily newspapers uses specialist arts public relations activity? Anecdotal evidence and working assumptions suggest that it is a good deal, but this has been an area of relative scholarly neglect within the journalism studies field.

METHODOLOGY; SEPARATING ARTS JOURNALISM FROM PR

A content analysis was conducted to establish the extent of "public relations activity" (Zawawi, 1994) in a one week sample of arts journalism in *The Age* and the *Herald Sun*[1] using Zawawi's definition of public relations as: "an organised effort by an individual or organization which specifically sets out to achieve media coverage either as part of a primary objective or as part of a wider communications strategy" (1994, p. 68). This definition has been recognized by other journalism scholars (Turner et al., 2000, p. 42; Macnamara, 2009, p. 7) as capturing a broader range of public relations activities than simply press releases, and also confirms that these activities are commonly identifiable in the stated sources of news articles (Zawawi, 1994, p. 71).

Sample: the sample for analysis was drawn from a seven-day date range in 2009 between Monday, March 9 to Sunday, March 15 inclusive; a period which was free from any of the arts events with which both papers have myriad sponsorship arrangements, ruling this out as a possible influence on public relations activity. The analysis was conducted on items published in the main news section of each paper, plus the specialist arts sections: weekday—'Metro' in *The Age* and 'Arts & Entertainment' in the *Herald-Sun*; late-week and weekend lift-outs–Friday's 'EG', Saturday's 'A2' and Sunday's 'M' in *The Age* and Thursday's 'HIT', Saturday's 'Weekend' and Sunday's 'Play' in the *Herald-Sun*.

Defining 'the arts': while the slippage between 'high' and 'low' culture in arts journalism is the focus of some research (see Janssen, 1999), in this study it was considered important to incorporate both 'high' culture and popular art forms in a definition of 'the arts'. Subjects that were considered 'the arts' were as follows: popular music, classical music, jazz or world music, theatre, comedy, dance, cabaret, musical theatre, opera, visual art (including craft and design), books, ballet and film. Editorial items were considered a unit of analysis if one or more of the above art forms were its primary topic i.e., it was about the practice or presentation of the art form, or a specific work of that art form, or a topic arising directly from it. Thus, an example of an article *not* considered a unit of analysis was a news story about a memorial service held in Melbourne's Princess Theatre after the sudden death of a leading cast member of the Melbourne production of *Wicked*. This article was not considered to be *primarily* about musical theatre. Similarly, and importantly, celebrity journalism that did not include an art form as its primary subject was not considered to be arts journalism, but an interview with a celebrity that focused on a newly released film or album *was* considered to be arts journalism.

Formats: arts reviews are a key constituent of arts journalism (Harries and Wahl-Jorgensen, 2008, p. 624) but in this study it was not considered possible to analyze arts criticism using the model proposed by Zawawi because of its fundamentally different protocols which as Forde (2001, p. 120) emphasizes: "all types of critic must be considered outside of the dominant models of news production." For this reason, arts reviews were not considered to be a unit of analysis. The 'capsule' article of less than 100 words, while not a traditional format for journalism, was considered important to count as a unit of analysis due to its prominent and increasing use in arts coverage that is part of the wider trend toward design-driven formats in print media (Franklin, 2008, p. 15). In this study, all capsule articles were considered as one unit of analysis each, in the same way as an entire news story or feature article, because each capsule featured a different arts event. Articles were also coded for word counts: <100, 100–500, 500–1000, 1000+.

This methodology was designed to give a broad quantitative indication of the amount of public relations activity contributing to arts journalism in these papers.

FINDINGS

A total of 233 published items were coded as arts journalism across the two papers during the sample week: 131 items were identified in *The Age*, and 102 were identified in the *Herald Sun*. The items were sorted into broad source areas that were evident from the content of the articles:

1. Events—the Sound Relief Concert for Victorian bushfire victims, Sotheby's auction, press conference by National Gallery Director Gerard Vaughn
2. New releases and new work—articles rising from new releases and openings, films, music, books, exhibition, concerts, and festival openings etc.
3. Artists/arts workers—articles based on interviews with artists/arts workers
4. Award winners/nominees—the Miles Franklin long-list, the Moran Prize for portraiture
5. Association reports and documents—Australian Records Industry of Australia yearly sales report, announcement by the Australian Institute of Architects
6. Acknowledged press releases or websites—upcoming and current programs of events, ticketing, and event information

7. Other articles—stories quoting from or referring to others
8. Syndicated/wire copy
9. Other—a film column based on answers to reader's letters, an undergraduate honors thesis

Eighty-four percent (84%) of items from the sample (109 items in *The Age*, and 87 in the *Herald Sun*) arose from events, new releases, openings, and interviews with artists and arts-workers about new works. Using Zawawi's definition, articles in these source categories were considered to test positive for public relations activity where dates, venue and ticketing information were included in either the body of the article or at the bottom. Where this information was not explicit (which was rare) public relations activity was considered to be present also if the article quoted only, or mainly, the primary artist or producer involved in the work being discussed. These sources were considered to have a vested interest in talking about their work in the media as part of a "wider communications strategy" for attracting audiences. Importantly, 50% of these items (65 in *The Age*, and 34 in the *Herald-Sun*) were 'capsule' articles of less than 100 words that did not include interviews or quotes, but printed basic event, ticketing, and other grabs of information alongside images.

The remaining source categories were almost negligible, with news of award-winners amounting to six items in *The Age* and four items in the *Herald Sun*. Three items arose from government and association reports in *The Age* (but none in the *Herald Sun*), and items drawn from stories published elsewhere occurring four times in *The Age* and three times in the *Herald Sun*. Two items in *The Age* and five in the *Herald Sun* referred to information available directly on websites, while three items in *The Age* (none in the *Herald Sun*) were syndicated from UK and US papers.

Using Zawawi's definition, all but eight items across the whole sample revealed the presence of public relations activity. The total percentage of published items which suggested an influence for public relations in the aetiology of the sample articles was 97% for *The Age* and 98% in the *Herald Sun*. The combined sample of one week's arts journalism in both papers showed total public relations activity of 97%.

Only eight items across the whole sample *could not* be immediately identified as having been derived from public relations activity, and of these, seven were 'capsule' articles of less than 100 words that appeared in weekly arts columns. These items were considered to be a small enough occurrence to be the exception rather than the rule. In *The Age*, two of these items were summaries of crime/court stories from other media outlets, another of these item referred to an undergraduate honors thesis on the concept of 'selling-out' in the music industry, and the last quoted the leaseholder of a famous rock music venue in Melbourne about the upcoming sale of the building. This last item appeared to be the only example of a local arts story making its way into *The Age* without a public relations intermediary.

Only one feature article in the whole sample, appearing in *The Age*, could not immediately be linked with public relations activity. This reported the growing community of Australian musicians living and working in Los Angeles, and although this article quoted a famous musician's manager and the Australian music representative in the office of Australian trade in the US, who might both be involved in public relations activity, neither of these sources appeared to have any particular interest in the main focus of the article, so it was considered to be not immediately recogniable as sourced from public relations activity. Of three items in the *Herald Sun* not clearly connected to public relations activity, two items were 'capsule' articles: one was a summary of a story from another news media source, and the other was about puppets melting during a rehearsal because of the hot weather. The third item in the *Herald Sun* was a film column based on readers' questions.

DISCUSSION: CHANGING ARTS NEWS VALUES— THE ARTS AS LEISURE IN THE CREATIVE CITY

The results of the content analysis confirm assumptions that public relations material is central to the production of arts journalism at these newspapers. Arts publicity is normalized in arts journalism in *The Age* and the *Herald-Sun* both implicitly, where messages are submerged in previews and news articles about arts events, but also explicitly where arts publicity has assumed the value of journalism itself. Evidently, arts publicity is not only an element of arts journalism in *The Age* and the *Herald Sun*—it is presented *as* arts journalism. This was the case in nearly half of the arts coverage sampled here, which took the form of 'capsule' coverage of less than 100 or even 50 words. Little or no conventional journalistic activity was evident in these colorful layouts made up of images, ticketing information, and grabs of commentary. Here, publicity and arts news values are inseparable.

Arts journalism has always been fertile ground for PR with publicity for openings and new work easily submerged in the newsworthiness of the event as something "timely" (Allan, 2004, p. 57). The feature story "The Fire Inside" (*The Age*, March 15, 2009), about a new production of the ballet *Firebird* by the Australian Ballet provides an example of this. Drawing on an interview with the Australian ballet's artistic director, the article focuses on the changing career trajectories for ballerinas that have replaced the iconic status of the prima ballerina. The publicity message for the production is submerged within this discussion, but fulfilled by the timely coverage, the large color production stills accompanying the article, and the name of the ballet featuring prominently in the headline. In these kinds of conventional arts previews there is a dovetailing of public relations objectives and the particular arts news values espoused by the respondents to Harries and Wahl-Jorgensen's interviews: both are concerned with communicating the meaning, intentions, and significance of the production, deepening the public understanding of ballet and generating interest in the upcoming work.

But the sample also shows that publicity is increasingly becoming explicit in arts journalism rather than submerged. Forty-two percent (42%) of the sample in this study was constituted by 'capsules' of under 100 or even 50 words, where publicity completely usurps the status of journalism. Running dates, venue and ticketing information, and images are no longer submerged within arts journalism, they are presented *as* arts journalism. This is something similar to what Turner et al. (2000, p. 56) identify as a "restructuring of news values" that has seen celebrity promotions and publicity come to be accepted as news.

This seeming restructuring of arts news values is a significant point for further research and here it is worth drawing together some threads that might offer a few leads. One of the changing news values in this kind of 'capsule' arts coverage seems to be that the arts are perceived predominantly as a consumer leisure activity, about which the only journalism required is to detail when, where and how much? A connection may be drawn between this and broader cultural shifts that have seen the arts take on a new popular appeal as a leisure time activity and a key part of Melbourne's attraction for tourists and weekend crowds.

Melbourne, perhaps more than any other Australian city, over the past decade has invested in the idea of a 'creative economy' with massive spending on arts infrastructure and employment.[2] Scott McQuire (2005, p. 206) points out how this kind of new economic harnessing of the arts "presages fundamental changes in contemporary art and cultural exchange" and that one of these changes is that the arts are now expected to "address multiple constituencies." It is this process that has seen the arts in Melbourne take on new popular appeal as a trendy inner-city leisure-time activity that is intricately connected to the identity of Melbourne as a Creative City[3] and Melburnians as cultured and creative people. It is in this construction of a "creative' identity—for the city and the 'creative class'" (Florida, 2002) of people who live in it—that we might identify a new function for arts journalism.

Here Hartley's idea of "Do-It-Yourself citizenship" is useful, building as it does on notions of 'cultural citizenship' that are commonly applied to discussions of celebrity media and identity politics, to a new citizenship "based not on an authenticist notion of cultural identity" but rather, on "mobility and choice in identity" (ibid., p. 210). The construction of identity through DIY citizenship is different to gendered and racial identities, here the consumer-media-citizen builds her own "semiotically self-determined" social identity through niche and specialist media consumption. This is a compelling idea to apply in further examinations of the shifting ground between the arts and changing journalistic practices, particularly in cities such as Melbourne where the arts have become a key marker of identity for the city itself and the people who live in it.

CONCLUSION

The results of this analysis point to an industry of arts public relations practitioners in Melbourne who are integrally involved in the production of arts journalism in *The Age* and the *Herald Sun*. The centrality of PR activity in arts journalism at these newspapers is particularly evident where publicity has assumed the value of journalism itself in 'capsule' articles of less than 100 words that reproduce basic information such as dates, venue and ticket prices. This phenomenon raises significant questions about the role and function of arts journalism, and here Hartley's idea of "DIY citizenship" (1999, p. 179) offers a useful lead for further considerations of the connection between arts journalism and the construction of creative identities.

NOTES

1. *The Age* is a local broadsheet with a peak Saturday circulation of 294,900. The *Herald Sun* is a local tabloid with a peak Saturday circulation of 515,000.
2. In 2006 arts and recreation services in the City of Melbourne grew faster than the food and beverage, retail, telecommunications, construction, and manufacturing industries (Melbourne City Council, 2006, p. 15).
3. In 2008 Melbourne was successful in its bid to be named a UNESCO City of Literature as part of the global Creative Cities network.

REFERENCES

Allan, Stuart (2004) *News Culture*, 2nd edition, Maidenhead: Open University Press.

Davis, Aeron (2008) "Public relations in the news" in Bob Franklin (Ed) *Pulling Newspapers Apart: Analysing print journalism,* London: Routledge, pp. 272–281.

Florida, Richard (2002) *The Rise of the Creative Class*, New York: Basic Books.

Forde, Eamonn (2001) "Journalists with a difference: Producing music journalism" in Simon Cottle (Ed) *Media Organisation and Production*, Thousand Oaks, CA: Sage, 113–131.

Franklin, Bob (2008) Introduction to "Newspapers: Trends and developments" in Bob Franklin (Ed) *Pulling Newspapers Apart: Analysing print journalism,* London: Routledge, pp. 1–36.

Harries, Gemma, and Wahl-Jorgensen, Karin (2007) "The culture of arts journalists: Elitists, saviours or manic depressives?" *Journalism* 8(6): pp. 619–639.

Hartley, John (1999) *Uses for Television,* London: Routledge,

Janssen, Susanne (1999) "Arts journalism and cultural change: The coverage of the arts in Dutch newspapers 1965–1990," *Poetics* 26(5): pp. 329–348.

Lewis, Justin, Williams, Andrew, Franklin, Bob, Thomas, James, and Mosdell, Nick (2006) 'The quality and independence of British Journalism', Report by Cardiff School of Journalism, Media and Cultural Studies, for Media Standards Trust. Available: http://www.mediastandardstrust.org/resources/media-research/researchdetails.aspx?sid=12914. Accessed May 16, 2009.

Melbourne City Council (2006) "Census of Land Use and Employment Brochure, Part II." Available: http://www.melbourne.vic.gov.au/info.cfm?top=91&pa=2089&pg=3679. Accessed August 3, 2007.

Macnamara, Jim (2009) "Journalism and PR: Beyond Myths and Stereotypes to Transparency and Management in the Public Interest," Address to the Public Relations Institute of Australia, May 6, 2009. Sydney.

Mcquire, Scott (2005) "Introduction: The burden of culture in the global city," in Scott McQuire and Nikos Papastergiadis (Eds) *Empires, Ruins and Networks: The transcultural agenda in art*, Carlton, Melbourne: Melbourne University Press.

Schultz, Julianne (1998) *Reviving the Fourth Estate,* Cambridge: Cambridge University Press

Szanto, Andras, Levy, Daniel S., and Tyndall, Andrew (2004) *Reporting the Arts II,* Report for the National Arts Journalism Program (NAJP), Seattle. Available: http://www.najp.org/publications/researchreports/rta2.html. Accessed January 16, 2009.

Turner, Graeme, Bonner, Frances, Marshall, P. David (2000) *Fame Games: The production of celebrity in Australia*, Cambridge: Cambridge University Press

Zawawi, Clara (1994) "Sources of news: Who feeds the watchdogs?," *Australian Journalism Review* 16(1): pp. 67–71.

Part III

Citizens and Sourcing

Finding a Way Forward

9 Are Citizens Becoming Sources?
A Look into the Professional Contacts of Flemish Journalists

Jeroen De Keyser, Karin Raeymaeckers, and Steve Paulussen

INTRODUCTION

Journalists' working routines in traditional newsrooms have had to adapt to new voices in the journalistic process in recent few years, as ordinary citizens have enjoyed a growing influence as new and active players in the field. The development of various digital technologies has made it relatively easy for anyone to disseminate information and to participate actively in the journalistic process (Bowman and Willis, 2003; Bruns, 2008; Gillmor, 2004). As a matter of course this also has an impact on newsroom routines, as some professional habits are bound to disappear in this new era of journalism. Among these routines, sourcing has undoubtedly been affected and this chapter describes these shifts in sourcing practices. Ordinary citizens in particular have assumed an added importance as sources, reflecting the tremendous increase in their capacities for disseminating information to the outside world. Our theoretical framework refers to Jürgen Habermas' model of arenas of political communication. This model serves as a starting point for an analysis of the appreciation of several types of information contacts, using data from a large-scale postal survey among Flemish (i.e., Northern Belgian) professional journalists. Our focus is on the perceived importance of elites and citizens as conveyors of information.

LITERATURE

Privileged Sources

When listening to, watching, or reading the news from several journalistic brands, one is confronted with a large number of names and faces. This could lead to the conclusion that journalists have an abundant list of sources. Reality, however, proves otherwise. Research indicates that journalists show a professional preference for sources with a certain level of authority (Ericson, Baranek, and Chan, 1989; Gans, 1979; Jha, 2008; Williams and Delli Carpini, 2004). They assume that by focusing on such elite sources they can reduce or even skip some of the (often basic) procedures of searching and checking information. As long ago as 1979, Gans (1979) described how the selection of news sources is driven by considerations of power and efficiency. In other words, "news workers must allocate scarce resources in producing their product, with due respect to the power structure within which they operate" (Reese, 1994, p. 14). This explains the eager use of ready-made press releases from professional communicators (O'Neill and O'Connor, 2007) that often reach the newsroom in a two-step process via wire services (Davies, 2008; Lewis, Williams, and Franklin, 2008; Chapter 6, this volume).

The common observation that "power elites" within society exert a major influence on news coverage (Helle, 2000) can be further explained by the immediate usability of the provided content. In the British context, for instance, Lewis et al. (2008) discern a hierarchy that grants citizens a lower level of access to the news making process than NGOs or business sources respectively. German research shows that wire services have been growing in importance, especially for the daily work at online news desks (Machill and Beiler, 2009).

Habermas' Model of Political Communication

Habermas (2006) offers a suitable theoretical framework for analysing sourcing practices that schematically shows how to assess the importance of different information actors. He sketches the different arenas of political communication, while taking into consideration how the different institutions and actors function within those environments (see Figure 9.1). An essential part of Habermas' model lies with the output that is generated by the institutions at the center of the political system. The actors situated within the confines of that same system use the news media as their communicative battlefield, with the dual intention of sparring with each other and influencing public opinion in general. These actors consist not only of politicians, but also of economic protagonists (i.e., lobby groups). In the past decades more and more special interest groups have been joining debates. This development has been fuelled by the bundling of forces of actors within civil society in order to speak with a louder voice and thus acquire a position of their own in the political system.

The ordinary citizen finds no direct forum in this system. The citizen could join one of the above-mentioned interest groups (see also Carpentier, 2008), or participate in opinion polls (elections being the ultimate example). Direct communication between citizens is only possible in the *discursive spaces* of the public sphere (Haas, 2007, pp. 41–42).

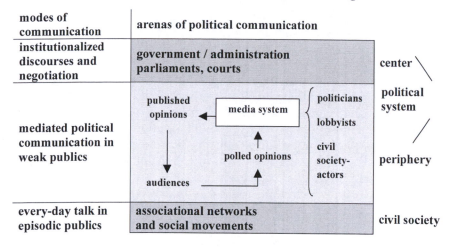

Figure 9.1 Arenas of political communication.

In this scheme Habermas explains the almost exclusive attention of professional journalism for the institutions and the actors in the political system. This relates to the above-mentioned 'usability' of this kind of information, which enjoys a growing impact because of the ever increasing professionalisation of lobbies and special interest groups (Feldstein, 2007; Lewis et al., 2008; Soley and Craig, 1992). The tendency to frame the news topic in a story-based journalistic form strengthens the journalist's reliance on elite sources even further.

A major drawback of Habermas model is its focus on political information. Even when taken in its broadest sense (i.e., including economic information or social problems and such like), it comprises only a fraction of the total news coverage. This theoretical restriction also limits its analytical possibilities. Nonetheless the field is broad enough for exploration, as Bennett (cited in Deuze, 2008, p. 14) affirms that "cooperation with (and pressures from) news sources, such as public relations officials, spokespeople for organizations, celebrities, and politicians" is part of the standardised journalistic news beat.

New Ways of Working in a New Context?

Apart from this topic-based limitation, Habermas' model further fails to take into account fully the opportunities the Internet offers to citizens for discussing political issues and ideas. A wide range of digital technologies have paved the way for the citizen to communicate with the outside world directly, rather than using the detour of special interest groups or opinion polls (Domingo, 2008; Oakham and Murrell, 2007). Examples of such technologies are Wikinews (Bruns, 2006; McIntosh, 2008) or Indymedia (see Chapter 4, this volume; Platon andand Deuze, 2003), although the latter bears the typical marks of special interest groups in some of its regional versions (Garcelon, 2006). In addition, citizens can use weblogs to publish news content. In many cases this remains limited to the role of "accidental" journalist, just being at the wrong place at the right time, i.e., when something spectacular happens (Campbell, Gibson, Gunter and Touri, 2007; Graves, 2007). But in general, bloggers tend to follow rather than lead the news: a lot of weblog coverage is influenced by, or even originates from, mainstream news media, which indicates that the professional media still play a dominant role in gatekeeping and agenda setting (Haas, 2005). Only the most successful bloggers have succeeded in putting certain topics on the general news agenda (Campbell et al., 2007; Messner and DiStaso, 2008). However, most of these A-list bloggers can be found in Anglo-Saxon countries, which suggests that this kind of agenda setting power is less strong or even non-existent in the rest of the world. Naturally, this does not exclude the possibility that professional journalists use citizen weblogs as sources (Neuberger, Nuernbergk and Rischke, 2007).

In short, disintermediation threatens to undermine the central role of professional journalism in the communication process within the confines of the political system. As early as 1996, Bardoel warned that traditional media might lose their controlling power in such a course of events. He suggested a different professional approach, with a more empathetic commitment to journalists' role as information filterers and a stronger focus on audience participation. These ideas have increasingly been up for discussion again in the past few years (see Chapter 12, this volume; Bivens, 2008; Deuze, Bruns and Neuberger, 2007; Gillmor, 2004). It follows that news workers may start regarding the public as "an army of researchers working for nothing" (Chung, 2007, p. 55). Such an assumption demands an adaptation of the model sketched previously. It implies that next to politicians, lobbyists, and special interest groups that emerge from civil society, individual citizens may also start supplying news input. This assumption is unrelated to the discussion concerning whether the internet is a useful platform for enabling or enhancing Habermas' concept of the public sphere (Dahlberg, 2007; Karakaya Polat, 2005). The fact that the media may start using ordinary citizens as active sources can be considered neither a confirmation, nor a denial, of Habermas' ideal platform for rational discussion.

Research Hypotheses

We propose four hypotheses concerning professional journalists' choice of information contacts: one comprehensive hypothesis and three hypotheses aimed at specific professional subgroups.[1] We put these hypotheses to the test using data from a large-scale postal survey conducted among Flemish professional journalists.

H1. Considering the recentness of the changes described above, the professional focus still remains on elite contacts, while information coming from the general public is also valued to some extent.

We assume that elite sources (i.e., representatives of the political or the economic world) are still more capable of presenting ready-made information. We also assume that a lesser importance is attributed to less elite sources such as NGOs or special interest groups, and still less to individual citizens.

We nevertheless believe that the Internet has had some influence on journalists' information contact preferences. That is also what our adaptation of Habermas' model implicitly predicts. Research has shown that the technological shift has indeed made ordinary citizens appear in journalists' contact lists, although the latter continue to prefer the traditional (i.e., official or elite) sources (Jha, 2008). However, not all scholars would agree. Some contend that professional caution applies in dealing with sources that could try to influence news content (Gieber, 1999/1964; Reader, 2008). On the other hand, some studies have noticed the contemporary erosion of this kind of professional caution (Deuze, 2008; Jha, 2008; Lewis et al. , 2008; Shin and Cameron, 2003).

H2. The perceived importance of the information contacts of journalists who are specialists in topics related to Habermas scheme can be linked to that same model.

After narrowing down the sample to specific journalistic specialisations, we take it that Habermas model can serve as a basis for interpreting the importance of information contact categories as perceived by journalists. This implies that sources closest to the center of the political system are most highly esteemed and vice versa, thus forming a source hierarchy (Reese, 1994).

H2 a   The source hierarchy is distinct among political journalists.

Information originating from elite sources, especially government representatives or politicians, is expected to be of much greater importance for political journalists. This may be obvious given the topic they are focusing on, but it can also be explained by the close connection between their societal position and Habermas model.

H2 b. The source hierarchy is distinct among economic journalists.

Economic journalists are expected to value elite sources above all others, since their specialisation also concentrates on elite doings and dealings. We logically expect other kinds of elite sources (i.e., special interest groups, economic actors, or NGOs) to stand out with economic journalists in comparison to political journalists.

H3. Online journalists prefer information contacts that supply easy-to-use information.

Research has shown that online journalists' professional views and habits differ from those of their colleagues (Cassidy, 2007; Cassidy, 2008; Paterson and Domingo, 2008). The former are arguably more intensely involved with new technologies, including those aimed at strengthening the bond with the public. Still, we do not believe that this will increase their preference for citizens as news sources, because of the already high workload in online newsrooms, which is multiplied by the perceived 'lost' time in moderating and verifying user-generated content (Hermida and Thurman, 2008; Paulussen and Ugille, 2008). On the contrary, we predict that online journalists will choose the most readily available news content, even if it means merely copying content from their offline counterparts (Erdal, 2009) or agency wires (Domingo, 2008; Machill and Beiler, 2009). Besides, the latter often simply replicate press releases from politicians or companies (Davies, 2008).

H4. Local journalists are more dependent on their own information contacts, which include citizens.

Local journalists face a high workload, if only because of the size of the geographic areas they are supposed to cover with a limited number of reporters (e.g., in the UK: Davies, 2008). Furthermore, the range of topics local journalists cover stretches much wider than just political news. Because their local focus makes it more difficult (if not impossible) for local journalists to rely on ready-made agency copy, it is reasonable for them to consult a broader range of first-hand information actors. These may also include ordinary citizens, as local journalists logically focus on stories that are closely linked with the daily lives of the common people. Nevertheless, research shows that even for local journalists, citizen sources remain of relatively less importance compared to other information actors (Harju, 2007; O'Neill and O'Connor, 2007).

RESEARCH

Method

The data underlying our research were gathered in a postal survey in 2008 by the Center for Journalism Studies (Ghent University) in cooperation with the Flemish journalists' association, VVJ/AVBB. All 2,230 Flemish professional journalists were invited to answer a questionnaire, either on paper or on a website. The response rate was nearly 31%. The survey was based on a similar survey from 2003, which in turn had followed the existing international tradition of sociological journalist surveys (see Weaver, 1998). In terms of age and gender, the 2008 survey respondents matched the population statistics perfectly. The 2008 questionnaire included three further questions concerning professional journalists' sources, in which we asked them about their appreciation of certain information actors (e.g., politicians or NGOs) and their use of certain source types (e.g., press releases or interviews). In our present study, we focus on the first question, with occasional references to the replies to the second. Unfortunately, as none of these questions had been included in the 2003 questionnaire, a comparison over time was not possible.

Results

In line with data from the international literature, Flemish journalists show a clear preference for sources with a certain level of authority (see Figure 9.2). Fellow journalists are considered (very) important (60.9%) sources while about two-thirds of Flemish journalists claim to use *other media* as a source every day (see Chapter 3, this volume), which signals a high level of self-referencing (see Deuze, 2008) or even intermedia agenda-setting (see Messner and DiStaso, 2008). Also, the authority of the government (59.9%) and of researchers (52.7%) is all-important for at least half of the respondents. Information actors that could try to use the news media as an outlet for communication management (i.e., companies (43.1%), special interest groups (40.4%), or NGOs (29.6%)) are deemed the least important. Politicians as sources (49.6%) are considered of medium importance, as they are not only representatives of the democratic system but also possible propagandists. Citizen sources (45.1%) also occupy a central position.

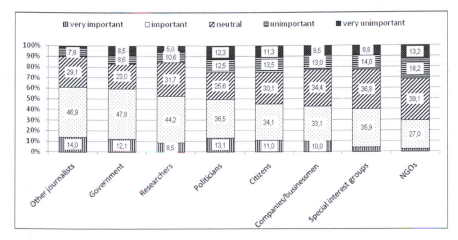

Figure 9.2 How important are different kinds of information actors for journalists?

Hypothesis 1: Given the above ranking, we can confirm some aspects of the hypothesis that predicts a preference for elite sources. Leaving journalists aside, the top three are undeniably elite sources (i.e., government, researchers, and politicians). As predicted, citizen input is similarly appreciated by a relatively large percentage of journalists. Citizen sources are even valued more highly than special interest groups, NGOs and even the business elite. As such, the hypothesis cannot be fully confirmed, as not all elite sources achieve top scores. This suggests that the readiness of the information offered by information actors is not the only factor that influences its actual use. It also indicates that professional caution towards possibly economically tainted information does indeed exist.

From the results in the specific journalistic subgroups in Figure 9.3, divergent patterns concerning their preferred information actors can clearly be distinguished. We shall discuss the remaining hypotheses using this graph and the results of T-tests[2] comparing the journalists belonging to the respective subgroups with their colleagues in our sample.

Hypothesis 2: We hypothesised a distinct source hierarchy in journalistic subgroups that are more closely linked to Habermas' model. This appears to be the case for political (H2a) and for economic (H2b) journalists, who both tend to prefer elite sources above citizen sources. Political journalists naturally rank governmental and other political sources first. But all other elite sources are also ranked highest, while citizens and NGOs come last. Analysis shows that this contact preference distinguishes these subgroups from the general group. Political journalists rank almost all elite contacts significantly higher. The results are statistically less manifest only for researchers (p=0.059). Surprisingly though, the T-test shows that political journalists do not appreciate citizen sources

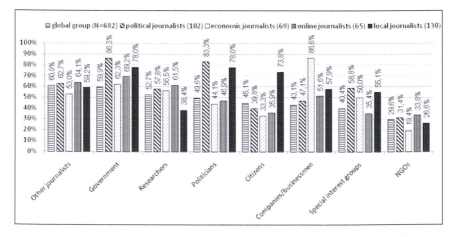

Figure 9.3   Percentage of very important information actors for various journalism sub-groups.

significantly less. The information actor preference of economic journalists shows a similar pattern. They, too, rank elite sources first, evidently preferring business people far above all others. Governmental sources come second, followed by researchers. Citizens and NGOs are at the bottom of the list once again. A T-test reveals that economic journalists have two significantly distinct preferences: they value businesspeople more and citizens less than do their colleagues. We can observe a tendency that special interest groups may be less important for them as well (p=0.067).

Hypothesis 3: The third hypothesis states that online journalists favour easy-to-use information, and consequently prefer information contacts that provide a kind of ready-made content. Figure 9.3 confirms this: the government, fellow journalists, researchers, and businessmen rank as important sources in that order, while citizens are valued to some extent but considered neither extremely important nor unimportant. Apart from the high ranking of business sources, this list may appear relatively similar to that of the preferences of the total group of Flemish journalists. However, a T-test provides extra evidence for H3. First, it shows no different evaluation of citizen sources by online journalists (contrary to what Figure 9.3 might suggest). It also shows that governmental and business sources are clearly more highly valued by the online subgroup. The same counts for researchers as a source, although this result is more doubtful (p=0.105). In other words, among online journalists the two information actors distributing the largest amounts of press releases get top rankings and are consequently valued more highly. A supplementary T-test concerning the reported use of press releases confirms that online journalists draw more intensely on this source type (p=0.079). Similar T-tests for the use of wire services show a significantly more intensive use of international wires, but no difference regarding national wires (the latter being the most popular both for online as well as other journalists).

Hypothesis 4: The final hypothesis predicts that local journalists have an extended and more diverse list of possible contacts. It also states that they deem citizen sources more highly. A T-test comparing local journalists with their non-local colleagues confirms both assumptions. Local journalists attach significantly more value to governmental sources, politicians, companies, special interest groups, and citizens. Figure 9.3 shows that especially politicians and citizens are of much greater importance to this journalistic subgroup. The figures for this group clearly contradict previous research (Harju, 2007; O'Neill and O'Connor, 2007), even though our survey merely measured the journalists' perception and did not consider the actual journalistic output. NGOs are the only information actor journalists value significantly less, possibly because the scope of this kind of actor is more often global than local. Local journalists do not differ significantly in their evaluation of other journalists or researchers as information contacts. These, too, do not generally provide local information.

CONCLUSION

One specific conclusion is remarkable because it had not been predicted. For no obvious reason, NGOs are rated lowest by all studied groups; their impact as information sources appears to be marginal. We cannot explain why this should be the case, especially in view of the fact that groups that evidently try to influence coverage on specific topics (i.e., commercial enterprises or special interest groups) do achieve higher scores.

As to the main question of this study, we can conclude that citizens score highly as journalistic information sources. Their perceived influence clearly goes beyond what traditional models, such as Habermas', would predict. Although the results of this kind of survey reflect perceptions rather than actual professional practice, we may assume that a change in practice can only be genuine if preceded by a change of heart. As such, the results of our research may announce more fundamental changes in newsroom organization in the future.

Conversely, some journalistic professional subgroups are found to adhere to their traditional sources. Unsurprisingly, these are the groups that are most closely associated with political or economic news content. The model of arenas of political communication fits political journalists best, for they are the 'purest' Habermasian journalistic subgroup. Also economic journalists clearly prefer elite contacts, even if they rank other kinds of elites first. Online journalists also rate citizen sources lower, albeit statistically speaking not as significantly different from the general professional group, and more than likely for different reasons (such as lack of time).

Unfortunately, as our approach did not allow for a comparison over time, it has left questions open about a further growth in the impact of citizens as news sources.

NOTES

1. The subgroups of "political journalists" (N=102), "economic journalists" (N=69) and "local journalists" (N=130) are based on the topical specialisations mentioned by the respondents. The subgroup of "online journalists" (N=65) consists of journalists who work for an online medium, even if only on a part-time basis. Similar tests for journalists who primarily work for an online medium (N=13) showed analogous results, but with lower significance figures because of the small group size.
2. All test results are significant at p ≤ 0.05 level, unless stated otherwise.

REFERENCES

Bardoel, Jo (1996) "Beyond journalism: A profession between information society and civil society," *European Journal of Communication*, 11(3): pp. 283–302.

Bivens, Rena Kim (2008) "The Internet, mobile phones and blogging: How new media are transforming traditional journalism," *Journalism Practice* 2(1): pp. 113–129.

Bowman, Shayne and Willis, Chris (2003) *"We Media: How Audiences are Shaping the Future of News and Information,"* Reston, VA: The Media Center at the Amercian Press Institute. Available: http://www.hypergene.net/wemedia/download/we_media.pdf. Accessed April 19, 2006.

Bruns, Axel (2006) "Wikinews: Towards multiperspectival, deliberative news reporting," *Scan Journal of Media Arts Culture* 3(1): n.p.

Bruns, Axel (2008) *Blogs, Wikipedia, Second Life, and Beyond: From production to produsage,* New York: Peter Lang.

Campbell, Vincent, Gibson, Rachel, Gunter, Barrie and Touri, Maria (2007). "News Blogs and the Future of Newspapers," Paper presented at the Future of Newspapers Conference, September, Cardiff, Wales.

Carpentier, Nico (2008) "The belly of the city: Alternative communicative city networks," *International Communication Gazette* 7(3–4): pp. 237–255.

Cassidy, William P. (2007). "Online news credibility: An examination of the perceptions of newspaper journalists," *Journal of Computer-Mediated Communication* 12(2): n.p.

Cassidy, William P. (2008) "Outside Influences: extramedia forces and the newsworthiness conceptions of online newspaper journalists," *First Monday* 13(1): n.p.

Chung, Deborah Soun (2007) "Profits and perils," *Convergence* 13(1): pp. 43–61.

Dahlberg, Lincoln (2007) "Rethinking the fragmentation of the cyberpublic: From consensus to contestation," *New Media & Society* 9(5): pp. 827–847.

Davies, Nick (2008) *Flat Earth News,* London: Vintage Books.

Deuze, Mark (2008) "Understanding journalism as newswork: How it changes, and how it remains the same," *Westminster Papers in Communication and Culture* 5(2): pp. 4–23.

Deuze, Mark, Bruns, Axel, and Neuberger, Christoph (2007) "Preparing for an age of participatory news," *Journalism Practice* 1(3): pp. 322–338.

Domingo, David (2008) "Interactivity in the daily routines of online newsrooms: Dealing with an uncomfortable myth," *Journal of Computer-Mediated Communication* 13(2): pp. 680–704.

Erdal, Ivar John (2009) "Repurposing of content in multi-platform news production: Towards a typology of cross-media journalism," *Journalism Practice* 3(2): pp. 178–195.

Ericson, Richard V., Baranek, Patricia M., and Chan, Janet B. L. (1989) *Negotiating Control: A study of news sources.* Maidenhead: Open University Press.

Feldstein, Mark (2007) "Dummies and ventriloquists: Models of how sources set the investigative agenda," *Journalism* 8(5): pp. 499–509.

Gans, Herbert J. (1979) *Deciding What's News: A study of CBS evening news, NBC Nightly News, Newsweek and Time,* New York: Pantheon Books.

Garcelon, Marc (2006) "The 'Indymedia' experiment: The Internet as a movement facilitator against institutional control," *Convergence* 12(1): pp. 55–82.

Gieber, Walter (1999/1964). "News is what newspapermen make it," in Howard Tumber (Ed) *News, A Reader,* Oxford: Oxford University Press, pp. 218–223.

Gillmor, Dan (2004) *We the Media,* Sebastopol: O'Reilly.

Graves, Lucas (2007) "The affordances of blogging: A case study in culture and technological effects," *Journal of Communication Inquiry* 31(4): pp. 331346.

Haas, Tanni (2005) "From 'public journalism' to the 'public's journalism'?," *Journalism Studies* 6(3): pp. 387–396.

Haas, Tanni (2007) *The Pursuit of Public Journalism: Theory, practice, and criticism,* New York: Routledge.

Habermas, Jurgen (2006) "Political Communication in Media Society—Does Democracy Still Enjoy an Epistemic Dimension? The Impact of Normative Theory on Empirical Research," Paper presented at the ICA Annual Convention, June 20, Dresden, Germany.

Harju, Auli (2007) "Citizen participation and local public spheres: An agency and identity focussed approach to the Tampere postal services conflict," in Bart Cammaerts and Nico Carpentier (Eds) *Reclaiming the Media: Communication rights and democratic media roles*, Bristol: Intellect Books, pp. 92–106.

Helle, Merja (2000) "Disturbances and contradictions as tools for understanding work in the newsroom," *Scandinavian Journal of Information Systems* 12: pp. 81–114.

Hermida, Alfred and Thurman, Neil (2008) "A clash of cultures: The integration of user-generated content within professional journalistic frameworks at British newspaper websites," *Journalism Practice* 2(3): pp. 343–356.

Jha, Sonora (2008) "Why they wouldn't cite from sites: A study of journalists' perceptions of social movement web sites and the impact on their coverage of social protest," *Journalism* 9(6): pp. 711–732.

Karakaya Polat, Rabia (2005) "The internet and political participation: Exploring the explanatory links," *European Journal of Communication* 20(4): pp. 435–459.

Lewis, Justin, Williams, Andrew and Franklin, Bob (2008) "A Compromised Fourth Estate? UK News journalism, public relations and news sources," *Journalism Studies* 9(1): pp. 1–20.

Machill, Marcel and Beiler, Markus (2009) "The importance of the Internet for journalistic research: A multi-method study of the research performed by journalists working for daily newspapers, radio, television and online," *Journalism Studies* 10(2): pp. 178–203.

Mcintosh, Shawn (2008) "Collaboration, consensus, and conflict: Negotiating news the wiki way," *Journalism Practice* 2(2): pp. 197–211.

Messner, Marcus and Distaso, Marcia Watson (2008) "The source cycle: How traditional media and weblogs use each other as sources," *Journalism Studies* 9(3): pp. 447–463.

Neuberger, Christoph, Nuernbergk, Christian, and Rischke, Melanie (2007). "Weblogs und Journalismus: Konkurrenz, Ergänzung oder Integration?," *Media Perspektiven* 2: pp. 96–112.

O'Neill, Deirdre and O'Connor, Catherine (2007) "The passive journalist: How sources dominate the local news," *Journalism Practice* 2(3): pp. 487–500.

Oakham, Katrina Mandy and Murrell, Colleen (2007) "Citizens at the Gate. But whose news are they peddling?" Paper presented at the Future of Newspapers Conference, September, Cardiff, Wales.

Paterson, Chris and Domingo, David (Eds) (2008) *Making Online News. The ethnography of new media production,* New York: Peter Lang.

Paulussen, Steve and Ugille, Pieter (2008) "User generated content in the newsroom: Professional and organisational constraints on participatory journalism," *Westminster Papers in Communication and Culture* 5(2): pp. 24–41.

Platon, Sara and Deuze, Mark (2003) "Indymedia journalism: A radical way of making, selecting and sharing news?," *Journalism* 4(3): pp. 336–355.

Reader, Bill (2008) "Turf wars? Rhetorical struggle over 'prepared' letters to the editor," *Journalism* 9(5): pp. 606–623.

Reese, Stephen D. (1994). "The Media Sociology of Herbert Gans: A Chicago Functionalist" Paper presented at the Annual ICA Conference, July, Sydney, Australia.

Shin, Jae-wha and Cameron, Glen T. (2003) "The interplay of professional and cultural factors in the online source-reporter relationship," *Journalism Studies* 4(2): pp. 253–272.

Soley, Lawrence C. and Craig, Robert L (1992) "Advertising pressures on newspapers: a survey," *Journal of Advertising* 11(4): pp. 1–10.

Weaver, David (1998) "Journalists around the world: Commonalities and differences," in David Weaver (Ed) *The Global Journalist*, Cresskill, NJ: Hampton Press, pp. 455–480.

Williams, Bruce A. and Delli Carpini, Michael X. (2004) "Monica and Bill All the Time and Everywhere: The collapse of gatekeeping and agenda setting in the new media environment," *American Behavioral Scientist* 47(9): pp. 1208–1230.

10 The Limits of Audience Participation
UGC @ the BBC

Andy Williams, Claire Wardle,
and Karin Wahl-Jorgensen

INTRODUCTION

This chapter provides a case study which examines BBC news journalists' attitudes to, and uses of, audience material or user-generated content (UGC). Our findings are based on a multi-method study of audience material at the BBC, co-funded by the Arts and Humanities Research Council (AHRC) and the BBC, which studied the ways in which BBC news journalism is affected by audience material, which audience members submit material, and what public attitudes are towards it. We focus here on the production element of the research, and use data drawn from newsroom observations and interviews with practitioners. Our guiding research questions were as follows: What are the attitudes of BBC news journalists towards the increased use of audience material in the news? How do journalists use audience material on a daily basis? Has the increased use of audience material changed journalism practice, and if so in what ways? What roles do the institutional frameworks set up by the BBC to elicit content from the audience, and to integrate it into news products, play in cementing or disrupting established journalism practice?

LITERATURE REVIEW: AUDIENCE PARTICIPATION
AND THE SOCIOLOGY OF JOURNALISM

Previous research into media organizations and the institutions of news production has consistently found that the norms and routines that underpin journalism are both extremely influential and difficult to change. A number of pioneering newsroom ethnographies in the late 1960s and the 1970s showed how important the institutional and professional routines of journalism practice are to the shape and content of the news (Gans, 1979; Golding and Elliot, 1979; Schlesinger, 1978; Tuchman, 1973, 1978; see also the Introduction, this volume). As Gaye Tuchman (1978, p. 12) argued, "Newswork transforms occurrences into news events." The routines associated with such work are durable partly because they are so central to the continuing authority of journalism: they not only construct external events as news, but they are self-legitimating practices. As Tuchman put it, "professionalism serves organizational interests by reaffirming the institutional processes in which newswork is embedded" (1978, p. 12). Such sociological research has also shown that this news work has often been characterized by indifference, and sometimes hostility, to the audience. For example, Gans (1979) established that journalists are largely dismissive of, and indifferent to, feedback from the audience because they see it as unrepresentative. To them, the mail comes from a particularly conservative segment of the citizenry, sometimes bordering on the lunatic (1979, pp. 230–235). This well-documented resistance to the audience is understandable given the fact that journalists' professional status and sense of autonomy often rests on their perceived ability to make more valid decisions than consumers of the news (Schlesinger, 1978, p. 111). It nevertheless clashes with a long-standing emphasis on participatory media formats as important to democratic responsibility, tied to notions of public service. Media organizations' interest in audience participation is not a new phenomenon, but rather as old as the media themselves. The desire for professional autonomy has always co-existed in tension with aspects of journalistic self-understandings which emphasize service to the public (e.g., Carey, 1987).

The recent rise of citizen journalism represents a significant leap forward in enabling new modes and genres of audience participation, however, and has been well charted since the turn of the century (Deuze, 2008, p.107). What unites most accounts is an emphasis on describing the increased role of the public in producing material that would formerly have been the preserve of professional journalists. Another common scholarly theme is the idea that communication is no longer a one-way practice, and is becoming more collaborative and consensual. To use a common metaphor, traditional journalism was like a lecture, but today's citizen journalism is more like a conversation (Kunelius, 2001; Gillmor, 2004). Put simply, the new journalism "must be seen as a praxis that is not exclusively tied to salaried work or professional institutions anymore" (Deuze et al., 2007, p. 323).

Unsurprisingly, given the potential threat to ingrained professional values and practices posed by these developments, research has also found that mainstream news organizations tend to approach the challenges of participatory journalism somewhat conservatively, and with continued recourse to existing routines (Deuze, 2003). Jane Singer has written persuasively about the ways in which the mainstream media have attempted to "normalise" participatory media formats until they become subsumed within "traditional journalistic norms and practices" (2005, p. 173). She has argued that some new media forms, such as weblogs, are a threat to longstanding traditional journalistic practices because of their dialogic, conversational, and collaborative nature as well as their emphasis on process and transparency.

More recently scholars have pointed out that the mainstream news media have been "slow to respond" to citizen journalism (Thurman, 2008, p. 139), and drawn attention to the often "sluggish adoption of interactivity in online journalism" (Paulussen et al., 2007, p. 146). Alfred Hermida, writing about blogging at the BBC, found that journalists still see blogs as "an extension of, rather than a departure from, traditional journalistic norms and practices" (2009, p. 2). Similarly, Singer (2010) suggested that UK local and regional reporters believe that unless it is carefully monitored UGC "can undermine journalistic norms and values," and Harrison (2010) discussed BBC journalists' continued perceptions of a "very real and quite genuine worry about the threat UGC poses to editorial values and ultimately to news standards." Others have found that opportunities for mainstream media audiences to participate in the processes of news production are often circumscribed. Much of the time participation is limited to providing comment on stories either in separate discussion boards or under already completed online news articles (Domingo et al., 2008, pp. 337–339). Another international comparative study demonstrated that "personal, or DIY, journalism is [. . .] strongly rejected as a form of 'real' journalism" by reporters (O'Sullivan and Heinonen, 2008, pp. 367–368). This finding was echoed in the work of Hermida and Thurman (2008) who stated that the limited experiments with audience interaction in UK online news have led to strict re-enforcement of strong gatekeeper roles for journalists.

METHOD

This research was conducted using multi-site newsroom observations, with a team of five Cardiff University researchers spending a total of 38 days in different newsrooms across the BBC, both at the Network and regional level. Access to newsrooms was facilitated by the fact the BBC co-funded the research. Researchers spent time at the following locations: BBC Devon Plymouth (10 days); BBC Cardiff (5 days); BBC Sheffield (10 days); BBC Leeds (3 days); the UGC Hub (6 days); *BBC Breakfast* (1 day); *News 24* (1 day); World Service *Newshour* and *World Have Your Say* (1 day); BBC College of Journalism "Have They Got News For Us?" course, and BBC Wales, Cardiff (1 day).

Before beginning our project we devised a research plan which included emphases on exploratory and semi-structured interviews, ethnographic mapping, and examination of day-to-day routines including shadowing exercises and observing meetings and exchanges between staff. The observations took place during the first two weeks of September 2007, and the research team was in frequent contact exchanging notes and observations. The design allowed us to track where and how audience material circulated both within and between newsrooms at regional, national, and network levels at the

BBC. This was particularly important because of the need to observe the centralized system for the management of audience material based around the 'UGC Hub' in Television Centre, London. As part of the observations, we completed interviews with 115 BBC journalists with varying degrees of experience and seniority. Six months after the observations, once the first stage of analysis was completed, we interviewed ten senior managers, including the Head of Global News, the Editor of BBC News, the editor of the BBC website and BBC Head of Editorial Development for Multimedia.

HAVE THEY GOT NEWS FOR US? USER-GENERATED CONTENT AT THE BBC

During our newsroom observations we found five different types of audience material at the BBC: Audience Content (including eyewitness footage or photos, accounts of experiences, and story tip-offs); Audience Comment (e.g., SMS, emails, bulletin board posts); Non-news Content (e.g., photos of nature, the weather, etc); Collaborative Content (offline collaborations between journalists and audience members such as web diaries or video nation); and Networked Journalism (online collaborative initiatives which tap into online communities within the audience to improve journalistic output; Wardle and Williams, 2009, p. 10). Broadly speaking, the first three categories in this typology fit most easily into established and long-standing journalistic practices, particularly reporter-source relationships. The final two examples are most disruptive of the traditional relationships between journalists and audience members, producers and consumers of the news. They are also the examples where most control over the production process is ceded to the audience member. These collaborative partnership-based journalistic projects were seldom found.

The most common form of audience material published or broadcast by the BBC is Audience Comment (Wardle and Williams, 2009, p. 55–58). Comment has, of course, long been a staple of local and network radio programs, and has recently proliferated in the form of texts and e-mails to television programs. It is on the internet, however, that possibilities for audience comment have proliferated most in recent years. Not only does BBC News offer the central *Have Your Say* website (active since 2005), but most high-profile news and current affairs programs on radio and TV also have some form of interactive discussion forum such as a blog or bulletin board (Wardle and Williams, 2009, p. 57–58). Of all of these forms of UGC, however, BBC News has most wholeheartedly embraced what we call Audience Content (eyewitness material including direct accounts of experiences, audio-visual material, and story tip-offs). Indeed, the editorial desirability of such content is so marked that the catch-all term 'UGC' has become almost synonymous with Audience Content at the BBC. This is unsurprising given the tone and content of the 'UGC' training offered to staff.

The BBC College of Journalism's bespoke 'UGC' training course is central to the corporation's institutional response to the rise of audience content. Entitled "Have They Got News For Us?" the course, which has been running since Spring 2006, acts as a primer for journalists who might come into contact with audience material. It is structured around a series of short films introducing the concept, a number of group role-playing exercises (which encourage attendees to reflect on the ethical, legal, and professional challenges of working with audience material), and examples of the ways in which user-submitted content might enhance BBC news output. Chris Walton, the BBC journalist who devised the course, told us, "It's [about] the idea that there's a whole new [. . .] media setup going on with journalism no longer being a one-way street, so to speak, that it was very much two-way. And interactive journalism was no longer a sermon but was more of a conversation."

Despite using the language of conversation and interactivity, the prospect for the kind of participatory relationships Walton describes are limited by the range of audience material covered by the course. Almost without exception, the examples of UGC invoked and the training scenarios encouraged by the two-hour session involve processing audience content as source material with a heavy emphasis on avoiding being duped by potential "UGC hoaxes." As the title of the course suggests, the BBC is more interested in showing its news journalists what they can get from the audience than it is in encouraging collaborative news journalism.[1]

In the vast majority of cases, the extent of the "conversation" mentioned by this trainer was limited to acts in which the audience submit raw material and the journalist processes it in the same way that they would material from other news sources. This emphasis was also echoed in our interview with Walton:

> The thing about user-generated content is that it's not new. None of this stuff is actually new. We've been dealing with material and responses from the audience for years. What's new is that it's coming very fast, instantaneously, and the volume is absolutely huge and coming via devices like the internet and mobile phones. [. . .] But still, in terms of how you process it, it shouldn't be any different.

Analogous statements that stress the importance of continuity in journalism practice, and play down the novelty of audience participation were common in our interviews. One might expect this from journalists working on established platforms such as radio and television at the regional and local peripheries of BBC News, or from older reporters skeptical of what they see as a new fad. But one might anticipate a different picture from newsrooms at the cutting edge of the BBC's engagement with its audience: the UGC Hub and its centerpiece, the *Have Your Say* news discussion forum.

SORTING THE WHEAT FROM THE CHAFF AT THE UGC HUB

But here too the dominant way of understanding audience material amongst BBC journalists involves seeing it as little more than another news source. Audience content is viewed by most journalists working at the UGC Hub as material to be processed, rather than as an opportunity for the public to retain creative control over their output, or a chance for journalists to truly collaborate with the public. These attitudes are continually re-enforced by the way the Hub is structured as an extension of the corporation's newsgathering machine rather than as a facilitator of sustained interaction between journalists and audience members. This is somewhat at odds with the new media values underpinning the rise of citizen journalism.

Set up in 2005, the UGC Hub is at the center of the BBC's response to the increase in citizen participation in the media. It currently consists of a team of 23 journalists based in the new multimedia newsroom in London, and has grown significantly in size in recent years (at the time of our research there were 12 journalists at the Hub, and when it was set up it had a workforce of just three). Hub journalists are responsible for the smooth running of the *Have Your Say* news discussion website, for eliciting and processing audience material in a number of other ways, and for distributing audience material to news teams across the BBC. On an average day the Hub receives around 10,000 to 12,000 emails, as well as hundreds of pictures and video clips, sent in by the public.

Peter Horrocks (then editor of the BBC's integrated newsroom, now Director of the BBC World Service) is clear about the need for the Hub to extract editorially useful audience content. He has repeatedly said that most of the comment-based material on *Have Your Say* debates are inconsequential compared with the few examples of eyewitness materials that are also sometimes posted. Citing a web discussion after the death of Benazir Bhutto he stated:

> The top 20 or 30 recommended posts all had variations on the theme, attacking Islam in comprehensive terms. [. . .] To be honest it was pretty boring wading through them. [. . .] Buried amongst the comments however, [. . .] were valuable eyewitness comments from people who were at the scene in Rawalpindi. Our team that deals with user content sifted through the chaff to find some excellent wheat. (Horrocks, 2008)

In common with many of the journalists we spoke to in newsrooms across the country and with the BBC's audience material-related training, this senior editor is keen to separate out editorially useful content (the wheat), from other (in this case opinion-based) material (the chaff).

Horrocks' emphasis on audience material as a news source is also evident in the Hub's position within the (then soon-to-be-opened) multimedia newsroom:

Close to the middle of that operation will be our user-generated content unit. It will be right alongside the newsgathering teams that deploy our conventional journalistic resources. And the UGC team will be deploying and receiving our unconventional journalistic resources—information and opinion from the audience. (Horrocks, 2008)

It is clear from both its physical position within the newsroom and the work done by journalists who work there that news gathering is the Hub's primary reason for existing.

MODERATING *HAVE YOUR SAY*: DEALING WITH THE CHAFF?

Moderating debate at the BBC is costly. To manage these costs most of the corporation's comment-based UGC is outsourced to third-party operators. The *Have Your Say* forum is an exception to this rule, however, and is moderated by a team of trained broadcast journalists and broadcast assistants at the UGC Hub. Under the supervision of the BBC's interactivity editor this team is responsible for setting the parameters for, and moderating debates on, the forum, setting up post forms inviting the audience to respond to various online news stories, monitoring other audience content (e.g., that submitted to the yourpics@bbc.co.uk email address), and distributing material to various BBC news outlets.

Most Hub journalists consider moderating debates to be an onerous job. As one told us, "We're all moderators. That's a task that never ceases. It just goes on and on. There are some debates where you will just see thousands and thousands of comments [. . .], and the task of moderation, [. . .] it just never stops." The majority of debates on the site are "fully moderated," meaning that posts not written by the 2000 or so registered users have to be checked before publication. The volume of responses to be dealt with is clearly a challenge. Readers regularly post 10,000 messages a day per topic, and this can rise to upwards of 30,000 on very popular debates. Because of this high response rate not all messages get published. During the week-long sample period covered by our content analysis, for example, 62% of posts were published (49,192 of 79,237 in total), 5% were rejected for breaking the rules (3,879), and 33% were left unpublished in the "moderation queue" (26,232; Wardle and Williams, 2009, p. 57).

Despite the time-consuming and sometimes tedious or frustrating nature of moderation, many journalists at the Hub express a belief that the BBC offering such a space for debate is a good thing. However, most also see any public service value as of secondary importance to the editorial value which is routinely garnered from material submitted to the site. As one journalist told us:

Have your say debates have to be the most important thing that we do. Because without them, we wouldn't get any content for programmes. From a purely selfish news point of view, we are not interested in what 90% of people have to say. [The] 10% of people who say something useful, or say something which could be interesting from a case study point of view, we would never get them if we did not have the other 90%, if you see what I mean. Whatever debate you do there will only ever be a very tiny proportion of people who will say something interesting from a newsgathering point of view.

This reporter sets up a dichotomy which emphasizes the instrumental value attached to certain kinds of audience comment, and this position was echoed by many hub journalists. There is a strong belief even amongst those who dislike audience comment that this "chaff" is needed in order to get to the "wheat." As one told us, "We do two things, you've got to remember, and sometimes they rub against each other. We offer the service, the discussion boards, but then we also get to use the interesting contacts. The more of a service we offer, the more and the better contacts we get." Moderation is seen as something which the team has to do to find the eyewitness content (tip-offs, stories, accounts, case studies, and contacts which could lead to audio-visual material) that they really want for their news output.

NEWSGATHERING AT THE UGC HUB: FINDING THE "WHEAT"?

What form does this "wheat" take? We identified three principal inter-related categories of Audience Content gathered at the BBC's UGC Hub: material that leads to the generation of new stories; eyewitness accounts and footage or stills of breaking or existing news stories; and case studies and contacts for people with experience or knowledge of already existing news stories. In all of these instances Audience Content is, in the main, treated as conventional source material.

Story Generation

Have Your Say has generated a limited number of high-profile news stories for the BBC. In this framework Audience Content takes the form of tip-offs, a long-standing form of public engagement with journalism. In some instances, an initial tip-off leads to a version of crowd-sourcing in order to add depth, weight, and detail to a story. The most commonly cited of these stories initially came from a *Have Your Say* debate which revealed low levels of morale among British soldiers serving overseas in Iraq and Afghanistan, "after the story led the *Ten O'Clock News* we were just inundated with responses and pictures. It ended up leading the *Ten O'Clock News* the second night as well, and that very rarely happens. And it was all down to user-generated content." Another high-profile crowd-sourced story we were told about on a number of occasions was one that dealt with lost or unclaimed luggage at Heathrow Airport in December 2006. Initially prompted by user-generated photographs emailed to the Hub, a *Have Your Say* debate was started on the subject, which in turn prompted thousands of audience members to contribute to the debate or send in their own stories and audio-visual material. Coverage on the website, *News 24*, the *One O'Clock News*, and all of the radio stations followed, and British Airways were forced to issue an apology (Taylor, 2007).

Eyewitness Material

As we have suggested, in many BBC newsrooms (especially online and television newsrooms) the term UGC is used primarily to refer to audio-visual material (video footage, photographs, etc.) of breaking or existing news events. It is unsurprising then that such Audience Content, described by one Hub employee as "nuggets of gold," is also highly valued at the Hub. One journalist explained why:

> That first hour before you get your resources to that story: this is where we come into our own. We will have access to people who are there and who are contacting us much quicker than any other news resource we can get there. When you think about it you have millions of people who have mobile phones in this country, and who can take pictures and video footage. And also because they're at the end of a phone they can do interviews.

The UGC Hub team was expanded in the wake of the London Bombings of 2005, largely to process the increasing amounts of material of this kind the public were submitting to the BBC. Much of this kind of material also comes from the pro-active cultivation of sources who have submitted comments online. Hub journalists routinely contact *Have Your Say* posters and "commission" them to send in original photographs or video footage before adding their details to a growing database of citizen news sources.

A steady stream of this kind of material flows into the Hub, and some of it is distributed to various news outlets across the BBC. But the Hub is at its most valuable during major UGC-rich stories such as terror attacks or extreme weather events. In such circumstances, day-to-day tasks get shelved in favor of dealing with the increased volume of eyewitness footage and photographs. The UK summer floods of 2007 were an example that came up frequently in our interviews, and was described as a period when hundreds of pictures and video clips were sent to the Hub every day.

During such big "UGC stories," as well as processing this audio-visual material, Hub journalists also contact submitters of UGC to ask them to talk about their experiences as guests.

Case Studies

Despite the editorial desirability of material in the first two categories, it appears relatively infrequently. Most of the "wheat" Hub employees find takes the form of what they call "case studies" or "contacts" for people with experience or knowledge of already existing news stories who are willing to act as guests or sources for relevant BBC news outlets. "Case studies," one Hub employee told us, come from "people whose views we should be interested in for a particular reason: because they have first-hand experience of the story; or they are at the location where the story is taking place. It's very rare that we'll have just general punters on air."

Most journalists found it difficult to estimate how many usable case studies they found, suggesting that it depended on what material had already been requested by news outlets, the kinds of debates that were running on *Have Your Say*, and how many post forms were in operation on different BBC news web pages. When asked how many of the case studies passed on by the Hub make it on air, one reporter told us, "out of 1000 messages on *Have Your Say* you may get around a couple of dozen case studies that could be used which we pass on to programs. The ones which actually get on air would be perhaps half of that."

Case studies are harvested in one of two ways: speculatively, in which case journalists trawl through material flowing into the Hub and log the details of contributors who seem like promising future contacts; or at the behest of particular editors or journalists who have requested contacts or material on a subject. They elicit content in a number of ways, either by starting a debate on *Have Your Say*, writing a promotional call to action (a 'promo'), or setting up a 'post form' at the bottom of an internet news story. We found evidence in regional newsrooms, as well as at outlets such as *Radio 5 Live* and the *World Service*, that the journalists who elicit material from the Hub are satisfied when they can effectively outsource some of their newsgathering activities in this way.

DISCUSSION: JUST ANOTHER NEWS SOURCE?

Harrison is sceptical of the broader civic value in the BBC's use of audience material. She believes that in the future "UGC" at the BBC will be limited largely to photos and videos shot opportunistically from a mobile phones "which can be used and stored as a repository of potentially useful sources" (2010). Our data suggests that she is right. With the exception of some marginal collaborative news projects (Wardle and Williams, 2009, pp. 26–30), rather than changing the way most news journalists at the BBC work the ways that BBC News processes audience material are firmly embedded within long-established practices relating to news gathering and sourcing.

Expressed differently, the BBC's embrace of the "audience revolution" has not notably disrupted the traditional roles played by consumers and producers of the news. The rise of UGC at the BBC has largely involved harnessing audience material to fit within existing routines of journalistic production. Reich (2009), in discussing online audience comment, has argued that the ways in which the mainstream media have embraced audience material often involve a "taming" of the power of the audience to produce its own content. We share this assessment. Of course the BBC has encouraged its audience to participate in many different ways, but the democratizing potential of increased citizen participation in news production has been blunted by the unwillingness of BBC News to accept models of engagement which emphasize partnership with the public.

Örnebring began a recent study of two European newspapers' uses of audience material by asking, "does the blurring of the producer-consumer represent a real shift in power away from traditional media/news organizations [. . .]?" (2008, p. 771). Implicit in this question is skepticism about whether the celebratory words of some journalists and editors about the rise of audience material really correspond with the emergence of a truly collaborative and participatory journalism. From our observation of day-to-day practices of news production in a range of different newsrooms, our interviews with journalists about their uses of (and attitudes to) audience material, and our scrutiny of the institutional structures put in place to deal with it, it is clear that any partnerships that do exist are usually very unequal. One might even say that in the "give and take" relationship which exists between the BBC and its contributors the public do most of the giving, and the corporation much of the taking.

We are conscious of the difficulty of making generalizations about a concept as multifaceted as audience material in any newsroom, let alone about numerous newsrooms at an organization as large as the BBC. Divergence in attitudes and practices will always be discernible between newsrooms which produce content for different platforms, and which exist in different geographical locations. A recent intervention from Quandt and Heinonen (2009) shows that even within individual newsrooms there are disparities in approach between journalists with diverse outlooks, experiences and approaches. They identify two broad attitudes that reporters hold when talking about audience material: a segregationist approach which favors leaving journalism to journalists, and an integrationist approach in which the public/audience are regarded as an ally in a journalistic process which is co-creative. Our own data shows how such attitudes are apparent not only within the same newsroom but sometimes also within the (at times contradictory) discourse of individual journalists.

Even so, close attention to the discourse and practice of a large number of journalists and editors, alongside observation of the institutional frameworks put in place to manage the flow of audience material, has allowed us to identify dominant trends at the BBC. The paramount value of Audience Content is apparent at senior managerial level (in the words of influential figures within BBC News), from the structures which have been put in place to elicit and process news-related audience material, and from the practices we observed and the interviews we conducted with newsworkers across platforms and geographic locations. To most news journalists "UGC" is little more than raw material which they turn into the news; grist to the journalistic mill. Of course, technology has enabled significant increases in the volume of content they get from the public and the speed with which it can be submitted. But such relationships with the audience have always existed.

Towards the end of his speech on audience material, Peter Horrocks was even more explicit about questioning the need to expend so much time and effort on dealing with audience comment that is not immediately editorially useful. "If we can free up effort from simply processing large volumes of opinion [. . .] our intention will be to enhance our efforts in getting real journalistic value out of this material" (Horrocks, 2008). Kevin Marsh, the Editor-in-Chief of the BBC College of Journalism (and former editor of Radio 4's *Today Programme*) was less certain about this pervasive way of understanding the role of UGC at the BBC. On his own blog he responded to Horrocks' words by calling them too "journocentric" and suggesting his view of what the audience can offer is too limited. "His vision of journalism," he wrote, "yields very little of the trade's role as the principal agent in the information business. Interacting with audiences isn't much more than a help and assistance in that. Not everyone would agree" (Marsh, 2007). The dominant way of understanding and using audience material at the BBC is undoubtedly too "journocentric." It discourages an understanding of how an "audience revolution" in the production of the news could lead to fruitful and creative collaborations and partnerships between journalists and audience members. One journalist at the Hub was aware of this, and talked about the limited opportunities members of the public have to act as anything more than a source of information. She admitted that the audience material passed on to BBC newsrooms is usually "turned around" with minimum input from the audience member.

The same journalist was keenly aware of the differential between her usual practice and participatory ideals, and was eager to point out that the BBC does aspire to produce more collaborative journalism, claiming that resource constraints are the primary reason why this does not often happen:

> That newsroom might also be interested in offering that person the time to go out and record some material themselves, or to go out and record some new audio and broadcast that on the radio, or to give them a camera and ask them to go out and shoot their own story in the style of *Video Nation*. [. . .] That happens less often in general newsrooms

because it's so labour-intensive, but that is the ultimate BBC vision of UGC because it gets so much control to the audience member. [. . .] I think there's a soft but genuine aim to do more of that sort of thing.

There is no doubt that the BBC aspires to provide more opportunities for truly collaborative journalism. This is expressed by some journalists and editors and to a limited extent it is evident in some output (Wardle and Williams, 2009, pp. 26–30). But these examples are mainly to be found either outside, or on the margins of, the BBC's news operation.

Audience material is often characterized as a democratizing force, allowing the audience to have an input into news production and eroding traditional distinctions between producers and consumers of the news. One current barrier preventing fuller participation from the audience is a dominant "journocentric" mindset among news journalists and editors that too often sees Audience Material only as a source of news. We do not wish to suggest that what is currently seen as "UGC" should not be integrated into existing news production processes. But we do suggest that seeing it only, or even mainly, as a news gathering opportunity limits the possibilities offered by the upsurge in submissions of audience material. For most news journalists there has been no radical upheaval in the way they work, and no great change in the structural roles played by traditional producers and consumers of the news. The corporation's training and guidance around audience material, as evidenced in its flagship "Have They Got News For Us" course, serves to perpetuate this pattern, as does the discourse and practice of most journalists and senior editors, and the role of the UGC Hub as a source-management and newsgathering tool.

Overwhelmingly, journalists have remained journalists and audiences are still audiences, and truly collaborative relations between the two groups remain rare exceptions. Until the institutional structures that underpin these relationships are challenged, the possibilities for truly participatory journalism at the BBC will remain marginal, and increased audience interaction will continue to be a euphemism for allowing the public to subsidize the corporation's newsgathering efforts.

ACKNOWLEDGMENT

A longer version of this chapter will appear as "'Have They Got News For Us?' Audience revolution or business as usual at the BBC?" in *Journalism Practice*, forthcoming. We are grateful to the publisher for allowing us to reproduce some materials here.

NOTES

1. The principal exception to this in the session we observed was a small final segment of the course in which journalists were encouraged to scan the internet for

useful blogs which could inform future BBC News content. In certain cases this could lead to examples of what we call Networked Journalism. Even this part of the course was mainly framed in terms of very traditional journalist-source relations, however, with the instructor suggesting, "an increasing number of journalists are learning to find the best blogs and to use them as sources. [. . .] Blogs can be good sources, but remember, they're just sources."

REFERENCES

Carey, James (1987) "The press and public discourse," *The Center Magazine* 20: pp. 4–32.

Deuze, Mark, Bruns, Axel, and Neuberger, Christoph (2007) "Preparing for an age of participatory news," *Journalism Practice* 1(3): pp. 322–338.

Deuze, Mark (2008) "The professional identity of journalists in the context of convergence culture," *Observatorio* 7: pp. 103–117.

Deuze, Mark (2003) "The Web and its journalisms: Considering the consequences of different types of news media online", *New Media & Society* 5(2): pp. 203–230.

Domingo, David, Quandt, Thorsten, Heinonen, Ari, Paulussen, Steve, Singer, Jane B., and Vujnovic, Marina (2008) "Participatory journalism practices in the media and beyond," *Journalism Practice* 2(3): pp. 326–342.

Gans, Herbert (1979) *Deciding What's News*, New York: Pantheon

Gillmor, Dan (2004) *We the Media*, O'Reilly: Available: www.oreilly.com/catalog/wemedia/book/index.csp. Accessed July 8, 2009

Golding, Peter and Elliott, Philip (1979) *Making the News*, London: Longman

Harrison, Jackie (2010) "UGC and Gatekeeping at the BBC" in *Journalism Studies*, 11(2): 243–256.

Hermida, Alfred, and Thurman, Neil (2008) "A clash of cultures," *Journalism Practice* 2(3): pp. 343–356.

Hermida, Alfred (2009) "The blogging BBC: Journalism blogs at 'the world's most trusted news organisation'," *Journalism Practice* 3(3): pp. 268–284.

Horrocks, Peter (2008) "The Value of Citizen Journalism," Available: www.bbc.co.uk/blogs/theeditors/2008/01/value_of_citizen_journalism.html. Accessed July 7, 2009.

Kunelius, Risto. (2001) "Conversation: a metaphor and a method for better journalism?," *Journalism Studies* 2(1): pp. 31–54.

Marsh, Kevin (2008) "Future(ish) News(ish)." Available: storycurve.blogspot.com/2008/01/recently-my-good-friend-and-head-of-bbc.html. Accessed July 7, 2009.

Örnebring, Henrik (2008) "The consumer as producer—of what?," *Journalism Studies* 9(5): pp. 771–785.

O'Sullivan, John and Heinonen, Ari (2008) "Old Values, New Media," *Journalism Practice* 2(3): pp. 357–371.

Paulussen, Seve, Heinonen, Ari, Domingo, David, and Quandt, Thorsten (2007) "Doing it together," *Observatorio Journal* 1(3): pp. 131–154.

Quandt, Thorsten and Heinonen, Ari (2009) "User-Generated Content as Challenge to Traditional Journalistic Ideology," Paper presented to the 2009 ICA Conference "Keywords in Communication," May, Chicago.

Reich, Zvi (2009) "Weaving the Thread," Paper presented to the 2009 ICA Conference "Keywords in Communication," May, Chicago.

Schlesinger, Philip (1978) *Putting Reality Together*, London: Constable

Singer, Jane B. (2010) "Quality Control" in *Journalism Practice* 4(2): 127–142.

Singer, Jane B. (2006) "Stepping back from the gate," *Journalism & Mass Communication Quarterly* 83(2): pp. 265—280.

Singer, Jane B. (2005) "The political j-blogger: 'Normalising' a new media form to fit old norms and practices," *Journalism* 6(2): pp. 173–198.

Singer, Jane B., and Ashman, Ian (2009) "User-generated content and journalistic values," in Stuart Allan and Einar Thorsen (Eds) *Citizen Journalism: Global Perspectives*, New York: Peter Lang

Taylor, Vicki (2007) "Lost Luggage Woes." Available: www.bbc.co.uk/blogs/the-editors/2007/01/lost_luggage_woes.html. Accessed July 7, 2009.

Thurman, Neil (2008) "Forums for citizen journalists?," *New Media & Society* 10(1): pp. 139–157.

Tuchman, Gaye (1973) "Making news by doing work," *American Journal of Sociology* 79: pp. 110–131.

Tuchman, Gaye (1978) *Making News*, New York: The Free Press.

Wardle, Claire, Williams, Andy, and Wahl-Jorgensen, Karin (2008) *UGC @ the BBC: Understanding its impact upon contributors, non-contributors, and BBC news,* report from a Knowledge Exchange project funded by the AHRC and the BBC.

11 The Scope of User-Generated Content
User-Contributions within Online Journalism

Annika Bergström

INTRODUCTION

New media techniques often form expectations in different ways. Since the new millennium, a new generation of Web applications have developed, sometimes gathered under the expression Web 2.0—an umbrella term for interactive possibilities characterized by the freedom of sharing content and participating (Limonard, 2007; Madden and Fox, 2006; OECD, 2007). Many examples of participatory media have emerged outside the existing media sphere, but the established media have also been affected by these digital developments. Blogs for example, are becoming regular sources in journalism, and online news producers are experimenting with user contributions and forms for user-generated content, both as a separate genre and as a source for professionally produced content (see Chapters 10 and 12).

The association of ordinary people with journalism has been evident since the first half of the 20th century in former Eastern Europe, where so-called 'Volkskorrespondenten' contributed news within desirable political frames. For decades, printed dailies have provided readers with opportunities to contribute debate articles and letters to the editor. However, the internet brings an infrastructure which facilitates the distribution of reader or self-produced content to a potentially larger audience (Croteau, 2006, p. 341). The internet enables *every* user to participate (Paulussen et al., 2007, p. 133). User-generated content (UGC) is a growing part of media content and the audience is becoming an increasingly common actor and source in news production (see Chapters 9 and 12, this volume). The public is expected to add value to traditional content, and journalists are no longer the only and obvious news producers. The user might be considered a companion, or even a competitor, in this sense.

Thus far, research has revealed a slightly reluctant attitude among publishers, as well as the audience itself, towards content provided by the audience. Editors in chief are reluctant to relinquish control, UGC is considered costly and unwieldy and consequently "mainstream media in Europe are still far removed from this ideal-typical model of 'networked' or participatory journalism" (Paulussen et al., 2007, p. 146. See also Chapter 10, this volume). The interactive audience seems to be most interested in expressing personal matters rather than debating. But studies of audience behaviour are rare, as are studies of the attraction of UGC from a user's point of view.

The purpose of this chapter is to outline the scope of UGC within newspaper journalism, to establish which areas engage the audience and to what extent they wish to contribute. The chapter addresses two research questions: first, how attractive is UGC in the eyes of the online news audience? Second, within which areas is the audience willing to engage, and which groups are more likely to contribute with different kinds of content?

User-contributions and journalists' uses of readers as sources are developing at a different pace in different countries. An American study suggests that a large number of American citizens have a positive attitude towards online news reporting, and that blogs and citizen journalism are considered vital and important (Chung, 2007). Because media structures differ between, for instance, Sweden and the US (see Hallin and Mancini, 2004) direct comparisons cannot be made. Sweden is an interesting case from this perspective. In contrast to the US and the UK, where a number of studies of UGC have been conducted, the Swedish press market is strong, and the Swedish press also dominates the online news market (Bergström, 2005; Weibull and Jönsson, 2007). Newspapers in print and online enjoy high credibility and competitors, in terms of new media features, seem to have had difficulties in breaking through within the news-reporting field. There is, however, an ongoing public debate tending to accredit UGC with great importance for democracy. This makes studies of user contributions important, in order to reveal the actual value for journalism as well as for society.

USERS AS SOURCES AND CO-PRODUCERS

According to Nip (2006), there are several models for participatory forms of journalism, reflecting both the degree and form of participation in the news process. Some have emerged and are maintained outside mainstream media, such as public journalism and citizen journalism. These forms are beyond the scope of this chapter. The focus here is on user participation taking place within journalism produced by professionals, where users are invited to interact and give feed-back on content which has already been produced, and journalists remain the central authority in the news-making process.

UGC includes a wide range of features (Gillmore, 2004: pp. 27ff; Hujanen and Pietikäninen, 2004; Örnebring, 2008). There are several Swedish examples of news sites offering tools to establish blogs, to enable comment on news articles and to contribute by answering Web polls that are sometimes turned into articles. UGC has become a service among others provided on the news site. It is sometimes thought of as additional value and a way of creating a bond with the audience but also to strengthen the brand and market position.

User contribution raises issues regarding different levels of interactivity (Rafaeli and Sudweeks, 1997; McMillan, 2002). Stromer-Galley's concept of medium interactivity and human interactivity are also applicable within the field of professional journalism (Stromer-Galley, 2000). Medium inter-activity is interactive communication between user and machine and is restricted by what technology allows, for instance downloads. Human interactivity is communication between users that takes place via a commu-nication channel, for instance e-mail links and chat features. Chung (2008) suggests a continuum of interactive features between the two. The different modes of interactivity mean different levels of control for the publisher. While medium interactive features are easier to control, human interactive features are more in the hands of the audience.

Many news organizations are characterized by their slow adaptation to interactivity and consumer participation (Domingo, 2008; Gillmore, 2004: pp. 112ff; Lasica, 2002; Limonard, 2007; Matheson, 2004; Thurman, 2008). Consumer empowerment has certainly increased, but the news production process and resources are highly controlled by someone other than the con-sumer or user. People are more often invited to react to existing content rather than to create texts and pictures of their own (Örnebring, 2008). The inter-nal context in which participatory journalism is supposed to evolve seems to present a number of barriers. The professional culture of mainstream jour-nalism still favours a top-down approach (Paulussen et al., 2007). Different studies show that news producers are interested in interactivity and UGC, but only to a certain extent, and only as long as they retain a strict editorial control (Hedman, 2009; Singer, 2006; Stromer-Galley, 2000).

Participating and contributing can take place in many different ways and for several reasons. It is evident that many of these activities in online environ-ments are motivated by individual interest and engagement. This is particu-larly evident in the blogosphere (Neuberger, 2007). Furthermore, it seems that a minority of users contribute a disproportionately large proportion of the overall amount of UGC (c.f. Limonard, 2007). Young people, for example, tend to generate more content than older people; uploading music and film are common activities. Women seem to be more active in expressing personal matters, while men are more likely to engage in public forum, political discus-sions and debates (Limonard, 2007; Nielsen, 2006; Tancer, 2007).

UGC has typically been studied from a producer perspective. There are, however, a few content studies illustrating that the actual user-contribution is minimal, and when published, UGC is strictly separated from journalist-pro-duced content. A British-Swedish study shows that only users' pictures achieve some kind of "journalist status" (Örnebring, 2008). A different Swedish study reveals a fairly considerable amount of UGC on many news sites, but further and more thorough analysis of the articles prompts reassessment to suggest that the interactivity with users is based on simply an e-mail or other link (Karlsson, 2006).

Online news audiences, moreover, seem reluctant to interact online. A study in six Swedish municipalities, for example, revealed that only 7% of readers had posted even a single comment to news articles within the previous year (Bergström, 2008). It was evident that such applications attracted younger people along with more frequent online news users (see Chapter 9, this volume). The study comes to the same conclusion for blog writing. An American study explored a wider range of UGC features within the journalistic field and similarly concluded that overall, the online news audience was using interactive features infrequently, while two-way communication features were used the least (Chung, 2008). Chung concludes that audience adoption of interactive features may be exaggerated.

To date, the internet has been considered to be a place where you can find and consume content provided by somebody else. Some argue that we are so used to framing ourselves as consumers, rather than producers, that we do not see the possibility of participating offered by the new technology. One reason for this could be, of course, that the news genre has traditionally been regarded as a restricted area intended only for journalists (Chisholm, 2004; Hujanen et al., 2004; Roscoe, 1999). Findings from an American study show that information seeking and entertainment are motivational factors for using online news, whereas socializing factors are of less importance (Chung and Yoo, 2008).

Related to this is the extent to which the audience values and ranks different kinds of news content. Some areas, such as local and national news, are considered more important in newspapers, while others, such as culture and entertainment, are considered less so. However, importance does not automatically generate use. Entertainment content is used frequently in newspapers. On the other hand, editorials are considered important but only a few read them (Strid, 2008). There is little research on how UGC is perceived, in terms of importance, by the audience.

METHOD

The results presented in this chapter are based on data collected within the framework of the annual national SOM (Society, Opinion, and Media) surveys. The SOM Institute at the University of Gothenburg conducts interdisciplinary research on the topics of Society, Opinion, and Media. The Institute is jointly managed by the Department of Journalism, Media and Communication, the Department of Political Science and the School of Public Administration (see www.som.gu.se). The SOM survey has been conducted as a national mail survey annually since 1986. Each year 6,000 people between the ages of 15 and 85 living in Sweden, receive the survey. The frequency of response is on average 65% divided in almost the same way as the Swedish population into age, gender, social class, education etc (Nilsson, 2009). The survey gives a statistically significant picture of Swedish media habits. However, it is important to be aware of some general limitations in using quantitative research techniques. Such a survey can provide statistically significant answers about people's habits, but it does not give more in-depth information about how and why audiences engage in different kinds of practice.

In the media section of the questionnaire, habits as well as attitudes towards different media are measured. The survey also contains demographic data, and interest and lifestyle data, which deliver good pre-conditions for the analysis of correlations and the comparison of different groups. Questions on attitudes towards UGC and participation within the professional journalistic field are posed in one of the 2008 SOM-questionnaires comprising a sample of 3,000 persons with a response rate of 59%.

In order to analyse the users' contribution on news sites, two different questions were posed. One dealt with attitudes towards UGC in general and included a four-grade scale from *not important at all* to *very important*. There was also a *no opinion* option. The design resembled the one used for measuring the importance of content in printed newspapers (Strid, 2008). Then the respondents were asked to indicate how frequently they use six interactive features on news sites. The items were chosen to cover the range of interactivity discussed above. The use of email links and personal customization was omitted. One single item was about the use of other peoples' contributions in terms of comments. The answering options were seven on an ordinal scale from *never* to *daily*.

The independent variables used in this analysis are mostly well known and unproblematic. Online news habits and political interest are measured on ordinal scales. The political interest item strongly correlates with several questions on civic engagement and has also turned out to be a good predictor for political engagement (see Bergström, 2005). Civic engagement was constructed by adding questions about involvement in different organizations such as church, sports and civil rights groups.

RESULTS

We know fairly well which types of content are considered important and what attracts larger audiences in print newspapers (Strid, 2008). But we know relatively little about the attraction of user-generated content. The first research question deals with attitudes to user contributions and attraction through the act of reading comments that others have posted.

The respondents were asked "How important do you consider content created by users on newspaper sites?" About a quarter—26%—find user contributions *very* or *fairly important*. Around 40% find them unimportant—*not very important* or *not important at all*. A rather large proportion of the population does not have an opinion in this question—34% . This indicates that user contribution achieves only slight approval among the public.

When comparing different demographic groups within the population, it is obvious that age plays an important role. Half of the respondents

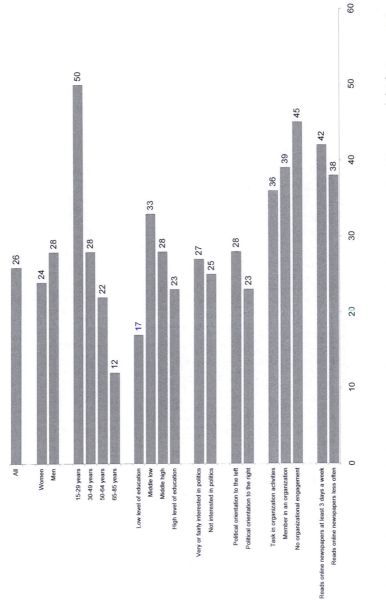

Figure 11.1   Attitudes towards the importance of user-generated content on news sites (% *very* and *fairly important*).

aged 15 to 30 agree on the importance of user-generated content compared to only 12% among the pensioners (Figure 11.1). Level of education is strongly correlated to age, which explains the low figures for persons with a lower level of education, as well as the higher rate for a middle-low level of education.

It could be argued that more politically interested respondents consider the opportunity to contribute to news sites more important than those who are less interested. We know from the printed papers that people with a strong political interest consider debate and letters to the editor to be fairly important (Strid, 2008). This is not evident for user-generated content, however, where about a quarter of the population consider it important regardless of political interest. Furthermore, it is possible to see a slightly greater disposition for people who place themselves politically more to the left to place greater value on UGC. Differences due to political interest and orientation, however, are not statistically significant. Up to date user-generated content does not seem to have any great political importance. More important is civic engagement, which seems to have the opposite impact than might be anticipated. Consequently, the less engaged respondent is likely to place a greater value on UGC. The findings might indicate that less engaged persons see the contribution possibilities online as a hypothetical possibility from a bottom-up perspective. It does not mean, however, that they are using them. Furthermore, there is a slightly more positive attitude towards user-generated content among those who regularly visit news sites, compared to less frequent users.

Another way of trying to frame the value of UGC is to see how it is actually used by the online news audience in terms of reading comments. About 30% of the population have read other users' comments on news sites in the 2008 study. This is three times as many as in the 2007 survey, which indicates a fast growing interest in reading and studying comment. However, users' postings do not draw large audiences on a regular basis: 1% read comments every day, 10% at least once a week.

Comment reading is far more common among younger persons (Figure 11.2). About half of the population aged 15 to 30 has read comments once or more, compared to 8% of pensioners. Reading posted comments also increases with level of education and is also more common among politically-interested respondents, where almost four out of ten have read comments compared to nearer 25% among less politically-interested people. Educational level and political interest strongly correlate with age. Attitudes towards UGC seem to matter to a certain extent: those who consider user contributions to be of *fairly* or *great importance* are more frequent comment readers. But of even greater importance are online news habits. Frequent users are also more frequent readers of comments.

To consider something as being important, however, does not mean that this is what you actually do. Many people find certain kinds of media

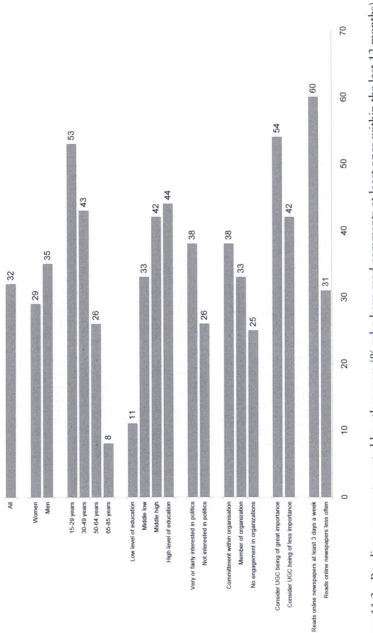

Figure 11.2 Reading comments posted by other users (% who have read comments at least once within the last 12 months).

content important but they hardly ever read them and vice versa. The second research question focuses on what kind of user contribution is taking place, how often and by whom. The respondents were asked how often they usually contribute with different kinds of user-generated content. When turning to actual participation, frequent use is rare. On a weekly basis, 4% claim to have answered a Web poll and 1% have done one or more of the remaining options posed in the questionnaire (Figure 11.3). Contributing with text and pictures is rare. It is the less interactive features, the reacting to existing content, which attract the largest audiences.

There may of course be several explanations for this rather reluctant audience behaviour. Earlier research points to the fact that editors are not encouraging the audience to any great extent. Users are typically empowered to create culture-oriented and personal-oriented content, whereas direct user involvement in news production is rare (Örnebring, 2008). One of the most common reasons for visiting news sites is the round the clock update in short user sessions (Bergström, 2005). The very context of online news might to a certain extent discourage popular and culture-oriented content provided by non-professionals regarding both contribution and reading.

It is a well-known fact that internet use differs when comparing different groups in society. UCG is no exception. Among the traditional demographic factors, age appears to be the most important. Young people contribute more frequently with different kinds of content than older people (Table 11.1). There are of course factors other than traditional demographics that can impact on user contribution. From political science, it is well established that those who are more politically interested typically participate more frequently in different political activities, not least online (c.f. Clark, 2002; Davis, 2005). It is reasonable to assume that these same correlations also hold for UGC, especially since comment and editorials are traditionally more attractive to politically- interested people. The findings here seem to support this assumption to a certain extent. Persons who are more

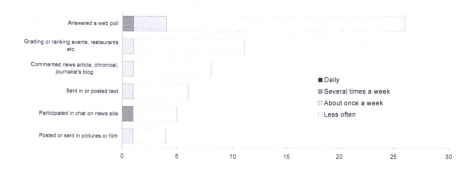

Figure 11.3 Contribution with different kinds of content on news sites (% of population).

Table 11.1   Contributors to News Sites: Their Demographic and Other Variables (% who have contributed at least once within the last 12 months)

	Commented news article/ chronicle/jour- nalists blog	Sent in/ posted pictures or film	Sent in/ posted text	Answered Web poll	Participated in chat	Graded or ranked events, restaurants etc.	n=
All	8	4	6	26	5	12	1661
Gender:							
Women	6	3	5	24	4	10	888
Men	10	6	7	29	7	14	773
Age:							
15–29 years	17	8	12	45	11	26	298
30–49 years	8	4	7	38	7	15	519
50–64 years	7	4	4	19	4	7	453
65–85 years	2	2	1	6	1	2	391
Level of education:							
Low	3	3	2	9	3	5	383
Middle low	10	5	7	29	4	14	525
Middle high	12	4	7	36	8	13	344
High	8	4	6	34	5	14	367
General political interest:							
Very or fairly interested	11	4	7	30	6	14	848
Not interested	5	4	4	23	4	9	779
Civic engagement:							
Commitment within org.	10	4	8	34	8	14	287
Member of organization	8	5	6	28	6	12	1076
No engagement in organization	6	4	4	16	2	9	255
Online news habits:							
Newspaper sites 3–7days per week	14	8	10	52	10	23	569
Newspaper sites less often	8	3	6	23	5	10	527
Attitudes towards UGC:							
Considered very or fairly important	15	9	12	44	12	24	421
Not considered important	10	6	6	35	7	12	644

interested in general politics engage more in co-creation on news sites. The same holds for respondents who have a higher level of civic engagement.

The findings clearly show that people with a more positive attitude towards UCG are more likely to contribute themselves. This is especially evident for posting, chatting and ranking, while answering Web polls is not affected to the same extent by attitudes towards UGC. The more regular online news users are also more likely and frequently to be content generating than sporadic users. The actual 'being there' seems to be important, just as it matters in other Web 2.0 contributor situations (cf. Bergström, 2008).

There seem to be several factors affecting user contribution on online news sites. The patterns are not unequivocal since some of these factors are related to each other. We know, for instance, that older persons have a lower educational level, that more highly educated people are more likely to be interested in politics etc. To establish which single factor matters most, a linear regression analysis was conducted (Table 11.2).

Table 11.2   Contributors to News Sites and Different Background Factors (regression coefficients, beta)

	Commented news article/ chronicle/ journalists blog	Sent in/ posted pictures or film	Sent in/ posted text	Answered Web poll	Participated in chat	Grading or ranking events, restaurants etc.
Gender	.059	.047	.042	.044	.044	.056
Age	-.074*	-.049	-.070*	-.147***	-.071*	-.149***
Level of education	.015	.013	.047	.030	-.021	-.025
Online news habits	.077*	.092***	.049	.296***	.105***	.145***
Attitudes towards UGC	.082*	.082*	.106***	.117***	.085***	.117***
Political interest	.083*	-.046	.025	.029	.008	.063
Civic engagement	.044	.034	.034	.060*	.086***	.070*
Adjusted R²	.031	.020	.024	.159	.031	.078

$^*p < .05$ $^{**}p < .01$ $^{***}p < .001$
Gender: dummy coded with female 1 and male 2.
Level of education: four-point scale from low level to high level.
Online news habits: four-point scale—never, more seldom, 1–2 days a week, 3–7 days a week.
Attitudes towards UGC: four-point scale from not at all important to very important.
Political interest: four-point scale from not at all interested to very interested.
Civic engagement: three-point scale—no engagement in organization, member of organization, commitment in organization.

The regression analysis shows that age, online news habits and, to a certain extent, attitudes towards UGC explain much of the user contributions on news sites, whereas gender and level of education turn out to be of little importance. There are some differences when comparing types of UGC. Political interest has a significant importance in explaining commenting, while civic engagement matters for answering Web polls, participating in chats and ranking material.

The findings from this survey point to a comparatively low level of user participation on professional journalistic news sites, which also means that the user as a source is used only to a modest extent. As already mentioned, the opportunities for participation are limited by the editorial staff for several reasons. If you widen the perspective outside the scope of the traditional journalistic context, it seems, however, that the general interest of creating content for the Web is limited. User-generated content within and outside traditional journalism has a relatively high reading value but only a few choose to contribute (Limonard, 2007). In a relatively strictly controlled environment such as professional journalism, it is not surprising that the overall level of user contribution is found to be at a modest level. In Sweden, the newspaper market is strong in print and online, and the audience seems, first and foremost, to visit news sites for reasons of updating, expecting to find the latest news gathered, produced and presented by professionals.

CONCLUSIONS

In spite of the low levels of participation found in this study, user contribution within professional journalism is a growing phenomenon. As outlined, it can mean a wide range of different things—from sending emails to editors to commenting on news articles. In many respects the former readers have been invited to participate and are being used as sources for journalistic content. This study has focused on two main issues: attitudes towards and the value of user-contributions, and the use of specific features that are published on news sites.

It is obvious that user contributions are not considered to be the most important content on news sites. Readers do not seem so interested in reading about other readers, and many do not even have an opinion about UGC. When asked how frequently they read comments posted by other users, the same pattern occurs. Other people's contributions are not as attractive as professionally produced content. In both cases it is mainly young people who are positive about user-contributions and read comments. For comment-reading, online news habits are significant. The actual being there is important.

In contrast to the impression from the public debate—where UGC seems to equal participation, which in turn is often considered positive—there seems to be much talk but little action. UGC to some extent appears to be an inflated bubble in the democracy debate, and also in the future-of-journalism debate. It is supposed to attract readers and is sometimes considered as the key for the future. Unfortunately, the debate seems to tilt in favour of the public and commercial benefits, and little is argued about whether professional journalism should actually let the users into news production, in what ways and to what extent. It is obviously unclear what the role of the user is: the role of source or the role of co-producer.

The findings from this study point to the fact that user contributions are rather moderate. The contributors are mostly young, and we know from previous research that most new online features attract young persons (Bergström, 2005). Some of them continue to spread into a larger public, but many fade as the young users move on to new features. It is reasonable to assume that UGC will henceforth be part of the news site offering, just as user contribution has always been in various ways. It seems, from a journalistic perspective, that users as news sources are a marginal phenomenon, most likely as a consequence both of what is actually asked for from the professionals and what is desirable from an audience point of view. New applications do not seem to change the role of the user as a source to any large extent—not at present.

Future research needs to emphasize the value to the audience of user sources and user contributions within different categories of online news content. It might be considered of high importance within certain areas but on the other hand relatively unimportant within others. Research also needs to address the question of *why* certain user contributions attract readers, and under what circumstances the audience is a desirable source for the professionals.

REFERENCES

Bergström, Annika (2005) "nyhetsvanor.nu: Nyhetsanvändning på internet 1998 till 2003" [News consumption practices on the Internet 1998 to 2003], Paper prepared for the Department of Journalism and Mass Communication, University of Gothenburg.

Bergström, Annika (2008) "The reluctant audience: Online participation in the Swedish journalistic context," *Westminster Papers in Communication and Culture* 5(2): pp. 60–80.

Chisholm, Jim (2004) "Question of news value driving papers," *Newspapers & Technology*, February.

Chung, Deborah, S. (2007) "Profits and perils: Online news producers' perceptions of interactivity and uses of interactive features," *Convergence* 13(1): pp. 43–61.

Chung, Deborah (2008) "Interactive features of online newspapers: Identifying patterns and predicting use of engaged readers," *Journal of Computer-Mediated Communication* 13: pp. 658–679.

Chung, Deborah, S. and Chan Yun Yoo (2008) "Audience motivations for using interactive features: Distinguishing use of different types of interactivity on an online newspaper," *Mass Communication and Society* 11(4): pp. 375–397.

Clark, Wayne (2002) *Activism in the Public Sphere: Exploring the discourse of political participation*, Aldershot: Ashgate.

Croteau, David (2006) "The growth of self-produced media content and the challenge to media studies," In *Critical Studies in Media Communication* 23(4): pp. 340–344.

Davis, Richard (2005) *Politics Online: Blogs, chatrooms and discussion groups in American democracy*, New York/London: Routledge.

Domingo, David (2008) "Interactivity in the daily routines of online newsrooms: Dealing with an uncomfortable myth," *Journal of Computer-Mediated Communication* 13(3): pp. 680–704.

Gillmore, Dan (2004) *We the Media. Grassroots Journalism by the People for the People.* Sebastopol-Farnham: O'Reilly.

Hallin, Dan and Mancini, Paolo (2004) *Comparing Media Systems: Three Models of Media and Politics.* Cambridge: Cambridge University Press.

Hedman, Ulrika (2009) Läsarmedverkan: Lönande logiskt lockbete [User-contributions as part of the company strategy], Gothenburg: Department of Journalism and Mass Communication, University of Gothenburg.

Hujanen, Jaana and Pietikäninen, Sari (2004) "Interactive uses of journalism: crossing between technological potential and young people's news using practices," *New Media & Society* 6(3): pp. 383–401.

Karlsson, Michael (2006) "*Nätjournalistik: En explorative fallstudie av digitala mediers karaktärsdrag på fyra svenska tidningssajter,*" [Net Journalism: An explorive case study of character of news sites], *Lund Studies in Media and Communication* 9. pp. 1–239.

Lasica, Joseph, D. "The promise of the daily me," *Online Journalism Review.* Available: httm://www.ojr.org/ojr/lasica/1017779142.php.

Limonard, Sander (2007) "Business Requirements and Potential Bottlenecks for Successful New Citizen Media Applications," Report prepared for the Sixth Framework Programme: Citizen Media Project.

Madden, Mary and Fox, Susannah (2006) "Riding the Waves of 'Web 2.0'," Pew Internet Project. Available: www.pewinternet.org. Accessed July 9, 2010.

Matheson, Donald (2004) "Weblogs and the epistemology of the news: Some trends in online journalism," *New Media & Society* 6(4): pp. 443–468.

McMillan, Sally J. (2002) "A four-part model of cyber-interactivity: Some cyberplaces are more interactive than others," *New Media & Society* 4(2): pp. 271–291.

Neuberger, Christoph (2007) "Weblogs und Journalismus: Konkurrenz, Ergänzung oder Integration?," *Medieperspektiven* 2. Available: charlottabaltazar. files.wordpress.com/. . ./bloggen-en-asiktsmaskin-av-c-baltazar2.pdf.

Nielsen, Jakob (2006) "Participation inequality: Encouraging more users to contribute," Jacob Nielsen's Alertbox. Available: www.useit.com/alertbox/participation_inequality.html.

Nilsson, Åsa (2009) "Den nationella SOM-undersökningen 2008 [The national SOM-survey 2008]," in Sören Holmberg and Lennart Weibull (Eds) *Svensk Höst* [Swedish Fall], Report no. 41, Gothenburg: The SOM-Institute, University of Gothenburg.

Nip, Joyce, M. (2006) "Exploring the second phase of journalism charlottabaltazar.files.wordpress.com/. . ./bloggen-en-asiktsmaskin-av-c-baltazar2.pdf *Journalism Studies*7(2): pp. 212–236.

OECD (2007) "Participative Net and User-Created Content. Web 2.0, Wikis and Social Networking." Available: http://www.oecd.org/document/40/0,3343,en_2649_34223_39428648_1_1_1_1,00.html. Accessed July 10, 2010.

Örnebring, Henrik (2008) "The consumer as producer—of what? User-generated tabloid content in *The Sun* (UK) and *Aftonbladet* (Sweden)," *Journalism Studies* 9(5): pp. 771–785.

Paulussen, Steve, Heinonen, Ari, Domingo, David, and Quandt Thorsten (2007) "Doing it together: Citizen participation in the professional news making process," *Observatorio Journal* 3: pp. 131–154.

Rafaeli, Sheizaf and Sudweeks, Fay (1997) "Networked interactivity"' *Journal of Computer-Mediated Communication* 2(4). Available at: http://jcmc.indiana.edu/vol2/issue4/rafaeli.sudweeks.html. (accessed June 2008).

Roscoe, Timothy (1999) "The construction of the World Wide Web audience," *Media, Culture and Society* 21. vol. 5, pp. 673–684.

Singer, Jane (2006) "Stepping back from the gate: Online newspaper editors and the co-production of content in 'Campaign 2004'," *Journalism and Mass Communication Quarterly* 83(2): pp. 265–280.

Strid, Jan (2008) "Morgonpressens innehåll—vad är läst och vad är viktigt 2007?" [The content in morning papers—what is read and what is important in 2007?], in Sören Holmberg and Lennart Weibull (Eds) *Skilda världar: Trettioåtta kapitel om politik, medier och samhälle* [Separate worlds], Report no. 44, Gothenburg: The SOM-Institute, University of Gothenburg.

Stromer-Galley, Jennifer (2000) "On-line interaction and why candidates avoid it," *Journal of Communication* 50(4): pp. 111–132.

Thurman, Neil (2008) "Forum for citizen journalists? Adoption of user generated content initiatives by online news media," *New Media & Society* 10. vol. 1, pp. 139–157.

Tancer, Bill (2007) "Measuring Web 2.0 Consumer Participation." Available www.hitwise.com/down-loads/reports/Hitwise_US_Measuring_Web_2.0_Consumer_Participation_June_2007.pdf.

Weibull, Lennart and Jönsson, Anna Maria (2007) "The Swedish Media Landscape," in Georgiao Terzis (Ed) *European Media Governance: National and Regional Dimensions*, Bristol: Intellect Books, The Mill. Avialable: www.som.gu.se/.

12 Citizen Journalism and Everyday Life

A Case Study of Germany's *Myheimat.De*

Axel Bruns

INTRODUCTION: BEYOND THE USUAL POLITICS

The impact of citizen journalism on the established journalism industry, and its role in the future news media mix, remain key topics in current journalism studies research, not least in the context of the current crisis facing many news organizations around the globe. The centrality of this issue is also reflected in the substantial number of 'citizen journalism' monographs and collections published across the last few years (see for example Paterson and Domingo, 2008; Boler, 2008; Allan and Thorsen, 2009; Neuberger, Nuernbergk, and Rischke, 2009; Gordon, 2009; Russell and Echchaibi, 2009; Meikle and Redden, forthcoming). With relatively few notable exceptions, much of the research and wider public discussion surrounding the citizen journalism phenomenon has employed a relatively narrow definition of the term, with many researchers focusing on citizen journalism projects that provide mainly *political* news and commentary, and on their role in influencing the political process especially in countries like the US.

This research has made important contributions by highlighting the role of citizen journalism publications as a corrective to mainstream news media especially on those occasions when the quality of coverage has been found wanting. But the research has also signaled the emergence of a younger group of news consumers who have turned away from print editions of newspapers, preferring to seek their news predominantly online, and here no longer necessarily only from 'reputable', well-established news organizations (see Chapter 4, this volume). But at the same time, this focus on political news has perpetuated an existing distinction between 'hard' and 'soft' news which has tended to privilege the political over most other forms of news reporting, and relegated to the background other areas of the news which may benefit just as much from a broader range of news outlets and contributions from non-professional journalists.

An unresolved contradiction, however, remains at the heart of the 'citizen journalism' concept. While on the one hand, citizen journalism has unquestionably enabled more 'citizens' (understood here in the first place as 'non-journalists') to participate in more journalistic processes, including especially news commentary, on the other hand this has so far failed to translate into participation by a more representative cross-section of the overall citizenry. The public and scholarly focus on citizen journalism as political news, moreover, means the majority of participants in citizen journalism appear to be what Coleman (2006) has described as 'political junkies' (PJs)—namely, citizens who already have a keen interest in political matters, and engage with citizen journalism projects as vehicles for their political participation and expression. While valuable in their own right, then, such citizen journalism sites mainly provide an outlet for the already converted—citizens already interested in civic participation—rather than introducing more previously uninvolved members of society to active participation in public matters.

Part of the problem in this context is likely to be that highly valued, 'hard' news topics provide only limited opportunity for meaningful participation beyond the mere voicing of personal opinion: 'hard' news is considered hard not least because an in-depth understanding of current political issues is required in order to contribute meaningful commentary or generate new insights from a close reading of existing information. In order to engage in this form, one must become a PJ, and preferably be embedded in a social milieu which guarantees access to other PJs. While detailed studies of the demographics of major citizen journalism Websites have yet to be undertaken, this suggests that active participants are likely to be drawn mainly from a relatively narrow group of participants, most likely based in state and national capitals.

One approach to broadening the base for citizen journalism beyond this group—especially also on a geographic level—has been to explore hyperlocal citizen journalism models. Internationally, several successful projects of this kind covering —local politics—are in train, and a recent venture in Australia, *Youdecide2007.org*, successfully deployed a platform enabling users to report on the individual local electoral races in the 2007 Australian federal election, providing coverage of the election well beyond the mainstream media's focus on the contest between the major party candidates for Prime Minister (see Wilson, Saunders, and Bruns, 2009).[1]

Such projects provide a space for citizen journalism participants who may be at a considerable remove from national politics, but nonetheless have meaningful contributions to make by reporting on (and from) areas of which they have immediate, first-hand knowledge. *Youdecide2007*, for example, was able to shine a light on political issues in highly remote areas such as the northwest Australian electorate of Kalgoorlie, which would otherwise be almost entirely absent from mainstream political coverage. Nonetheless, even projects such as this perpetuate the privileged positioning of political news over other topics. A citizen journalism that aims for a truly broad-based level of participation by the citizenry may need to explore other avenues.

FROM CITIZEN JOURNALISM TO COMMUNITY NEWS?

The German participatory news Website *myHeimat.de* provides a useful—and importantly, successful—model for another form of citizen journalism. Launched in its present form in 2005, the site is structured as an aggregated hyperlocal news site. Users specify their home location (their *Heimatort*) as they register for the site, and are presented with recent user-generated news items from their local area on subsequent logins. They are also able, however, to search for content from other regions, or to browse site content by topic and other characteristics rather than by location. This provides a space for the development and maintenance of multiple on-site communities around shared local origins, but also offers a platform for the nationwide coverage of news and events from diverse local perspectives, and for the development of interest groups based on shared interests beyond local identity. Developed and launched in Augsburg near Munich, *myHeimat* retains a strong focus on this region as well as on a number of other areas where it partners with local print outlets, although it has been able to attract some 20,000 users who are distributed across nearly all of Germany. The following analysis of the *myHeimat* project is based substantially on interviews which were conducted in October 2008 with *myHeimat* founder Martin Huber, CEO of Gogol Medien (the company operating *myHeimat*), and Peter Taubald and Clemens Wlokas, editor and deputy editor-in-chief of the *Heimatzeitungen*, a group of local newspapers based in Garbsen near Hannover that are produced by the Madsack publishing house which is a publishing partner for *myHeimat*.[2]

Compared to the sites which are more commonly studied by citizen journalism researchers, *myHeimat* at first appears decidedly apolitical—in keeping with the (hyper) local focus of the site, its user-generated content ranges from news reports about local events and community activities to stories on local history and photojournalism from the region, but also addresses topics such as local planning, council services, and related themes. *myHeimat* may therefore be better described as 'community news' than 'citizen journalism' in the sense that has been established in recent publications—but as Huber notes,

> we have discovered that it's often those themes which are simple, but relevant to everyday life, which are crucial to people in the region, and so ultimately we have a very user-oriented approach. . . . We don't so much have a journalistic perspective, under an assumption that we know what is of interest to the people, but we trust in the fact that the wisdom of the many, in the respective regions . . . will know best what is relevant.

This, he notes, also helps ensure the quality of the content contributed by *myHeimat* users:

we really want those topics, too, which are specific to the [local] microcosm, because: the further away from the everyday world those topics
are, the harder it is for the citizen reporter to communicate them. If I
step outside my door and go to the next playground, and it's dirty and
not serviced by the council, then I can communicate that very well; even
as a lay-person, especially as someone affected by it, I have a strong incentive to address the topic—. . . ultimately I don't need the aptitudes
and abilities that a journalist has. The further it is away from me, and
at least when it's Obama-McCain, then perhaps I can have a personal
opinion, but the question is, in competition with other offerings, can
I reach a certain level with that topic, or does it remain a subjective
individual opinion as it's already available in a thousand blogs in the
long tail?

Where higher-level politics does appear on *myHeimat*, is where it inter-
sects directly with the local—most of all (in parallel with projects such as
Youdecide2007) in the context of local elections or the local contests in
state elections. In Bavaria, Huber notes,

this has worked very very well, and we had a few mayors and mayoral
candidates who ran their political blog through *myHeimat*, which we
were very happy about, because a debate and a dialogue took place
on a small scale, which ultimately is part of our vision . . . . That's an
approach which has something of a basic democratic element, and an
inclusion [of citizens]—or a revival of inclusion, of participation, of
self-expression—in all things, including in politics. If not on an everyday basis, then at least at key points, like mayoral elections.

Everyday community reporting is more typical of *myHeimat* rather than
these isolated 'one-off' political events—Huber's vision was to create a site
"which is entirely made by the region for the region." As is the case with
many other citizen journalism initiatives, this is also a response to perceived shortcomings in the established media landscape:

Germany in particular is for the most part very monopolistic, as far
as local media are concerned . . . and that carries the threat that some
user needs, some reader needs aren't . . . attended to or regularly incorporated into products in the way the customer would like it to. In the
past, there were relatively high barriers to entry to creating a proper
product—at the local, daily level.

Notably in this context, the *myHeimat* initiative originated not with a
local newspaper, but with Gogol Medien, an Augsburg-based IT company.
This lack of journalistic background helped rather than hindered the site's
development, Huber believes: "journalistically, content-wise, we stay out

of it, and merely offer a platform which provides for elegant community exchange." He sees his staff as moderators, facilitators and animators of the community process, especially in its early stages, who "time and again accompany, advance, enable, and nudge . . . users, but . . . on the other hand never predetermine content aspects." This community-building process is crucial:

> simply to make clear, 'this is open and anyone can participate', that's something that you have to impress [on users] and for which we have to give an appropriate push. You have to set a very low threshold, so that users don't need to start with a contribution consisting of a page of text—plus ten images, ready to print with a gripping headline—but can begin simply with a snapshot, with a brief impression.
>
> And we notice clearly that people follow a learning curve on the platform, where they do in part begin with a snapshot, with an impression, with an image, and then step by step learn to operate [the system] and gain confidence. . . . And that really needs to be supported, that's nothing these people are familiar with from 30 to 40 years of media consumption. . . . That's a very different approach or a very different understanding of such a product from what a traditionally educated journalist does.

As participants have followed that learning curve, however, quality content and a strong sense of community have emerged, most of all in those regional *myHeimat* communities where a substantial, critical mass of users is active on the site. Huber describes a typical distribution of activity across the community:

> there are people who are relatively rarely or very moderately active, there's a third who are moderately active, there's a third or a quarter who are hyperactive, sometimes with an enormous amount of articles—a distribution that is similar to what's known in many communities.

Once a critical mass of highly active local users has been reached (which Huber sets at around 1 to 5% of the total population, that is, above 100 users for most small German towns), community dynamics tend to set in which for the most part enable the community to take care of its own affairs. "Once the community has internalized" *myHeimat*'s overall rules and values, Huber says,

> its self-cleaning (i.e., self-managing or self-policing) powers come into force, and more and more controversial topics can be dealt with . . . . And we see very clearly by now that it works very well to let controversial topics run their course. But you have to understand this very clearly, it simply needs some time until this works—I would be very

sceptical, I don't think this would work right from the start when the community isn't large enough yet and doesn't have the momentum.

The ability of the mature *myHeimat* communities in various localities to manage their own affairs and police their interactions with minimal moderating interference from *myHeimat* staff—which stands in stark contrast to perceptions of social media especially in the mainstream media industries—stems in good part from two key factors: the online community's overlap with the local *offline* community, and the fact that the overwhelming majority of *myHeimat* users are registered under their real names rather than under a pseudonym. "One of the fundamental values of a community is transparency, authenticity, openness," Huber notes, and estimates that

> 90 to 95% of the people are there with their real names, with their photos . . . And additionally, of course, there's a possibility in the regional community, when you're stepping outside your door in the real world, that you're confronted with [the things you've written], and have to stand for it just as if I'm telling someone face to face or at the pub. The central point is not to create a virtual community, but to represent a real existing one and to achieve a connection with reality. . . . And so we have far fewer disruptive people here than in classical [pseudonymous, online] fora.

FROM ONLINE TO PRINT

Another substantial incentive—especially so perhaps in smaller regional towns—which may encourage constructive community participation is the possibility that users may see their content in print. In a number of German regions where *myHeimat* has been able to attract a critical mass, Gogol Medien and its regional partners now regularly publish local magazines and newspaper inserts which use the content contributed through the online platform. According to Huber—who suggests that "the real excitement comes from the attached print component", as on October 2008,

> in Bavaria and Swabia . . . there are 18 magazines, with a circulation of 138,000 copies, then there are the pages in the local newspapers around Hannover [in Lower Saxony], which have a circulation of 130,000 copies, and by now the third or fourth magazine in Hannover . . . . The newspapers in the city of Hannover, *Hannoversche Allgemeine* and *Neue Presse*, are also starting to publish content . . . on Thursdays, and that's another 100,000, 150,000, or for the *Neue Presse* 200,000 units, but only once a week.

Additional print publications have been added since the time of the interview. This is a remarkable development especially since Gogol Medien had not been a newspaper or magazine publisher in its own right, and initially began publishing these local magazines without backing from an established print publisher.

A number of different publishing models exist for these publications. In *myHeimat*'s home state of Bavaria, Gogol pursued a free publication model which saw magazines distributed directly to households or made available at newsagents and other collection locations—"the approach is relatively open, and deliberately open, in terms of conversion into print, which means that you can explore the whole bandwidth" of possible models, Huber notes. Much as their content is drawn from hyperlocal communities and consequently these magazines are financed in part by what could be described as hyperlocal advertising: they provide an advertising venue for local businesses for whom even city and regional newspapers reach a too wide targeted and nondescript audience. Larger businesses also advertise in these publications, however. What remains important in this step from online to print, Huber points out, is that

> this maintains certain fundamental elements: that transparency is maintained; that it remains visible somewhere where it all comes from, so that the user or author is acknowledged appropriately, and feels valued; but that the feedback loop is closed, too, and that the understanding is maintained that things which are posted to *myHeimat* may potentially go to print.

Another model for print publication has emerged from *myHeimat*'s growing cooperation with existing news organizations—and here in particular with the Hannover-based newspaper publisher Madsack and the editors of its local newspapers for the region surrounding Hannover, the *Heimatzeitungen*. This cooperation emerged from an initiative to develop an online presence for the various papers published by the *Heimatzeitungen*, and has subsequently been further cemented with the Madsack group becoming a shareholder in Gogol Medien. As editor-in-chief Peter Taubald describes it,

> we thought, if we don't create a classic news portal, under the masthead of the newspaper, then maybe it would be good if we place all the reader contributions—. . . mainly from clubs and associations—. . . on the Internet, and create something like a reader newspaper in our newspaper. The working title was *meineheimat.de*, but that was already taken . . . , and we were looking for domain names [and found *myHeimat*] . . . and then we cried "it's been done already, damn . . ."
>
> And most of all, we found that they were doing a good job. . . . We had plenty of ideas, like everyone else, but it all costs money . . . and that's exactly what Gogol Medien does: create [print] magazines from the Internet content and earn money in the conventional advertising

market, and we thought that's great. So first we met with them and agreed to cooperate, and now the shareholdership.

Launched on April 23, 2008, cooperation between *myHeimat* and the *Heimatzeitungen* has been mutually beneficial. In the first place, the newspaper has served as a suitable vehicle for promoting participation in the online platform, leading to some 5,000 user registrations within the first six months of operation alone (some 1,200 of these registered users had contributed content by late October 2008). Similar to the magazines in Bavaria, regular *myHeimat* pages in the various editions of the newspaper, which are published for different towns in the Hannover region, re-publish the best user-generated online content from the region, and thus provide further motivation for participants. In selecting this content and organizing local advertising around it, the project is also able to draw on the journalistic and business expertise of the *Heimatzeitung* organization.

But the journalistic aspects of this collaboration needed some time to get underway, as Deputy Editor-in-Chief Clemens Wlokas notes:

> our colleagues watched this with a sceptical eye especially during the first months. . . . We had something in Burgdorf where a street had subsided. This wasn't a small corner, but a larger area, because a water mains had broken and a lot of water had escaped, and that story was in the [online] community first. So in the editorial meeting we said, we should have a look, and why didn't we find out about this before? But it still took two, three days until it was properly in the paper—and then on the title page, because it really was headline news. A huge story.
>
> But our colleagues said, we can't look at the [online] community as well—we have the press release, police meetings and so on; to check the community for what they're posting, to evaluate this, is it a topic for us or not . . . Why are they forcing another type of reality on us?
>
> So we said, this *is* reality—if the users think this is important, then we have to check for ourselves, is this an interesting piece that we need to redevelop? Not just the way the community see it, of course—we have the chance to research, to interview others, to evaluate, to comment; we have our journalistic means of dealing with it.

Taubald adds:

> we think it's great that we have our discussion, because we say that it doesn't matter whether we do *myHeimat* or not, because the phenomenon that people are communicating in this form is there anyway, and we must respond to it in some way. If the result is that you can read things which are of local interest, and of interest to a [local] newspaper, online first, and then later they show up in a daily newspaper, then the

daily newspaper loses its value. This means that we must produce content of a quality that is clearly distinct from anything else. . . .

I'm glad that we've done what we've done, because this requires us in our role as editors-in-chief, with the newsroom staff, to much more strongly think about how to deal with these times. I think this is a debate which touches all newspapers . . . and which we must lead intensively.

But, Wlokas notes,

for us there are always two pillars, community and competence, which complement one another, which influence one another, but which do not replace one another. This was a concern in many newsrooms, that publishers who no longer want to spend money on expensive newsrooms now take citizen journalists as *ersatz* content producers to obtain content cheaply and put papers on the market without employing a newsroom. That's not at all what we do—we wouldn't even think about it, because the connection, the cross-fertilization, the two pillars, that's important, that's essential.

What Taubald and Wlokas describe here, then, is a live example for a hybrid pro-am model of journalism (cf. Bruns, 2010) that draws on crowdsourcing to identify stories and brings to light further background information, but which further enhances this material through journalistic processing. As Huber describes it,

if there are 300, 400 citizens in the region [who are registered on *myHeimat*], and they only need to be dormant, but if something happens, then there's a network of correspondents, that's amazing for such a region, and it's fast and it's authentic.

The content generated by this network of citizen reporters, then, is processed by journalists who are acting in a curatorial role at least as much as they work as reporters in their own right, in line with Taubald's definition of the role of the journalist in today's media environment: "journalists are there to cut an aisle of understanding through the jungle of information."

THE LIMITS OF *MYHEIMAT*'S HYPERLOCAL MODEL

To date, *myHeimat* has been most successful in developing a critical mass of community participation in a number of regional areas in Germany—first of all around Augsburg, where it was founded, and in neighboring regions in the state of Bavaria, and in the region around Hannover in Lower Saxony since early 2008, through the efforts of the *Heimatzeitungen* team. Additional Madsack publications in other German states have also begun to pursue the *Heimatzeitung* model, but are at earlier stages of development.

While it is possible to observe a tendency for participation in the site to develop gradually, both within individual towns and villages and by skipping from one town to its neighbours, a number of limits to such growth have also become obvious. *myHeimat* has so far failed to attract a substantial level of participation in major cities—notably including the state capitals Munich and Hannover in spite of their central location within the site's two most active regions. Site-staff note that at present, the site is most successful in attracting contributors from regional and rural areas, and suggest that for residents in such areas there is a very different sense of local connection than for the inhabitants of major cities. In the regions, residents identify strongly with *their* town or village—and, as Taubald notes,

offline the perception of Hannover is of course also divided into different suburbs, relying on this suburban identity alone online doesn't seem to me to be working—because interestingly, those people who are from Hannover or write content about Hannover are writing very warmly about Hannover *in general*. Nice things about Hannover for them are for the most part those things which people from Hannover or many tourists also find nice—city hall, the Berggarten, the Maschsee lake. How do I find out about the playground in [the suburb of] Bothfeld? . . .

You can't do what you do here in the [Hannover] region, where the communities are more closed and unified. People in these communities think, first of all I'm from Burgdorf, then nothing, and then to some extent perhaps I'm from Hannover. It's not the same in the city, they're all from Hannover, and there's no-one really from Bothfeld.

Anecdotally, Taubald and Wlokas also point to marked differences even in the Hannover region itself, outside the city: here, take up of *myHeimat* has been notably greater in the older, more organically grown surrounding cities than in those communities which over the past decades have developed mainly as leafy estate villages for Hannover's upper classes. Speaking for Munich, Huber agrees that these different levels of identification with the local area impact on the viability of the *myHeimat* model:

in our opinion, of course the effects and the microcosm in a small town are different from a metropolis. If I look at Munich, there are significantly more new residents, who may only be here for some time and who have newly arrived; there is more fluctuation and change; and there is significantly more nomadism and cosmopolitanism, so that there are different effects than in a small town of 20,000 inhabitants, which is at the upper level of a size where everyone knows everyone else. . . . We're in the process of looking at this, can it be translated to city quarters, to suburbs; where is the analogy to the metropolis?

At the same time, even if widespread take-up in the major cities so far remains out of reach for *myHeimat*, then, this still leaves substantial room for growth for its community, he notes:

Germany is a very attractive market, because Germany has some 80 million inhabitants, of whom 30 million live in cities of up to 30,000 inhabitants—this means that this is a very attractive segment.

A different question, however, is whether it will be possible to translate the *myHeimat* model to other, differently structured nations—for example to Australia, where the vast majority of the population is concentrated in a handful of major cities.

CONCLUSION

myHeimat presents one of only a small number of successful examples of broad-based citizen journalism (or perhaps more appropriately, community news) projects which have emerged internationally. The viability of this model—at least for regional and rural communities—is demonstrated not least by the growing support and cooperation between *myHeimat* itself and the *Heimatzeitungen* and other journalistic publications; indeed, late in 2008, the *Heimatzeitungen* won a European Newspaper Award for their role in this initiative (Warnecke, 2008).

Most centrally, the project points to a possible future beyond the repetitive journalist vs. blogger wars that continue to plague journalism practice as well as journalism studies—it provides a model for pro-am journalism approaches in which both sides have valuable contributions to make. Such new models will take some time to establish, as the *myHeimat* experience itself demonstrates, and Huber's appreciation for his collaborators in Hannover is instructive in this context: "if they were all like this in the industry, the structural transformation would happen much more quickly."

What was already evident even before the current financial crisis, but what has been made even more urgent by it, is that for better or for worse the transformation must, and will, happen. At worst, it may lead to the disappearance of many professional journalism institutions without sufficient replacement, a future where—as Wlokas has described it—citizen journalists are harnessed as cheap *ersatz* content producers by commercial news operators; at best, it may lead to the development of sustainable hybrid models which combine the best of professional and citizen journalism to free up paid journalism staff to create content, add value to citizen journalism content, and curate the combined product.

From this perspective, the fact that Gogol Medien has recently licensed out the platform which is used to run *myHeimat* as a basis for the 'participatory newspaper' *Gießener Zeitung* may be seen as the first step towards a broader proliferation of *myHeimat*'s and similar pro-am models. As Huber puts it:

> It's a very interesting aspect that . . . the effect of this approach reaches much further than only to the original products which are based on it. . . . A single citizen reporter on *myHeimat* probably doesn't even know how they indirectly manage to make the newspaper better, by creating competition or introducing new thinking.

ACKNOWLEDGMENTS

The author wishes to thank the interviewees, Peter Taubald and Clemens Wlokas at the *Heimatzeitungen* and Martin Huber at *myHeimat*, for so generously making themselves available for the interviews on which this chapter is based.

NOTES

1. Axel Bruns was a chief Investigator of the ARC Linkage project which developed *Youdecide2007*, in partnership with public broadcaster SBS, *The National Forum*, and Cisco Systems.
2. Interviews were conducted in German and translated to English by the author.

REFERENCES

Allan, Stuart, and Thorsen, Einar (Eds) (2009) *Citizen Journalism: Global perspectives*, New York: Peter Lang.
Boler, Megan (Ed) (2008) *Digital Media and Democracy: Tactics in hard times*, Cambridge, MA: MIT Press.
Bruns, Axel (2010) "News produsage in a pro-am mediasphere," in Graham Meikle and Guy Redden (Eds) *News Online: Transformations and continuities*, London: Palgrave Macmillan.
Coleman, Stephen (2006) "How the other half votes: *Big Brother* viewers and the 2005 general election," *International Journal of Cultural Studies* 9(4): pp. 457–479.
Gordon, Janey (Ed) (2009) *Notions of Community: A collection of community media debates and dilemmas*, New York: Peter Lang.
Huber, Martin (2008) Interviewed by Axel Bruns. Munich, Germany, October 29.
Meikle, Graham and Redden, Guy (Eds) (2010) *News Online: Transformations and continuities*, London: Palgrave Macmillan.
Neuberger, Christoph, Nuernbergk, Christoph, and Rischke Melanie (Eds) (2009) *Journalismus im Internet: Profession—Partizipation—Technisierung*, Wiesbaden: VS-Verlag.

Paterson, Chris and Domingo David (Eds) (2008) *Making Online News: The ethnography of new media production*, New York: Peter Lang.

Russell, Adrienne and Echchaibi, Nabil (Eds) (2009) *International Blogging: Identity, politics, and networked publics*, New York: Peter Lang.

Taubald, Peter and Wlokas Clemens (2008) Interviewed by Axel Bruns. Garbsen, Germany, October 23.

Warnecke, Sven (2008) "Der europäische Zeitungs-Oscar gebührt allen," *myHeimat.de,* November 24. Available: http://www.myheimat.de/global/beitrag/61531/der-europaeische-zeitungs-oscar-gebuehrt-allen/. Accessed July 20, 2009.

Wilson, Jason, Saunders, Barry, and Bruns Axel (2009) "'Preditors': Making citizen journalism work," in Janey Gordon (Ed) *Notions of Community: A collection of community media debates and dilemmas*, New York: Peter Lang, pp. 245–270.

Contributors

Chris Atton is Professor of Media and Culture in the School of Arts and Creative Industries at Edinburgh Napier University, Edinburgh. His research specializes in alternative media and he is the author of four books, including *Alternative Media* (2002) and *Alternative Journalism* (2008, with James F. Hamilton), as well as over 50 articles and book chapters. He is particularly interested in questions of democratic access to the media and the social value of participatory media. He has made special studies of fanzines, the media of new social movements and popular music journalism.

Annika Bergström is Senior Lecturer in Media and Communication Science at the Department of Journalism, Media and Communication (JMG), University of Gothenburg. She holds a PhD in Journalism and Mass Communication. Her dissertation focused on internet news habits from 1998–2003. For the last few years her research has dealt with user participation in political contexts and user contributions within traditional journalism.

Axel Bruns, PhD, is a Senior Lecturer in the Creative Industries Faculty at Queensland University of Technology in Brisbane, Australia. He is the author of *Blogs, Wikipedia, Second Life and Beyond: From Production to Produsage* (2008) and *Gatewatching: Collaborative Online News Production* (2005), and the editor of *Uses of Blogs* with Joanne Jacobs (2006). He blogs at snurb.info and contributes to the Gatewatching.org group blog with Jason Wilson and Barry Saunders. Bruns has undertaken extensive research on citizen journalism in Australia and elsewhere, and is a Chief Investigator of an ARC Linkage project which developed the *Youdecide2007.org* hyperlocal citizen journalism Website for the 2007 Australian federal elections, in collaboration with SBS, Cisco Systems, and the *National Forum*.

Matt Carlson is Assistant Professor of Communication at Saint Louis University, US. He is author of *On The Condition of Anonymity: Unnamed*

Source and the Battle for Journalism (2011). His work has appeared in numerous journals, including *Critical Studies in Media Communication, New Media & Society,* and *Media, Culture & Society.* He has also presented papers at conferences both in the US and Europe. Carlson holds a PhD from the Annenberg School for Communication at the University of Pennsylvania and previously worked at the Project of Excellence in Journalism in Washington, DC.

Jeroen De Keyser is a member of the Center for Journalism Studies (Ghent University). He is a researcher for an FWO (Research Foundation— Flanders) project that investigates emerging forms of citizen journalism and their interaction with traditional journalistic models

Bob Franklin is Chair of Journalism Studies and Director of the Journalism Studies Research Group at Cardiff University, UK. He is the Editor of *Journalism Studies* and *Journalism Practice* and co-editor of the series *Journalism Studies: Key Texts.* Publications include *Journalism Education, Training and Employment* (2011); *The Future of Journalism* (2011); *The Future of Newspapers* (2009); *Key Concepts in Public Relations* (2009); *Pulling Newspapers Apart, Analysing Print Journalism* (2008); *Local Journalism and Local Media, Making the Local News* (2006); *Television Policy, The MacTaggart Lectures* (2005); *Key Concepts in Journalism Studies* (2005); and *Packaging Politics: Political Communication in Britain's Media Democracy* (2004).

Steve Paulussen is Senior Researcher at the IBBT research group for Media & ICT (MICT) in Ghent. He is also a member of the Center for Journalism Studies (CJS) at the Department of Communication Sciences at Ghent University, where he teaches journalism studies. Further, he is a part-time lecturer in journalism theory at the Vrije Universiteit Brussel (VUB).

Julian Petley is Professor of Screen Media and Journalism in the School of Arts at Brunel University, UK and Chair of the Campaign for Press and Broadcasting Freedom. His most recent publication is *Censorship: A Beginner's Guide* (2009). *Film and Video Censorship in Contemporary Britain*, and *Pointing the Finger: Muslims and Islam in the British Media* are both currently in press. He is a member of the editorial board of the *British Journalism Review*, and of the board of *Index on Censorship.*

Angela Phillips is responsible for undergraduate 'text' journalism and convenor of the MA Journalism at Goldsmiths, University of London where she teaches feature writing and journalism studies. She is interested in critical journalism research from a practitioner perspective. She works with the Leverhulme funded research group: "Spaces of the News," contributed to Natalie Fenton (Ed) *New Media: Old News*, (2010) and was co-editor, with Elizabeth Eide and Risto Kunelius of *Transnational Media Events: The Mohammed Cartoons and the Imagined Clash of Civilizations* (2008). She is currently working on a further book based on the Leverhulme research.

Karin Raeymaeckers is the Director of the Center for Journalism Studies (Ghent University). She teaches media structures, journalism, and political communication in the Communication Sciences Department of the University of Ghent. She is a member of several international research groups including the Euromedia Research Group.

Zvi Reich, PhD, combines rich journalistic experience as a former senior editor with extensive research activity in journalism and the sociology of news. His book, *Sourcing the News,* was recently published and his work has been published in *Journalism Studies, Journalism and Mass Communication Quarterly* and *Journalism.* Dr. Reich is a Lecturer at the Department of Communication Studies, Ben-Gurion University of the Negev, Beersheva, Israel.

Lucinda Strahan studied at Melbourne and Sydney Universities. She teaches media writing at the Royal Melbourne Institute of Technology (RMIT) where she is also an academic advisor. She trained in news journalism as a cadet at *The Melbourne Times* in 2001 before working extensively as a freelance print journalist specializing in arts and culture. Her work has been published in major daily newspapers, fashion and street magazines, online, and in many Australian arts journals. She has also collaborated with contemporary artists in creative writing projects. Her current research interests include arts journalism and the representation of arts and culture in the print news media, and the common areas between creative and professional media practices.

Tom Van Hout is assistant professor in the Humanities Faculty at Leiden University and visiting lecturer at the Department of Management at the University of Antwerp. He holds a PhD in linguistics from Ghent University and specializes in the ethnography of institutional communication. He has recently published work on intertextuality, journalism practice and newsroom ethnography.

Karin Wahl-Jorgensen, PhD, is a Reader at Cardiff University's School of Journalism, Media and Cultural Studies. She is interested in the relationship between citizenship, democracy, and the media. She is generally interested in how citizens are represented in news forms and genres, including vox pop interviews, letters to the editor, disaster coverage, and user-generated content. She is the author of two books, *Journalists and the Public* (2007) and *Citizens or Consumers?* (2005; co-authored with

Justin Lewis and Sanna Inthorn). She is editor of the *Handbook of Journalism Studies* (Routledge, 2009, with Thomas Hanitzsch) and *Mediated Citizenship* (Routledge, 2007).

Claire Wardle, PhD, is a Lecturer at Cardiff University's School of Journalism, Media and Cultural Studies. Her research examines the ways in which social and political issues are represented in different media formats. She recently led the knowledge exchange project co-funded by the BBC and AHRC (Arts and Humanities Research Council) which explored the ways in which BBC news and current affairs output includes user generated content. Her forthcoming book, *Reporting the Unimaginable* is a historical cross-cultural comparison of press coverage of child murders, considering the context for the most recent moral panic about pedophiles in society.

Andy Williams, PhD, is the RCUK Research Fellow in Risk, Health and Science Communication at Cardiff University's School of Journalism, Media and Cultural Studies. His research interests are media convergence (including the political economy of convergence, the effects of multiplatform news provision on news quality and journalists' pay and conditions, and the rise of user generated content), the role of public relations in the UK media, and media representations of health and science (particularly journalist-source relations and the relationship between science journalism and PR).

Index